Praise for *Community-Based Global Learning*

"Many colleges and universities claim to graduate 'global citizens' from their programs, but studies reveal that few accomplish this lofty goal. Grounded in decades of research, *Community-Based Global Learning* unpacks terms like *global citizen* and *transformative learning* and presents an alternate vision of *critical global citizenship* made accessible through a concrete toolbox of activities. This practical, hands-on approach will help higher education professionals conceptualize and develop equitable partnerships and successful global learning endeavors. This is an essential handbook for creating and sustaining community-based projects at home and abroad and will benefit seasoned and new practitioners alike."—***Ann Warner Ault***, *Assistant Professor of Spanish, Department of World Languages and Cultures, The College of New Jersey*

"A thoughtful, well-informed analysis of the promises and pitfalls of engaging in ethically sound community-based global learning. With examples and insights, the authors examine the core topics of good engaged pedagogy: learning objectives like global citizenship, reflection, intercultural communication, partnerships, and practical issues of implementing community-based global learning courses. Simultaneously applied, theoretical, moralistic, critical, and visionary, this book is a must-read for practitioners of not only community-based global learning but also community-based experiential learning."—***Robert G. Bringle***, *Chancellor's Professor Emeritus of Psychology and Philanthropic Studies, Indiana University-Purdue University Indianapolis*

"Grounded in development theory and fair trade learning principles, this book provides actionable strategies and tools for building meaningful community-based global learning programs in a variety of forms and within a variety of institutional frameworks. More importantly, however, the authors challenge us to think critically about our motivations for designing programs and push us toward a broader interrogation of higher education's role in championing peace and social justice and educating for social change. Bringing the same cultural humility we look to develop in our students, the authors encourage us to join them in cocreating a community of practice that advances the democratization of knowledge."—***Rachel Helwig***, *Director of Programs, Health & Safety, BCA Study Abroad*

"This book provides a useful definition of *community-based global learning* and ample evidence of its positive uses throughout the world. Through multiple examples, Hartman, Kiely, Boettcher, and Friedrichs prove that community-based global learning must be grounded in mutual respect for the learner. What's more, in their careful and meticulous descriptions of people involved in ethical engagement activities at home and abroad, the authors display the utmost respect for the learning process itself."—*Hilary Landorf, Executive Director, Office of Global Learning Initiatives, Florida International University*

"As a (global) service-learning scholar–practitioner located in the Global South, I am deeply gratified to read a book that is reflexive and aware of the inherent power dynamics in the practice of community-based global learning (CBGL) and in the understanding of global citizenship as a commitment to fundamental human dignity. There are many strengths to this publication. Most noteworthy for me is the idea that it is impossible to be a development agency without a theory that directs action to the underlying causes of underdevelopment. If universities are partnering with development agencies in CBGL, then aren't they taking on the role of a development agency, thus needing a theory of development as institutions? This is a profoundly new way of thinking about the university and its role in a broader sociopolitical context. In this way, the book makes visible many invisible processes, inequities, and positionalities—all of which without critical, thoughtful reflection, can contribute to reinforcing Global North-South divides. The text—which is both practical and theoretical (an achievement in itself)—should be required reading for anyone interested in the practice of CBGL and the role of universities in international education, global citizenship, and social justice."—*Janice McMillan, Associate Professor and Director, University of Cape Town Global Citizenship Program*

"This is an important book on community-based global learning. The authors, all leading thinkers and practitioners in the field, have written a unique volume that sits at the intersection of theory and practice and thus will be of immense value to both practitioners and scholars. Perhaps most importantly, this volume uses an informed critical lens and does so in a way that will not paralyze practitioners who seek to do this work but will instead free us to do it better."—*Eric Mlyn, Peter Lange Executive Director of DukeEngage; Assistant Vice Provost for Civic Engagement, Duke University*

"The authors invite readers to reimagine global service-learning through a lens of community-based global learning (CBGL), and they do this by putting criticality at the center. This book creates a space for the tension that CBGL educators and practitioners confront and experience when engaging in global community-based learning programs. It offers strong theoretical insights and practical tools to go deeper with our students and ourselves, especially as it relates to reflective practices and intentional program design. It's a strong resource for doing CBGL with critically reflective intentionality."—*Marisol Morales*, *Vice President for Network Leadership, Campus Compact*

"While we continue to debate the relative merits of two physically 'distanced' and generic models of education—the first is safely sequestered within walled and gated campus compounds, and the second asks students to stare at flickering pixels for hours on end—Hartman and colleagues reveal a deep and transformative 'third way'—a way that invites a new generation of students and educators to learn in and with and for global communities. May their tribe increase."—*Richard Slimbach*, *Azusa Pacific University*

"Writing with deep knowledge, experience, passion, and conviction, Hartman and colleagues provide an essential resource for study abroad faculty, community engagement staff, or anyone wishing to engage in effective, ethical, cross-cultural service and learning. Their arguments and program examples, theoretically contextualized and practice focused, advance frameworks for integrating any discipline with global learning and achieving learning and assessment outcomes desired by universities. They attend to challenges of power, privilege, and positionality, which flow throughout this work, as well as safety and risk management. This book will become a classic in the field."—*Timothy K. Stanton*, *Senior Consultant/Engaged Scholar, Ravensong Associates*

"*Community-Based Global Learning* raises the bar on what it means to offer quality and responsible off-campus, community- and partnership-based programming in higher education. The authors achieve an impressive balance between reviewing foundational theoretical work and sharing instructive cases and numerous examples of approaches and resources that can be readily adapted and applied across diverse community and organizational settings."—*John G. Tansey*, *Executive Director, The Frank J. Guarini Institute for International Education, Dartmouth College*

"*Community-Based Global Learning* combines rich theoretical analyses and conceptual material with scenarios, practical examples, and toolboxes. Throughout the book, the authors advance the scholarship in critical development studies and global citizenship education in a profound, yet accessible, way. The result is a highly effective facilitator's guide for developing students' global competency skills, critical reflection, cutting-edge learning experiences, and lifelong reflection, while simultaneously challenging us to reimagine the role and impact of institutions of higher education."—*Rebecca Tiessen, Professor and University Chair in Teaching, School of International Development and Global Studies, University of Ottawa, Canada; Author of* Learning and Volunteering Abroad for Development *(Routledge, 2018)*

"This is an essential book for community-based global learning practitioners and scholars at all levels. The authors effortlessly make the case for ethical community-based learning in global contexts while providing tools for campus-based leaders to ensure ethical engagement and appropriate preparation for students before they enter a community. This is an ideal book for communities of practice focused on community-based global learning, campus-based education abroad, service-learning, and global service-learning. The book would also be a great spark to encourage interaction and concrete connections on individual campuses between international offices or centers and service-learning or civic engagement centers. It is the new primer for engaged learning in a global context."—*Dawn Michele Whitehead, Senior Director for Global Learning and Curricular Change, Office of Integrative Liberal Learning and the Global Commons, Association of American Colleges & Universities (AAC&U)*

COMMUNITY-BASED GLOBAL LEARNING

COMMUNITY-BASED GLOBAL LEARNING

The Theory and Practice of Ethical Engagement at Home and Abroad

Eric Hartman, Richard Kiely, Christopher Boettcher, and *Jessica Friedrichs*

Foreword by *Rafia Zakaria*

STERLING, VIRGINIA

Published by Stylus Publishing, LLC 22883 Quicksilver Drive
Sterling, Virginia 20166-2019

Library of Congress Cataloging-in-Publication-Data
Names: Hartman, Eric, 1976- author.
Title: Community-based global learning : the theory and practice of ethical engagement at home and abroad / Eric Hartman, Richard Kiely, Christopher Boettcher, Jessica Friedrichs.
Description: First edition. |
Sterling, Virginia : Stylus Publishing, 2018. |
Includes bibliographical references and index.
Identifiers: LCCN 2017056046 (print) |
LCCN 2018011351 (ebook) |
ISBN 9781620360897 (Library networkable e-edition) |
ISBN 9781620360903 (Consumer e-edition) |
ISBN 9781620360873 (cloth : alk. paper) |
ISBN 9781620360880 (pbk. : alk. paper)
Subjects: LCSH: Community education. | Community and school. |
Service learning.
Classification: LCC LC1036 (ebook) |
LCC LC1036 .H37 2018 (print) |
DDC 371.19--dc23
LC record available at https://lccn.loc.gov/2017056046

13-digit ISBN: 978-1-62036-087-3 (cloth)
13-digit ISBN: 978-1-62036-088-0 (paperback)
13-digit ISBN: 978-1-62036-089-7 (library networkable e-edition)
13-digit ISBN: 978-1-62036-090-3 (consumer e-edition)

Printed in the United States of America

All first editions printed on acid-free paper
that meets the American National Standards Institute
Z39-48 Standard.

Bulk Purchases
Quantity discounts are available for use in workshops and for staff development.
Call 1-800-232-0223

First Edition, 2018

CONTENTS

FOREWORD

In 2014, I wrote an article titled "White Tourist's Burden" (Zakaria, 2014) that detailed my frustrations about well-intentioned but self-absorbed White westerners going into areas of the developing world with the intention of "helping" communities. The deliberate embrace of poverty and discomfort, I noted, had become a sort of virtue-signaling through which those who partook could say to others of their kind that they were better, more altruistic, nobler, so to speak, than others who opted for beach vacations where they lazed about. Pictures of the hapless Brown and Black impoverished people they helped were splashed across their social media, and some even made formal presentations to their friends, family members, and educational institutions. They had, in turn, become "inspiring"; the people they helped, of course, were just props in the process, often unnamed, the details of their lives and poverty exposed to the world often entirely without their consent.

I was writing then about adult *voluntourists* who took breaks from jobs and otherwise hectic first-world lives to engage in this kind of experience, but I knew that the operative moral logic, with its attached condescension and self-serving flavor also applied to international student programs. In many of these programs, some operated by elite colleges and universities, students were taken to countries in Africa or Asia or Latin America, where they would engage in a project often of their own devising and unconnected to the needs of the community. Once there, self-absorbed students would undertake this project, the schoolhouse or the latrine trenches or the well, while locals watched. Then they would leave, armed with self-congratulatory tales; many, many pictures; and a story they could tell at parties for the rest of their lives.

I did not include student groups engaging in service-learning abroad in my article because I was afraid that such a critique could have the effect of throwing the baby out with the bathwater, convincing an increasingly globally unengaged American student population that, since they could make a mess of things, they should do nothing at all. What they *could* learn, and the potential that they had to make things actually better, would not hold sway and the entire endeavor would be abandoned altogether. The entire forum for meaningful exchange thus could or would be discarded based on the premise that it could not be improved. I knew that global service-learning could be improved, but I could not articulate what the steps would be. It was a dilemma with vexed strands that I wanted very much to disentangle but could not figure out how.

This book, penned by the inimitable Eric Hartman, Richard Kiely, Christopher Boettcher, and Jessica Friedrichs, is the answer to all the vexing questions that I confronted. In *Community-Based Global Learning: The Theory and Practice of Ethical Engagement at Home and Abroad*, the authors, all of whom have extensive experience in administering and running study-abroad programs, lay out, piece by careful piece, how an ethical basis of engagement between two markedly different populations can be made fruitful and positive for both. While some forms of service-learning, such as working with children at orphanages and preprofessional medical service-learning by undergraduate students, are always wrong, almost all others can be structured and prefaced by classroom learning to enable both sides to learn.

The value of this volume is the care it takes in explicating the theory, the larger ethical universe, in which we all operate, and applying it to the dynamics of the service-learning encounter. It does not shy away from the problematic moments, such as when a community leader asks a team of newly arrived students and professors what exactly they mean by *community development* and what exactly the youth of this community would get from hanging out with a bunch of privileged kids from America.

There are, however, many reasons for hope, many ways of restructuring programs and ensuring there is attention paid to both sides, the students and the receiving community; the very reformulation of the operative terms *global service-learning* as *community-based global service-learning* reflects this ethic. The task of structuring a program can be daunting for even the most committed professors and administrators, but the care this book takes in presenting a thorough and step-by-step approach, never leaving the larger theoretical concerns behind, illustrates how it can be done and that it can be done well. As Hartman shows in one example, a student trip can become the basis of an evaluation that can facilitate the community's access to funding from the United States Agency for International Development; good things are indeed possible, but nothing good comes without effort.

Discarding engagement and global service-learning because it is hard, because it requires care and extra work, in compassion and in consideration, in theory and in practice, in arrangement and in execution, is easy. Grabbing the conundrums by the horns, insisting that engagement is more than taking pictures or setting up the poor as props is hard to do, but, as this book proves with such acuity, it is something that can definitely be done.

Rafia Zakaria
Columnist, Dawn (Karachi)
The Baffler

ACKNOWLEDGMENTS

With Deepest Gratitude: A Book Is Done

When did this book first emerge? Certainly not when I sent in the formal proposal. I have deep gratitude for the many muses named in this section and numerous collaborators not named here. In 2006, I copresented with Richard Kiely, Jessica Friedrichs, and Christopher Boettcher at an Amizade–West Virginia University (WVU) global service-learning institute in Oglebay, West Virginia. At the end of the multiday retreat, Kimberley Colebank, then the director of civic engagement at WVU, pointed her finger in our direction, circling the four of us and searching for words, "You all . . . you all . . . you all need to write a book about this." That was the first moment I felt confident that a book might emerge through our work.

But the formative learning came much earlier. In 2001 I was in Pittsburgh, Pennsylvania, looking for work at the intersection of political inquiry and civic practice. Michael Sandy, then executive director of Amizade, took me on as a volunteer, then an hourly employee, then a full-time staff member. That office was where I met Jessica Friedrichs and Christopher Boettcher, both of whom have become lifelong friends. Every day, one way or another, we worked on connecting Amizade's original ethos as a community-driven cross-cultural volunteering program with the insights of the civic education landscape and the contributions of scholars and activists working to advance global citizenship and ethical engaged learning.

It was not in the office or in the classroom, however, that most of the central ideas in this book were born. Matthias Brown in Petersfield, Jamaica, leveraged his role as the founder of a community development organization to envision an approach to global learning partnerships that would come to be known as Fair Trade Learning. Along with Brown, a vast network of community organization leaders taught all of the authors a great deal about walking humbly and with openness to others; diverse ways of being and knowing; and the hard work of attempting to build more inclusive, just, and sustainable communities.

These contributors and collaborators are quite literally too numerous to name, but some of the carriers of kindness include Patrick Sandoval and Sharron Etcity of the Navajo (Diné) Nation; Wayne Goutermont, JoLynn Sharrow, and Patrick Hoppe of Gardiner, Montana; Joseph Sekiku and Juma Massisi of Kayanga, Tanzania; Billy Kane and Derick Wilson of Northern

Ireland; Jean Carla Costas of Bolivia; and, of course, Dan and Geli Weiss of Brazil. Dan Weiss founded Amizade and sparked this network in 1994. Several faculty members, instructors, and facilitators also played key roles "from the inside" in ensuring that Amizade and our work were never co-opted by institutional and bureaucratic logics. Deep thanks to David Brumble, Monica Cwynar, Monica Frolander-Ulf, Reinhard Heinisch, and Jen Saffron for their insights and commitments. None of this work at and through Amizade would have been possible without a continuously dedicated and dynamic office staff, including—at different times—Marcedes Minana, Rebekah Harlan, Katie Baucco, Anna Ciaccio, and Sarah Orgass. Amizade students and interns have deeply influenced our work and thinking, sometimes quite formally, as in the case of Chad Martin, who rose from student to intern to program facilitator, board member, and finally board chair.

Richard Kiely also began his journey with this work in 1994 with a collaboration between Tompkins Cortland Community College (TC3) and Puerto Cabezas, Nicaragua. Richard extends his appreciation to Donna Nielsen and Paula Moore, professors of nursing at TC3, and Earl Bowie, Puerto Cabezas community leader and pastor, along with an extensive network of community collaborators, all of whom have sustained a vision for social change in Puerto Cabezas that continues to inspire and deliver quality community-driven partnership work. Their lifelong friendships and mentorship have led him on a deep personal and intellectual journey that has sparked numerous contributions to this field.

In 2003 Chris Boettcher and I presented at the International Association for Research on Service-Learning and Community Engagement in Salt Lake City, Utah, where Richard was presenting some of the many lucid concepts in his dissertation, including an articulation of transformational learning in global service-learning and the notion of the chameleon complex. We knew immediately that we and Amizade would benefit from more collaboration with Richard, and we were thrilled when he accepted Michael Sandy's invitation to present at Amizade's retreat for global service-learning instructors and facilitators later that winter. The community gathered at that rural retreat center was inspiring and included Lina Dostilio, Karin Cotterman, Joseph Croskey, and several other folks who have continued to advance ethical and inclusive work in higher education. I have been fortunate to have Richard as a friend, colleague, and mentor ever since.

In the fall of 2004, I enrolled as a doctoral student in the University of Pittsburgh's Graduate School of Public and International Affairs (GSPIA). GSPIA proved to be a place that offered me significant training in development studies; human rights thinking; and critical, participatory perspectives, while also allowing me the freedom to develop a wide-ranging, interdisciplinary dissertation on the topic of ethically educating for global citizenship. Paul Nelson and (upstairs, in political science) Michael Goodhart were both instrumental in my journey there and in the years that followed.

As I was writing my dissertation, Michael Sandy moved on from Amizade, and I was honored to find myself in the executive director role. Following three years as executive director of Amizade, I stepped down, supremely confident that Brandon Blache-Cohen, the person I hired as chief operating officer, would steward the organization to new heights as its fourth executive director. He most certainly has. I left for love, following Shannon Wheatley to Arizona State University (ASU), where she was a lecturer in political science and I was able to find a role in global studies. This continuous movement between scholar and practitioner roles is foundational in my worldview and critical to the genesis of this volume.

On January 18, 2011, from an ASU e-mail address, I sent a proposal to Stylus Publishing, imagining a book that would convey what colleagues and I had learned about community-based global learning through research and practice, from community, individual, nonprofit, and university perspectives. Since that proposal was submitted and accepted, I have lost both parents; gotten married to Shannon Wheatley Hartman; served in visiting, tenure-track, and administrative positions in higher education at diverse institutions all across the country; and—with all credit and gratitude to Shannon—become the father of two extraordinary daughters.

There is a great deal of change and transition, as well as sources of steadiness in the preceding paragraph. Some of the transitions are relevant to this volume. Though I now work at one of America's leading liberal arts institutions, I have also worked at rural and semi-urban Flagship R1 institutions, a community college, a private master's institution, and anchor institutions in urban environments. My coauthors also represent extraordinary institutional diversity. What our work reveals is that it is not institutional type or student population that matter here. What matters is the existence of a critical mass of campus and community collaborators who are committed to working through shared inquiry and action with integrity and coleadership. Professionally, I have been fortunate to be part of several such sustaining networks.

In addition to formative work with Amizade, I had the opportunity to serve as a visiting professor for two years in Providence College's (PC) global studies program. Drawing on several years of foundational work that Rick Battistoni, Keith Morton, Joe Cammarano, and others put into building the first public and community service studies major in the country, Nick Longo and Nuria Alonso Garcia now work with other collaborators to advance a community-engaged, local and global, four-year global studies experience. Those two programs at PC stand out as programs that have clarified how community-based learning and collaboration can become part of institutional fabric and institutional commitments. It was through one such commitment that I was fortunate to work with Michelle Carr on a campus–community oral history collaboration that celebrated Rhode Island's diverse and inclusive community.

I left PC for a tenure-track role in the Staley School of Leadership Studies at Kansas State University. Remarkably, the Staley School works with nearly 1,000 leadership studies minors from across the institution. They work with anthropologists and engineers, biologists and business majors, in an interdisciplinary space dedicated to better understanding personal leadership roles and responsibilities in a manner that fosters more diverse and inclusive communities. The Staley School showed me an impressive model for reaching high numbers of students, carefully and intentionally, across disciplines, backgrounds, and perspectives. With deep thanks to the leadership of Mary Tolar and Trisha Gott, as part of the Staley School's first Leading Change Institute, I was able to convene practitioners and scholars from around the world in a weeklong dialogue on ethical partnerships, a dialogue that has continued to spark publication, collaboration, and application. It would not have been possible without the support and collaboration of Lori Kniffin, as well as several dynamic and insightful students, including Hannah Carlgren, Olivia Harding, Nicole Kraly, and Garrett Wilkinson.

Even as this book was proposed, Richard Kiely and I were talking about ways to put portions of it online. Those ideas were the genesis of globalsl, which now operates as an online knowledge hub and multi-institutional network. It is a network of individuals who are relentless in their efforts to responsibly leverage higher education resources to support social change advancing more inclusive and sustainable communities. Through that network I have worked with and learned from Jessica Evert, Brian Hanson, Ben Lough, Florence Martin, Anna McKeown, Janice McMillan, Eric Mlyn, Amanda Moore McBride, Nora Reynolds, Rachel Tomas Morgan, Richard Slimbach, Cynthia Toms, Rafia Zakaria, and many other inspiring innovators.

Today, I am grateful to serve as executive director of the Haverford College Center for Peace and Global Citizenship, a campus-wide center dedicated to fostering ethical global learning since 2000. As this book goes to publication, we have just completed an interactive, inquisitive, inspiring, and intellectually stimulating symposium on Seeking Global Citizenship. We were fortunate to gather for more than a week with visionary community-based leaders and social change makers with whom the college has partnered for several years and sometimes more than a decade. Though we had never all met together in person before, we now see one another's strengths, stories, and depths of complexities in a way that would have been impossible without sustained and diverse forms of being in real, person-to-person community with one another.

I have certainly failed to name individuals who have been instrumental in my growth in this work. I imagine that the amount of life lived and lost in the seven years from proposal to publication makes writing acknowledgments especially difficult.

As coauthors, we wish to honor and remember a friend who was our first external reader, Susan Hicks. Susan was killed by a vehicle as she commuted home on her bicycle. She was a dedicated international educator and careful collaborator. She was thoughtful and humane and filled with exuberance for a life well lived. Her review restructured this book and made it better.

I suppose nearly everyone who completes a book must view his or her project as a unique product of community support, with deep thanks to broad networks of persons near and far, sped and slowed by the quotidian and critical moments of life and death. But I have tried to name the kindnesses and collaborators who have sustained me and us in this life and work.

Any successes I can claim track back to my good fortune of an extraordinary family, led by a mother and father who believed in the fullest potentials of their children, held them to high standards, and—at every stage—seemed to find ways to love and nudge forward without smothering. With my brothers and our wives—and in the case of our father, along with Andie, our half-sisters, and their families—we were able to share our love and thanks with our parents before they left. This will forever be one of the things for which I am most grateful. Without the confidence and drive instilled in me by my parents, I have a hard time imagining this book emerging as it did. That they each managed to live full lives and be good parents is something I appreciate more and more every day, and I am thankful to have in Shannon a partner who embodies deep love for our children, intellectual curiosity and playfulness, and compassionate commitment to all persons.

This book is, at best, one stepping stone on a journey toward a version of higher education that is more clearly supportive of the cocreation of just and sustainable communities. Critics will find flaws in it, as do I, on rereads and reconsiderations. These flaws sit with me, of course, more than anyone else. But I am grateful for the opportunity to present this work in this way, and thankful to Stylus Publishing for that opportunity. As we move forward together, my hope is that readers will engage critique in the spirit of steady, loving confrontation (Martin Luther King Jr's articulation of nonviolence), so that we may all continue to see one another and collaborate with one another in this shared journey toward more just possibilities.

Eric Hartman
Haverford College Center for Peace and Global Citizenship
April 2018

PHOTO ACKNOWLEDGMENTS

In the center, DukeEngage independent project student Alex Saffrit collaborates with a community member, Moses, in Nkokonjeru, Uganda, on a solar cooker project (© DukeEngage).

Clockwise from top left, MUDELFU Women's Cooperative President Araceli del Carmen Bonilla Hernandez (left) and Foundation for Sustainable Development intern Ellen Duvall (right) cooperate to advance sustainable, community-driven development in Tola, Nicaragua (© Foundation for Sustainable Development).

Community maintenance leader Ernesto Alaniz, Villanova University civil engineering student Allie Braun, and Water for Waslala program manager Iain Hunt cooperate to inspect a new water tank near Santa Maria Kubali, Nicaragua (© Water for Waslala).

Women's Emancipation and Development Agency (WOMEDA) executive director Juma Massisi (seated, center) facilitates conversation among women and Amizade students in Kayanga, Tanzania, as part of research that supported a successful United States Agency for International Development grant award for WOMEDA (© Eric Hartman).

DukeEngage students Jeline Rabideau and Jenny Denton work with middle school girls, such as Katie, in western North Carolina to enhance literacy skills through digital storytelling projects focused on their families (© DukeEngage).

The Challenge and the Journey

In the Navajo Nation, a sociology professor visits from the East Coast with her students. Her relationships in the community extend back many years. She is a longtime friend of the first person to receive tribal permission to write down the Diné (Navajo) creation story. As the program begins, two of her friends from the community lead classes. Natalie[1] instructs the students in Diné language learning. Karen shares her life story. It includes her personal experience of involuntary sterilization, a widespread experience for Native American women through the 1960s and 1970s (Lawrence, 2000), as well as participation in the American Indian Movement (AIM). The students are confused. They are rendered speechless by the landscape, a deeply troubling lens on recent and distant American history, and the attempt to understand the importance of extended family, nonlinear time, and the protection of the four mountains. They struggle; they grow. They see the Milky Way stretching across the southwestern desert sky. When they return to their East Coast communities, they fulfill the request made of them by several community members and nonprofit partners as they make presentations about Diné history, The Long March, and the many kinds of beauty still present in the Navajo Nation today.

A public health program in rural Tanzania joins two Tanzanian students with two U.S. students to investigate public health policy challenges. The teams present sustainable health policy options after a month of inquiry. During that time, faculty members guide them through systematic reflection on high-performing cross-cultural teams and the role of public health in resource-limited communities. Following the policy presentations, the students engage in direct service with local public health education efforts. In another part of Tanzania, a similar program draws on faculty and student presence to support a women's rights organization through a program evaluation. The organization uses the resulting evaluation as part of a grant application with the United States Agency for International Development (USAID), thereafter receiving USAID funding.

Near Philadelphia, students enroll in a course focused on cosmopolitanism, migration, and political action. Throughout the semester, the instructor guides them through engagement with various theoretical approaches to cosmopolitan thought, while also offering opportunities to meet with and learn from a variety of regional advocates for migrant rights. Even as the antimigrant rhetoric of the Trump administration continues unabated, students learn from representatives of the New Sanctuary Movement, *Puentes de Salud* (a Philadelphia-based public health initiative serving undocumented persons), and a husband–wife team who have made their prominent restaurant business a rally point for migrant rights activism. As the semester closes, students prepare for winter break travel that will include opportunities to learn from a migrant-serving organization in Mexico City, *La Casa de los Amigos*; visit Puebla, one of the primary sending communities for Philadelphia's Mexican population; and learn from human and migrant rights activists working at the U.S.–Mexico border. Their course is designed as an early introduction to later opportunities to intern with migrant rights organizations during summer breaks or to further focus their studies around rights and migration.

A group of adults signs up for a continuing education experience guided by a community-based organization. They help with historical preservation near the Holocaust death camp known as Auschwitz. Their volunteer service entails physical labor supporting preservation, but the broader goal is to promote remembrance and make real the cry: "Never again." A U.S. World War II veteran and the grandson of a survivor are both participants. This is the veteran's first return to Europe. It is the grandson's first experience of the historical sites of a death camp. This program is challenging for everyone. The physical service accompanies a learning experience that is profoundly unsettling and painful. The group facilitator leads structured dialogue about common human dignity and thoughtful approaches to consequential action. She pulls the group members from a disposition of overwhelming horror to a consideration of their past and present roles in stopping genocide. The veteran leaves the program saying he understands more about his military service now, early in the twenty-first century, than he ever had before. The grandson leaves with a renewed vigor to end contemporary crimes against humanity.

In Rhode Island, students in an introductory global studies course find a considerable portion of the course focuses on human migration as a global phenomenon. While holistically studying migration, they learn about local immigration through presentations from Welcoming Rhode Island, a non-profit with a mission that includes "bridging the divide between foreign-born newcomers and U.S.-born Rhode Islanders" (www.welcomingri.org/about-us). They learn they will conduct structured interviews with local migrants, asking about their lives before migration, during migration, and now in Rhode Island. An oral historian visits the class to provide an orientation to the process. At the end of the semester, Welcoming Rhode Island facilitates a celebration dinner. Local businesses donate food, local elected representatives visit the event—including Governor Chaffee—and the new Rhode Islanders are recognized through student presentations and certificates of welcome from the state legislature. In anonymous feedback after the course is completed, participating students report strongly positive experiences, with several students explicitly admitting they moved from negative to positive views of migrants broadly understood. Students from families who have migrated in recent generations feel safer sharing their experiences and insights in class. The collected histories are gathered online and periodically appear around the state as part of public art installations (Welcoming Rhode Island, 2017).

A political scientist and an English professor agree to lead service-learning programs in Bolivia through a nonprofit partner organization. Neither instructor has been to Bolivia, but the political scientist's area of expertise is Latin American politics, and the English professor specializes in indigenous literature. They work with a trusted organization with a strong track record in facilitating programs for universities. The political scientist is thrilled as he and his students meet in person with the head of the Coca Growers' Union, Evo Morales, who several years later becomes president of Bolivia. The English professor finds that many of her assumptions about indigenous communities, class, and Evo Morales are challenged through conversation and dialogue with Bolivians. She and her students leave with a substantially more robust sense of the diversity and nuance in both indigenous life and Bolivian life. Both courses support the construction of a rural elementary school through direct physical service and material donations during the students' time in Bolivia.

A rural Jamaican community implements a model of community-based tourism in partnership with multiple international volunteer and learning organizations based in the United States and Europe. Soon the community finds itself overrun with visiting high school and college students who set bad examples for the community youth and abuse the community's hospitality. The community stops the program. Years later, it skeptically partners with a global service-learning effort. The community begins hosting visitors again, but this time only those visitors engaged in community-driven service-learning and volunteer projects are welcomed. As the partnership deepens, the council of host families dialogues with its U.S. partners and decides that it will democratically determine compensation rates for homestays. Increasing numbers of visitors come, providing a sustainable revenue stream for host families while also offering a cross-cultural service-learning experience for community members and visitors. The initiatives lead to an improved annual summer camp, supplemental tutoring for many local children, an updated community center and community garden, and much more.

What do these examples have in common? Learning is community based, applied, reflective, connected, visceral, integrative, and engaged; it is locally contextualized, historically informed, and theoretically grounded. Participants cross many borders: political, cultural, socioeconomic, environmental, and national. They undergo disruptive experiences that often trigger a reevaluation of closely held assumptions and understanding. They are guided through this disruption[2] through reflective learning experiences with skilled facilitators. Community organizations have a clear role, relationship, and voice in designing the learning and—if applicable—development or service initiatives participants undertake. Any such experiential or community-based initiatives are enabled and strengthened through processes that grow depth of relationships and mutual understanding, enabling participants to more clearly see one another's worldviews and experiences. All of the relationships are informed by a deep and abiding respect for individuals and communities, along with an imaginative orientation toward future possibilities. The initially negative example from Jamaica points to the cultural humility, dialogue, care, and critically reflective practice that must support program design and evolving partnerships. These essential dimensions underpinning community-based global learning (CBGL) drive much of the rationale for this book.

We have gathered and developed theoretical insights and practical tools to support ethical global learning through community–campus partnerships like those we described earlier. We draw on research and insights from several academic disciplines and community partner perspectives, along with decades of applied, community-based development and education experience. We began this journey as university faculty and staff members engaged in what was then called global service-learning (GSL).

As will be clear throughout this book, we have strong roots in experiential learning and democratic education. Our original entry point for this work was through international and domestic community–campus partnerships advancing various approaches to community engagement and service-learning. Yet we also have theoretical and applied roots in international and community development and have come to see the ways in which many of these personal learning processes advance partnerships and outcomes from a community and international development perspective as well (Chambers, 2012; Farmer, Gutiérrez, Griffin, & Weiss Block, 2013; Korten, 1990). Furthermore, we have seen and appreciate many of the important critiques of a focus on "service" as opposed to learning, partnership, or community development. Our terminology has therefore evolved from *global service-learning* to *community-based global learning*, as well as *fair trade learning*, which will be discussed later in this book. While we moved away from the term *global service-learning*, we developed with it and recognize its location within existing fields of practice. Where sensible, on the basis of antecedents and field development, we continue to use *global service-learning*, albeit with heightened attentiveness to the ways in which the term itself may reassert hierarchies and call attention to existing inequities in terms of deficits rather than shared strengths.

It is not just the authors who have evolved their thinking in the nearly 15 years we have been working together. The fields of community engagement, service-learning, and international education, as well as their integration, have all developed rapidly—within an increasingly uncertain higher education landscape. Simultaneously, shared global challenges have become more evident, through growing migrant and refugee crises, widening inequity, ecological instability, and a terrifying nativism in many of the globe's most successful economies. This book is offered as one stone along the path that is the ongoing struggle to bring the best of higher education capacities into productive engagement with the grave challenges facing communities nearby and farther away. In many ways, this book emerged as a response to the questions presented by the increasing propensity of higher education institutions, at the dawn of the twenty-first century, to insist that they educate for global citizenship.

A basic interrogation of the concept of global citizenship reveals it to be a thorny, distant, and complicated ideal. Yet its aspirational qualities—that more of us in this world might learn to live well together, flourish, be in harmony with the environment that supports us, and be at peace in our profound and beautiful diversity—motivate this book. We see our work as practitioner-scholars not in the naming of a final theory of global citizenship but in the productive engagement of the processes, theories, habits, and partnership commitments that may support more educators, students, and citizens everywhere in the important journey of seeking global citizenship.

This volume includes functional tools, organizing tips, and aspirational challenges. We move from theoretically grounded teaching or partnership techniques that have worked well in previous programs and courses through engagement with Fair Trade Learning (FTL) principles that offer numerous challenging questions for higher education in its contemporary formulation, before closing with some imaginative engagement of what may be yet to come. Our field and our work will continue to evolve.

We write from local and more distant partnership insights in a variety of communities and with the lessons learned from extensive nonprofit and community organization work and service. Collectively, we have led courses and programs on six continents, scores of times, with a broad network of partners. Our strongest identities, however, are as people, humans, global citizens if you like, engaged in fallible yet important efforts to build more equitable and sustainable communities. Although we have had rewarding experiences teaching globally engaged courses locally and internationally, for formal academic credit, we also realize that students, families, college and university staff members, faith groups, and nonprofit organizations frequently act independently to advance service and learning programs across boundaries. We hope to contribute to their work as well. Our hope is to support anyone who is interested in developing and leading ethical experiential learning opportunities that highlight our global interdependence.

International education, volunteerism, service-learning, and CBGL programs are robust with potential (Bringle, Hatcher, & Jones, 2011). They can positively affect communities (Irie, Daniel, Cheplick, & Philips, 2010), achieve broad community support for partnerships (Hartman, 2015c; Larsen, 2015; Toms, 2013), grow civil society networks and advance human rights norms (Lough & Matthew, 2014; Reynolds, 2014), and have transformative effects for students (Kiely, 2004, 2005, 2011; Monard-Weissman, 2003) who become more globally aware and more engaged in global civil society (Hartman, 2014a). Yet they are also packed with peril.

Some efforts to engage in GSL—or at least international volunteering— have been reckless, harmful, and rightly criticized (Arends, 2014; Ausland, 2010a, 2010b; Holligurl, 2008; Illich, 1968; Larsen, 2015; Madsen-Camacho, 2004; Zemach-Bersin, 2008). Clear evidence indicates that these poor forms of programming have negative impacts on vulnerable persons, including medical patients (Evert, 2014; Lasker, 2016) and children (Punaks & Feit, 2014; Richter & Norman, 2010); cement stereotypes (Arends, 2014; Hartman, 2017a; Nelson, 2010); and reinforce patterns of privilege and exclusion (Andreotti, 2014; Crabtree, 2008). Important criticisms will be considered and discussed in the chapters that follow. These dangers can be mitigated, however, through collaborative planning, design, and evaluation that advances mutually beneficial community partnerships, critically reflective practice, dialogue, thoughtful facilitation, and creative use of resources (Chisholm, 2003; Hartman, Paris, & Blache-Cohen, 2014; Jacoby & Associates, 2003; Kiely & Nielsen, 2003; Sandmann, Kiely, & Grenier, 2009; Stoecker & Tryon, 2009; Tonkin, 2004).

Our efforts reside at the intersection of theory and practice. We are conscious that the two are intertwined and profoundly dependent on one another. We represent the work of several different disciplines here, and we work to do so in a theoretically grounded and academically rigorous manner. Yet we do so—as you have already noticed from our language— while recognizing that we are embedded within a community of CBGL practice. Our individual backgrounds—as community activists, nonprofit staff members, committed CBGL practitioners, university administrators, scholars, and educators—give us a reflective practitioner's sensibility.[3] We are therefore working to apply an important set of ideals while retaining a critical disposition; our praxis takes place at the intersection of critical inquiry and consequential action. This book therefore includes ongoing theoretical discussion and attendant encouragement of dialogue and questioning. Yet it also offers numerous clear pieces of advice for readers who are interested in applying our best theoretically informed and empirically validated insights now.

Community-engaged learning and research embraces the decentering of authority and the democratization of knowledge and power (Chambers, 1997; Deshler & Grudens-Schuck, 2000; Freire, 2000; Greenwood & Levin, 1998) to create spaces where multiple and diverse stakeholders are better able to participate in dialogue on what it means to be a healthy, prosperous community. Our commitment to community-engaged learning leads us to explicitly encourage everyone interested in carefully and conscientiously cooperating in engagement and learning (even if not accredited) across culture and difference. This work will advance faculty members in their course design and leadership and strengthen CBGL activities that do not have an explicit academic connection. In this way we embrace the variety of promising cocurricular programs, such as alternative spring breaks or extended summer service and learning programs, that have emerged outside the domain of explicitly academic, course-based programming. A growing body of research and our collective experience suggest good programs have a common core of best practices (Bringle, Hatcher, & Jones, 2011; Hartman & Kiely, 2014b; Sumka, Porter, & Piacitelli, 2015).

Recent research in the field of international education has indicated that facilitation by trained and experienced faculty is better at advancing student intercultural learning than those same facilitation practices when peer led (Vande Berg, Paige, & Hemming Lou, 2012). Yet other research on alternative spring break programming (Niehaus & Crain, 2013; Sumka et al., 2015) has suggested that best practices in peer-led and peer-facilitated programs can clearly support student and community development to a greater extent than is true for student-led programs that lack such attentiveness to best practice. It is also clear that poorly run programs can cement stereotypes and burden community organizations (Arends, 2014; Nelson, 2010; Stoecker & Tryon, 2009).

The opportunity for positive impact weighed against the perils of poor community-based programming presents a challenge for all educators and practitioners. We hope that you will learn from our experiences, successes, mistakes, compiled research, and time on the ground in diverse communities. We also hope that you will contribute to the effort to build a shared resource base by cataloging your ideas and program examples online with globalsl .org, a website that amasses and mobilizes peer-reviewed research and tools to support partnerships for global learning and community development (Campus Compact, 2017a). Ultimately, we hope to inspire you to take up the following challenge: Engage these highly nuanced and complex processes with conscientiousness and care so that together we manage to do more collaborative good than unintended harm.

Real Risks: Cementing Stereotypes and Harming Vulnerable Populations

We write this book in part because we have seen so many disturbing attempts related to CBGL. Particular categories of international volunteering have emerged as practices that should never be engaged, such as orphanage volunteering and preprofessional medical volunteering. A global movement of child rights professionals has organized to stop orphanage volunteering, which is harmful to vulnerable children in numerous ways, including heightened risk of abuse, increased likelihood of institutionalization until adulthood, and repeated experiences of abandonment (Punaks & Feit, 2014; Rotabi, Roby, & Bunkers, 2016; van Doore, 2016). Similarly, a coalition of global health and medical professionals has emerged to stop uncredentialed volunteering in clinical health environments, a practice that puts patients at unnecessary, preventable risk (Lasker, 2016; Sullivan, 2016). (For a brief and accessible online explanation of these two phenomena, see Hartman, 2016b.) Other community-based programming can be harmful in ways that are more nuanced.

The first example is of a university program in which a faculty member offered a traditional classroom course on international economics, then simply went along for the ride with students as they were later immersed in nominal service in a Ghanaian community. The faculty member joined students in exciting experiences in tourist markets and in other areas where the economy was highly dependent on tourist activity, but the experience was not connected to explicit intellectual inquiry. Course members seemed to be merely tourists, and community members had yet another experience of unprepared and curious students visiting to take away ideas, experiences, and trinkets with very little direction, supervision, or mentorship.

With thoughtful planning, a similar course might be more rewarding for all participants. An economics professor involved in such a course could cooperate with community members and students to reflect on lived experience in that same region of Ghana. They might have, for example, talked together about how the popularity of microfinance, which was just beginning to enter the host community, affected rural farmers' position and opportunities in the global economy. Students, community members, and faculty members could have worked to better understand the ways in which popular development concepts affect community members locally. They could have, through these investigations, more deeply recognized their interdependence. Major global corporations and development agencies were setting up various kinds of microfinance schemes while this idea became more popular in the Global North. All partners could have cooperated to build opportunities for rural farmers to have stronger voices in relation to the global market forces and ideas that affect their lives. When well prepared for teaching and learning in evolving and dynamic environments, faculty members and student leaders are in a strong position to facilitate powerful learning opportunities that surface such profound interconnections and may even move to serve community-articulated needs and goals.

Preparation, commitment, and collaborative planning are essential across responsible partnerships (Kiely & Nielsen, 2003). A second example is of a school of public health engaging in ultimately irresponsible "relief" service-learning in Haiti following the 2009 earthquake. As it began its effort, the school did not triage in a way that allowed for consistent record keeping among patients. Beyond the initial poor beginning of this institution's service work, it pulled out of Haiti months in advance of its initial commitment with the government and communities. Professors and administrators sitting in some of the most reputable institutions of higher learning in the world must recognize that if they choose to expose their students to the learning opportunities that come with such efforts, their programs may also quickly become one of the primary relief agencies in particularly stricken or especially rural communities. We must be acutely conscious of how our students' learning opportunities affect the dignity and rights of all community members.

A third example is found at an institution in the northwest United States, where the director of a nearby youth enrichment program expresses only frustration toward the nearby university. She sees students stream by the building where she works every day. She sees the university's lofty claims about service on the local news. Every year she attempts to figure out how to cooperate with the institution's orientation in August and MLK Day of Service activities in January, which send more than 500 students into regional nonprofits and government agencies as part of each semester's "service plunge." On the same campus, hundreds of first-year students arrive every August with an interest in making a difference, but they frequently have trouble figuring out how to connect that desire with sustained activity.

These three broad examples illustrate real situations in which opportunities for mutually beneficial partnership were squandered. In the Ghanaian example, these kinds of missteps can leave students in the location of potentially unreflective travelers. They may have a new experience, yet allow themselves the luxury of skipping deep inquiry into our profound global interdependence, such as consideration of the roles that Global North ideological framing, market desires, and policies play in influencing Global South structures, opportunities, and limitations. In the Haitian example, the active steps to engage in "service" were performed ineffectively and abandoned early, clearly causing irreparable community harm. The third example, from the United States, represents an instance in a pattern of service-learning arranged on university timelines and without real engagement with community-driven desires or articulated needs (Stoecker & Tryon, 2009). In all cases, better preparation and program management would ensure improved outcomes for student learning, intercultural connection, and community development. This book provides faculty members, staff members, administrators, and student leaders with the theoretical and practical resources necessary to engage in responsible and effective CBGL.

Organization of This Book

This book is arranged around the CBGL components articulated in chapter 1. After reading chapter 1, you will be familiar with the central points, practical resources, literature, and debates that animate CBGL theory and practice. By writing this book and engaging in these practices, we are testifying through our actions and commitments that we believe the work can be done ethically and well. There are, however, numerous reasonable critiques of domestic and international volunteerism (if not necessarily CBGL) and their position within U.S. civil society (Eliasoph, 2013; Poppendieck, 1999) and international development discourses (Andreotti, 2014; Crabtree, 2008; Hartman & Kiely, 2014b; Sexsmith & Kiely, 2014).

We do not sidestep these important critiques but engage them throughout the book. After exploring the foundational component of global citizenship inquiry in chapter 2, we illustrate the ways in which the reflection and critical reflection literature structures our inquiry on all topics in chapter 3. Toolbox I.1 presents an overview of the book through reflective and critically reflective frames. These reflective frames are further elaborated in chapter 3.

Chapter 4 reviews what international education and related fields have contributed to better understanding students' intercultural experiences during the past half century of research. We share this context and how it intersects with power and critical reflection to suggest how your program may maximize your students' movement toward deeper intercultural learning and cultural humility.

TOOLBOX I.1
Anticipating the Book

Chapter Topic	Reflective Questions	Critically Reflective Questions
1: CBGL	What are your goals for the CBGL program you oversee or are developing?	In what ways will your or your institution's assumptions need to change in order to develop increasingly robust and equitable global learning opportunities for all stakeholders in your CBGL work?
2: Seeking global citizenship	What are your goals regarding global citizenship education?	How does the global citizenship discourse privilege Western notions of the human experience and marginalize indigenous worldviews?
3: Critically reflective practice	How will reflection support participants' cognitive learning and skill development? How should these activities be staggered before, during, and after the travel experience?	How can reflective practice privilege Western ways of knowing and provide opportunities for rationalizing existing injustices?
4: Intercultural learning and cultural humility	How can your group systematically learn from cultural differences and communicate well as visitors?	How does the intercultural competence discourse trivialize meaningful difference and relativize worldviews? What dominant cultural values, norms, and institutions are simultaneously taken for granted and oppressive? How do you resist dominant cultural norms that are harmful?

(Continues)

TOOLBOX I.1 (*Continued*)

Chapter Topic	Reflective Questions	Critically Reflective Questions
5: Community-driven partnerships	What is your theory of development, and how does it relate to your community partnerships, program planning, and course approach?	How has the development discourse constrained your ability to see assets and strengths in communities in the Global South?
6: Immersive CBGL program design	What CBGL model is most appropriate for your course or program?	How do existing models of experiential education privilege institutions and students over communities?
7: Planning for immersive global learning	How can you plan your course to maximize student learning?	How does your discipline privilege detached expertise and marginalize situational expertise and other community voices, historically and currently?
8: Health, safety, and security	What are the best practices to keep all program participants safe, healthy, and happy? How can you best prepare for uncertainty?	How does the liability discourse fortify existing privileges and ensure that programs focus on Western students' education first and foremost?
9: Stepping forward	How will the final portion of your CBGL process support participants' movement toward related learning and action?	How are you an active cocreator of your community, institution, and broader culture in ways that honor the integrity of all persons and make progress toward a more just and sustainable world?

Chapter 5 draws on planning, international development, public health, and service-learning literatures to explore best practices and common challenges in advancing community-driven development. We include insights applicable for direct service and labor (school or home building), professional services (developing a documentary, writing a strategic plan, tutoring, and supporting public health education initiatives), and community-based research (determining rates of disease, documenting local history, and measuring pollution rates in streams). The chapter closes with discussion of FTL and the ways in which it operates as a strategy for addressing the extraordinary inequity in which CBGL programs often take place. As the book proceeds, it builds on the theoretical foundations reviewed in the first five chapters to apply program and course planning insights throughout chapters 6 and 7.

Program models, institutional relationships, and program sustainability are considered in chapter 6. That chapter includes discussion of the policy environment in which immersive CBGL programs are developed, sustained, and evaluated. As has been demonstrated through our discussion and examples thus far, we engage all of this work through a global frame. Although we believe that partnership principles and pedagogy practices apply with equal relevance to domestic and locally proximate engagement, it is also clear that the act of immersive travel adds different preparatory and logistical challenges. These differences are most apparent in chapters 6, 7, and 8, which provide many planning and instructional tools that are primarily intended for individuals working through the challenges of immersive programs, though several of the techniques and strategies are helpful for locally rooted CBGL as well.

Chapter 7 addresses the reality of the immersive CBGL experience as unpredictable, unfamiliar, and especially dynamic. We advance a course structure that harnesses the typical flow of CBGL experiences. The structure we identify provides faculty members and program leaders with a clear framework through which to integrate any discipline or community engagement experience. The framework articulates a design process for advancing learning and assessment of outcomes typically desired by universities, including development of intercultural communication capacities, discipline-specific academic learning, enhanced commitment to global citizenship, and development of skills in critical reflection and dialogue.

We turn in chapter 8 to a concern that will make or break CBGL with any institution: safety. Particularly in regard to international programs, parents, spouses, children, and friends are curious and concerned about their loved ones who are traveling to distant places for global learning experiences. The seriousness of that should be apparent long before a crisis in which you talk with one of these loved ones from halfway around the world. We share best practices gathered from trusted institutions and provide several immediately applicable tips for keeping program participants happy, healthy, and safe.

In addition to the discrete topics explored in the chapters already mentioned, two strands are woven through the book. The first, deliberate learning, demonstrates how we work to continue to understand and evaluate the influence of specific program factors on participant and community member learning and outcomes. Second, the challenges of power, privilege, and positionality are omnipresent and inescapable. As practitioners of CBGL, we must continuously and honestly engage positionality if we hope to ameliorate some of the gravest repercussions of unconsidered assumptions and embedded privileges. This surfaces in our critical approach to global citizenship, our embrace of cultural humility, our understanding of critically reflective practice, and our approach to community-driven development through FTL. Although the chapters stand alone and focus on specific content areas in a conventional sense, CBGL is complicated, nuanced, and interdependent. It is a profoundly interdisciplinary arena for the integration of research and practice. Choosing chapter order therefore caused us considerable consternation. The whole of CBGL should become much clearer as each component part is added.

Chapter 9 weaves these components together in a discussion of the principles and practices that encourage healthy reflection, community connection, and ongoing learning after CBGL experiences. This process is about both reconnecting and reimagining. We therefore close with reflections on *what is* and imagine *what could be*. We consider how our institutions and assumptions may constrain collaboration, community development, and people-powered peace building around the world. We share steps we can all take, within our institutions and professional and personal lives, to not merely shake up perceptions once a year but be part of a growing transformative movement.

We insist we will not simply globalize but globalize ethically; we will not educate parts but engage whole people; we will not pass through communities as if they are simply dynamic laboratories but create collaborative partnerships that transcend traditional boundaries in order to build a better world together. We begin with an exploration of the community–campus contribution to engaged, embodied, cross-cultural, and community-driven learning in chapter 1.

Notes

1. Pseudonyms are used to protect anonymity throughout the book, unless otherwise noted.

2. There are many terms used to describe experiences that are incongruent with one's existing experience and frame of reference, including *culture shock, dissonance, disorienting dilemma, disjuncture,* and even *simply the experience of being outside of one's comfort zone* (see Kiely, 2005, 2011).

3. As will be clear throughout this book, we have all worked with numerous nonprofit organizations and institutions of higher learning. The work we have in common, however, has largely occurred through Amizade, a Pittsburgh-based nonprofit with a mission to "inspire empathy, catalyze social action, and link diverse communities through Fair Trade Learning" (Amizade, 2017). We have worked with Amizade as staff members, volunteers, board members, faculty leaders, and institutional partners during the tenures of three of the organization's four executive directors. We hold it in the highest regard as an organizational network steeped in a community-driven ethos from its founding in Brazil in 1994.

I

DEFINING *COMMUNITY-BASED GLOBAL LEARNING*

The Community–Campus Contribution

At the campus–community nexus, CBGL[1] developed partly as a social movement (Swords & Kiely, 2010), partly as a pedagogical innovation (Bringle & Hatcher, 2011; Crabtree, 2008; Green & Johnson, 2014; Kiely & Kiely, 2006; Tonkin, 2004), and partly as an approach to community-driven development partnerships (Hartman, Paris, & Blache-Cohen, 2014). To situate the conversation, we begin with two prominent definitions of *academic service-learning*. Kiely and Kiely (2006) drew on existing research to suggest,

> International service-learning[2] is a course-based form of experiential education wherein students, faculty, staff and institutions: (a) collaborate with diverse community stakeholders on an organized service activity to address real social problems and issues in the community; (b) integrate classroom theory with active learning in the world; (c) gain knowledge and skills related to the course content and advance civic, personal, and social development; and (d) immerse themselves in another culture, experience daily reality in the host culture, and engage in dual exchange of ideas with people from other countries.

More recently, Bringle and Hatcher (2011) suggested international service-learning is

> a course-based, credit bearing course or program (educational experience) in another country where students:
>
> - participate in an organized service activity that addresses identified community needs;
> - learn from direct interaction and cross-cultural dialogue with others;
> - reflect on the experience in such a way as to gain further understanding of course content, a deeper understanding of global and intercultural issues, a broader appreciation of the host country and the discipline, and an enhanced sense of their own responsibilities as citizens, locally and globally. (p. 19)

17

Both of these definitions reflect a commitment to campus–community part-nerships primarily through course-based service-learning in international, cross-cultural contexts. Alternatively, we do not preclude the possibility of extremely important, thoughtful, and productive learning and partnership across cultures absent academic course integration. The essential compo-nents of responsible CBGL apply as much to faculty-led university courses as they do to any group that wishes to engage in ethical cross-cultural learning and community-driven development.

In this text, unless we say otherwise, we are referring to accredited learn-ing experiences (Howard, 1998). Those readers advancing other efforts will find useful advice and resources in all chapters but may prefer to skim the sections on integrating academics. When we refer to other efforts, however, we should also make clear that we are referring to structured programming that meets accepted international education or volunteer sector standards for integrating community voice, preparing program participants, ensuring health and safety, and engaging volunteers in critical reflection (Comhlámh, 2014; The Forum on Education Abroad, 2018a; International Volunteer Program Association, 2016; Sumka, Porter, & Piacitelli, 2015), practices that are further discussed in the following section.

The close reader will have noticed that both Kiely and Kiely (2006) and Bringle and Hatcher (2011) chose *international* rather than *global* in their original definitions. We believe strongly that *global* is the appropriate term. We choose *global* because the implicit and sometimes explicit values of this global orientation express universalistic aspirations, such as acceptance of human dignity or respect and concern for others regardless of citizenship status. One need not, to put it another way, cross a national border to exer-cise ethical global engagement (Hartman & Kiely, 2014b, 2017; Longo & Saltmarsh, 2011; Sobania, 2015; Whitehead, 2015). Indeed, one of the man-ifestations of thoughtful global partnership is supporting local engagement with global issues. Such engagement offers opportunities to better under-stand the globally complex, interdependent nature of socioeconomic, politi-cal, and environmental challenges, including the ways in which local practices and policies may negatively affect others around the world (Cameron, 2014). In addition, faculty members and program leaders should encourage partici-pants to engage with local and national global justice advocacy after their return from experiences abroad.

We do not choose the language and conceptual framing of *global* simply because of the allusion to universalistic values of global citizenship, however. Many years of work with domestic and international service-learning pro-grams led us to recognize that much of the emphasis placed on intercultural exploration and exchange in international programs is necessary and relevant for domestic conversations, both on campus and in community–campus engagement. Thoughtful consideration of culturally contingent assumptions and growing understanding of oneself as a historically and culturally formed being is equally important on campus, in nearby communities, and farther away.

Student diversity is also rapidly increasing (Institute of International Education, 2016), a fact that brings more nuance and complexity to intercultural border crossing (Kiely, 2005) and increases the need for care, awareness, and self-reflexivity among faculty and staff (Willis, 2015). Our experience and broader research (Bringle, Hatcher, & Jones, 2011; Brownell & Swaner, 2009) suggest that all students profit considerably from learning about their own and others' cultural traditions and conceptions of service and how they affect the needs, interests, relationships, and outcomes of partnerships (McMillan & Stanton, 2014; Reynolds, 2014). The teaching, learning, and partnership processes shared here, therefore, are equally relevant for domestic programs, which may take the form of domestic immersion experiences; on-campus courses with local partnerships; global citizenship workshops and related activist opportunities; campus clubs; and much more.

We do understand that there are vital logistical and educational differences between immersive programs and courses that involve community engagement experiences between typical work and school obligations. In the latter case, participants experience much less disruption of expectations and assumptions because they may regularly retreat to the familiar comforts of home. Nonetheless, we follow a number of scholars of service-learning to note that such domestic practice can be profoundly antifoundational (Butin, 2008) and counternormative (Ash & Clayton, 2009; Howard, 1998; Whitney & Clayton, 2011). We argue that the experiential reflective practice that is central to CBGL extends the antifoundationalism of more conventional forms of domestic service-learning in that it provokes students to radically question additional contingent assumptions, including nationality and citizenship (Hartman & Kiely, 2014a, 2014b; Kiely, 2004). In this way, undertaking domestic engagement with a global framing may have an inherently disruptive, counterhegemonic quality, moving the civic education emphasis away from a national citizenship and toward questions of shared dignity and a shared planet (Hartman & Kiely, 2017; Korten, 1990).

Understanding domestic engagement within a global frame is increasingly widespread among individuals and institutions working to build inclusive and just communities (Alonso García & Longo, 2013, 2015; Battistoni, Longo, & Jayanandhan, 2009; Hartman & Kiely, 2014b, 2017; Longo & Saltmarsh, 2011). There has also been a shift toward cooperative engagement across local and international spaces in the field of study abroad and international education. In addition to the traditional focus on language and intercultural learning, problem-solving and civic engagement in the communities students visit have been identified as important learning outcomes (Deardorff & Edwards, 2013; Landorf & Doscher, 2015; Tiessen & Huish, 2014; Whitehead, 2015). Landorf and Doscher (2015) provided a more recent definition that represents the study abroad field's growing recognition of global learning as embracing collaborative learning and engagement with local and international communities. They referred to *global learning* as "the process of diverse people collaboratively analyzing and addressing complex problems that transcend borders" (Landorf & Doscher, 2015).

Numerous higher education associations and scholars based in the United States have been moving away from international lenses on the world and toward global and intercultural ways of thinking. The leading national association concerned with the undergraduate liberal education experience, the Association of American Colleges & Universities (AAC&U), has for several years focused specifically on social responsibility and integrative liberal learning in a global context. The AAC&U (2014) integrates key components of intercultural competence and civic development through its global learning rubric, where it suggested,

> Through global learning, students should (1) become informed, open-minded, and responsible people who are attentive to diversity across the spectrum of differences; (2) seek to understand how their actions affect both local and global communities; and (3) address the world's most pressing and enduring issues collaboratively and equitably. (p. 1)

Integration of intercultural competence or attention to diversity with a focus on individual actions and attention to pressing issues, along with the development of critical thinking, is also featured throughout *A Crucible Moment: College Learning and Democracy's Future* (National Task Force on Civic Learning and Democratic Engagement, 2012), a document prepared at the request of the U.S. Department of Education. Campus Compact is the leading U.S. association advocating that universities serve public, civic purposes. Campus Compact responded to *A Crucible Moment* with a policy brief calling for higher education institutions to, among other things, "advance a contemporary, comprehensive framework for civic learning that *embraces U.S. and global interdependencies*" (Campus Compact, 2012, p. 8, emphasis ours). Meanwhile, the AAC&U cooperated with NAFSA to develop *Global Learning: Defining, Designing, Demonstrating*, a publication that again emphasizes that twenty-first-century graduates must integrate local and global civic knowledge and engagement, intercultural knowledge and competence, and ethical reasoning and action (Hovland, 2014). Here and elsewhere (Hartman & Kiely, 2014b; Sobania, 2015; Whitehead, 2015), it is clear that theorists and civic actors are working to integrate the local and domestic aspects of global citizenship and learning (Hartman, Lough, Toms, & Reynolds, 2015).

Although the CBGL practices we outline in this book are informed by the respect for all persons inherent in global citizenship traditions, our understanding of global citizenship itself is also informed by applied community practice and critical theory (Andreotti, 2006; Cameron, 2014; Hartman & Kiely, 2014a). Writers increasingly have recognized the role of critical service-learning (Mitchell, 2008; Porfilio & Hickman, 2011; Yoder Clark & Nugent, 2011), critical study abroad (Reilly & Senders, 2009), and critical reflection and engagement (Kiely, 2015) in moving participants to see new pathways and possibilities rather than falling into old patterns and paternalism. By claiming the category of "critical global citizenship" (Hartman & Kiely, 2014a) described in the conclusion of this chapter and beyond, we are claiming support for common dignity and respect for every person, advanced within a critical awareness of ideology, hegemony, and unequal power relations (Brookfield, 2000).

Synthesizing the concepts we introduced previously, CBGL must thoughtfully integrate seven basic components: (a) community-driven learning and/or service; (b) development of cultural humility; (c) seeking global citizenship; (d) continuous and diverse forms of critically reflective practice; and (e) ongoing attention to power, privilege, and positionality throughout programming and course work. These first five components should be carefully integrated and facilitated to ensure (f) deliberate and demonstrable learning within (g) safe, transparent, and well-managed programs.

By increasing emphasis on community voice, critical reflection, and attention to the power and privilege that enable us to be CBGL practitioners— themes that will become clearer throughout this book—we suggest that CBGL[3] is a community-driven learning and/or service experience that employs structured, critically reflective practice to better understand global citizenship, positionality, power, structure, and social responsibility in global context. It is a learning methodology *and* a community-driven development philosophy that cultivates a critically reflective disposition among all participants.

CBGL frequently includes academic credit for study within a particular discipline that is deepened through integration of experiential learning and reflective practice. But it is neither the particular content area nor the accreditation that makes a practice CBGL. Rather, the seven components listed previously are the essential elements that may qualify a course, a student affairs program, or a community development initiative as CBGL. Specific institutions remain the arbiters of what kinds of learning experiences deserve academic credit.

Figure 1.1 depicts the diverse and essential components that compose quality CBGL practice. Some of the components, such as health and safety, refer primarily to logistical arrangements, whereas others draw heavily on concepts and theories from particular areas of scholarly literature, such as critical global citizenship, critical reflection and intercultural learning, community development, and power and privilege. Yet these logistical arrangements and theoretical and philosophical underpinnings all act on and influence one another through CBGL practice. Each element is essential in a unique way, and no one component can be said to be entirely dominant. Some of the elements overlap or blend into one another, like colors in a spectrum, but they all have distinct identities that ultimately form CBGL as a whole.

Figure 1.1 Components of CBGL.

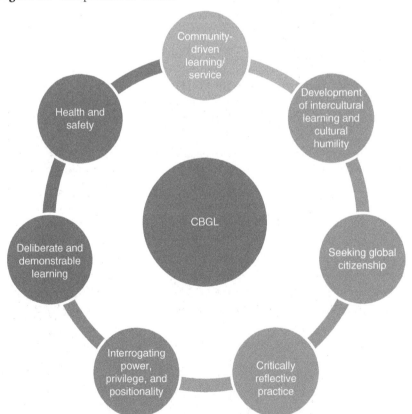

A Unifying Theme: Critical Global Citizenship

Through decades of work with CBGL, GSL, international education, community organizations, and political theory traditions, we have developed an understanding of critical global citizenship that serves as a unifying theme throughout our work (Hartman & Kiely, 2014b). We will return continually to consideration of critical global citizenship as this book proceeds, as it is both an object of intellectual inquiry and a motivating rational for our teaching, learning, and community partnership principles.

Community organizations, private travel and tour companies, and especially institutions of higher education claim to develop "global learners," "global leaders," and "global citizens." Yet this global learning or global citizenship is frequently undertheorized and often not even explicitly conceptualized. In *Assessing Global Learning: Matching Good Intentions With Good Practice*, the AAC&U asserted, "A large (and growing) number of liberal arts colleges specifically indicate in their mission statements that their graduates should be prepared to thrive in a future characterized by global interdependence" (Musil, 2006, p. 2). However, research on practices at 100 liberal arts colleges revealed that "there is little evidence that students are provided with multiple, robust, interdisciplinary learning opportunities at increasing levels of intellectual challenge to ensure that they acquire the global learning professed in mission statements" (Musil, 2006, p. 2).

More recently, Morais and Ogden (2011) noted that *global citizenship* is a term widely used in international education, but it is "rarely conceptually or operationally defined" (p. 445).[4] Apart from these conceptual inadequacies, several theorists have pointed out how dominant practices in study abroad (Reilly & Senders, 2009; Zemach-Bersin, 2008), international volunteerism (Nelson, 2010), and alternative travel and tourism (Higgins-Desbiolles & Russell-Mundine, 2008) serve to reify disturbing patterns of difference and inequity, against the ethos of common community implied by global citizenship assertions in each sector. Indeed, the term has been used so often it has been arguably emptied of meaning. Yet rich understandings of global citizenship exist (Andreotti, 2014; Andreotti & de Souza, 2008; Carter, 2001; Dower & Williams, 2002; Lewin, 2009).

There are two dominant strands of global citizenship theorizing in the philosophy and political theory literature: *moral cosmopolitanism* and *political cosmopolitanism* (Kleingeld & Brown, 2013). Moral cosmopolitanism insists on a global duty to support basic human rights and justice, whereas political cosmopolitanism attempts to imagine the structure of global political institutions that will uphold and guarantee such global ideals (Kleingeld & Brown,

2013). We are focused on thick approaches to moral cosmopolitanism (Cameron, 2014) where global learners develop their sense of agency not only as "do-gooders" but also as critical global citizens who at least attempt to "do no harm" and continually examine their complicity in, relationship to, and responsibility to address harm caused by others. Understanding and enacting critical global citizenship is no easy feat; international service and global citizenship efforts too frequently result in reinforcing inequities rather than decolonizing perceptions, advancing solidarity, and moving forward shared progress (Andreotti, 2014; Larkin, 2015).

As educators and community activists, we are interested in developing individuals' empathic capacities to see, appreciate, and commit to holding up the dignity of every person in common community as a lifelong endeavor. Just as is true in the human rights community (Donnelly, 2003), foundational rationales for this moral commitment to one another, and to cocreating communities that support individual and collective flourishing, may be less important than the commitment itself. Whether the commitment comes through rights-thinking (Donnelly, 2003), Ubuntu (Larkin, 2015), liberation theology (Farmer, Gutiérrez, Griffin, & Weiss Block, 2013), or another tradition entirely, we are interested in holding up that commitment and challenging ourselves to better understand what it requires of us as educators, learners, development professionals, and citizens. We are interested in understanding how that commitment leads us toward consequential action. And yet the roots of the commitment to common human dignity must also be considered and subjected to critical inquiry. As several scholars have observed, global partnership inquiry frequently sparks an "ontological project" (McMillan & Stanton, 2014) that advances inquiry into our ways of being and commonly held assumptions. As practitioner-scholars, we are both interested in the commitment to common dignity and to intellectual inquiry regarding the manner in which distinct traditions assume it and advance it.

As Richard Falk (2000) wrote, global citizens are like citizen pioneers on a journey to an as-yet unimagined tomorrow. We can build that tomorrow only if we can see how the dignity in each person (and, perhaps, our ecologies) requires us to reimagine our assumptions and recreate our organizing institutions. Against a popular discourse in which, for example, many news outlets recently referred to undocumented human beings simply as "illegals" or "illegal aliens" (the connotation here is that undocumented immigrants are not even human), we are encouraging an embrace of the dignity of every person. In times of war and conflict, we grieve all deaths and harm. We are enraged by structural violence that leaves children without access to safe water, food, shelter, health care, or the opportunity for basic education. We are equally angered by the cultural assumptions and structures of oppression that lead to a global pandemic of violence against women (Alter, 2014; Kristoff & WuDunn, 2009). Although we appreciate that many, if not most, people assert belief in human equality, the historical and contemporary record on that ideal moves us to inquire about better structures, consider alternative possibilities, and—most important—learn from and collaborate with individuals and communities who have been historically marginalized. CBGL pedagogy and partnership principles aim to elevate the concerns and insights of those who have been most negatively affected by dominant historical and cultural assumptions that undermine shared dignity.

Today, our policies often seem to be interpreted through a national rather than a cosmopolitan gaze. In respect to human migration, moving the dialogue to focus on responsibly managing flows of inherently dignified people would signal a radical departure from the current emphasis on keeping "our" borders safe and protecting "our" jobs. Considering global citizenship commitments in respect to unaccompanied children at the U.S.–Mexico border, Hartman (2015b) wrote, "It's not a question of efficaciousness (How can we most expeditiously process the minors at the border?). It's a question of ethics (How do we help the babes on our doorstep?)" (p. 79).

When people are undocumented or otherwise "othered," they become invisible. And when people are invisible, the voting public frequently fails to consider the effects of policies on those people. This is true whether the "invisible" person is making one's clothing halfway around the world, picking one's produce hundreds of miles away, or working in a coffee shop that one frequents every morning. The critical and cosmopolitan gaze combats invisibility by calling attention to the full humanity of each individual and challenging policies, practices, individuals, and institutions that dehumanize. Each person's dignity is a central organizing assumption (Kateb, 2014). This does not suggest that all cosmopolitans will or should think the same way about policy decisions or political preferences. It does suggest that there are cultural practices throughout the world that continuously undervalue many persons' inherent dignity, and these practices must be understood and addressed. We are on a journey to grow our and others' abilities to see the fullness in each person; this is the aspirational possibility presented by a critical global citizenship and CBGL.

When conceptualizations of global citizenship have been advanced, they have typically been foisted down from above rather than developed through grounded theory, ethnography, or practice (Crabtree, 2008; Hartman & Kiely, 2014b; Plater, Jones, Bringle, & Clayton, 2009). Our articulation of critical global citizenship, alternatively, is grounded in theory and informed by scores of dialogic partnership efforts to advance global learning, mutual respect, and community development (Hartman & Kiely, 2014a).

We largely agree with one of the most widely read theorists of global citizenship, Martha Nussbaum, while suggesting a different, more grounded, and critical lens. In *Cultivating Humanity*, Nussbaum (1997) called on universities in the United States to educate for world citizenship through emphasis on three commitments: common recognition of the value of human life, nurturing of empathy or the "narrative imagination," and something Nussbaum termed *critical distance*—the ability to recognize and analyze one's cultural biases and predispositions. Yet our research and experiences suggest Nussbaum has not gone far enough with her cultivation of critical distance (Hartman & Kiely, 2014a). Informed by critical traditions in adult education (Brookfield, 1995, 2000; Friere, 2000; Mezirow, 1991, 1995) and service-learning (Kiely, 2004, 2015; Mitchell, 2008; Yoder Clark & Nugent, 2011), as well as critical and postcolonial approaches to global citizenship education (Andreotti & de Souza, 2008), we embrace a deeper form of critical reflection, akin to what Burbules and Berk (1999) referred to as "criticality."

We emphasize criticality for two reasons. First, we are impressed by the increasingly strong and extensive literatures articulating the limitations of conventional forms of study abroad, service-learning, global development, and global citizenship theorizing. Study abroad has been labeled "instrumental, prosaic, and nationalistic" (Reilly & Senders, 2009, p. 251) in terms of its role in producing an elite mobile social class and advancing U.S. interests abroad (Kiely, 2011; Plater et al., 2009). International education has also been criticized for being increasingly commodified (Jenkins & Skelly, 2004), creating "colonial students" who want to be abroad to improve their career prospects and experience new cultures "in just the same way as new commodities are coveted, purchased, and owned" (Ogden, 2007–2008, p. 38).

In a related way, our research surfaces a concern that GSL is arguably more susceptible to the critiques leveled at "traditional service-learning," including that it can be patronizing and colonizing and that it can cement structures of power and privilege when, depoliticized, it serves simply as a "glorified welfare system" (Mitchell, 2008, p. 51). Many service-learning practitioners and researchers are rightly concerned by simplistic, charity-focused versions of service-learning that focus on individual relationships only, with no attention to broader systemic pressures (Hartman & Kiely, 2014b; Mitchell, 2008; Westheimer & Kahne, 2004). As these concerns have developed in the service-learning literature, they have advanced similarly in the alternative tourism and volunteerism literatures (Hammersley, 2014; Higgins-Desbiolles & Russell-Mundine, 2008) and scholarship in critical thinking and critical pedagogy. (See Burbules and Berk, 1999 for an excellent comparison and discussion of the concept of criticality.)

The second reason we emphasize criticality stems from our experiences working with diverse people, communities, and organizations around the world. Deeper criticality is required because students and faculty often work with community partners who, because of their positionality and lived experience, may understand the world in radically different ways. They often understand rationality, service, and community development through different frames of reference, according to different value systems, and in light of different beliefs. It is not enough to merely engage in a style of rational thinking premised on hundreds of years of Euro-American theorizing that has often viewed academia, philosophy, and insight as developing away from human interaction. Rather, we propose an embrace of a critical global citizenship that suggests substantially greater awareness of the continuously evolving and temporally and culturally contingent nature of concepts such as rights and citizenship (Donnelly, 2003). This critical global citizenship suggests an ongoing struggle aimed at questioning and transforming historical, linguistic, structural, cultural, political, economic, and institutional arrangements that cause harm and perpetuate inequality (Hartman & Kiely, 2014a). In this way, critical approaches to global citizenship draw on the critical reflection tradition to critique ideology, hegemony, and relations of power (Brookfield, 2000). Specifically, Brookfield (1995, 2000) and others (Kiely, 2005, 2015; Madsen-Camacho, 2004; Mitchell, 2008; Yoder Clark & Nugent, 2011) have used the term *critical* to indicate the essential role of examining power, ideology and hegemony, and agency-structure relationships and their relationship to any problem or social issue being discussed or acted upon in educational institutions and through service and learning contexts. Here too, CBGL is continuously engaged in an "ontological project" (McMillan & Stanton, 2014) that considers "what it means to be human and to be in relationship with an-Other" (Larkin, 2015, p. 256). And, importantly, in terms of one's moral obligation to advance equity and human and environmental rights, the cultivation of criticality in CBGL necessitates participants' deep epistemological shift in understanding "whose reality counts" (Chambers, 1997). In relation to the development of South–North partnerships, our embrace of criticality aligns with that of Larkin (2015), who asserted, "Without rebuilding global epistemologies, social justice will not be attained" (p. 254).

A critical approach to global citizenship is a commitment to fundamental human dignity, couched in a critically reflective understanding of historic and contemporary systems of oppression, along with acknowledgment of positionality within those systems; it connects with values, reflection, and action. Our critical understanding of global citizenship calls us all to humble, careful, and continuous efforts to build a world that better acknowledges

TOOLBOX 1.1

Considering and Contrasting International Education, Civic Education, and a Critical Global Citizenship

	International Education	Civic Engagement	Critical Global Citizenship
Purpose	Individuals able to function in a foreign nation in a variety of metrics (e.g., business skills, social interaction)	Educate citizens to fulfill civic obligations and build a more just national society	Promotion of the notions of equity, environmental justice, and fundamental human equality; critically understood in the context of efforts to collaboratively build a more just world
Knowledge	Utilized to learn customs, norms, and language and adapt to habits of host culture	Focus on institutional arrangements, citizen rights and responsibilities, democracy, rules, laws, and possibly pressing social issues	Emphasis on praxis, critique, and collaborative learning experiences to generate knowledge of sources and solutions to social and environmental challenges and focus on identifying and critiquing assumptions aimed at transformational learning
Questioning	Typically confined to consideration of home and host cultures' differing assumptions and how to navigate and adapt to those differences	Frequently not included; if included, often confined to justice-seeking within recognized state borders	Central to experience and analysis of how educational, social, institutional, cultural, political, and economic structures do or do not promote equity and the ethic of fundamental human equality
Culture shock, reverse culture shock, dissonance	To be processed to permit adaptation abroad and at home	Often not included	Vital learning moment; opportunity to examine distorted and harmful assumptions and work (an ongoing struggle) against unjust global realities

Emotion	Not typically included as part of learning process; emphasis is on cognitive understanding and communication skills	Connection with other citizens is emphasized and considered in light of civic responsibilities, duties, and national health	Embraced in connection with other individuals and emphasized and considered in light of concepts related to care, empathy, equity, human equality, reflection, and learning
Institutions and policies	Accepted for facility of travel, logistics, and exchange	Government institutions central as mechanisms to allow "our" public voice and governance	Questioned and considered in respect to their relevance to equity and human dignity
Spirituality and morality	Often not explored	Often not explored	Encouraged as part of dialogue on the integral nature of thinking, being, feeling, and doing
Core learning goal	Depth of knowledge in history, religion, culture, economic and political systems, social and international relations; skill and competency in language, observation, and cultural norms and practices	Responsible citizens with the knowledge, skills, and efficacy necessary to engage in debate on issues and participate in local, state, and national politics	Transformational learning that is critically reflective and dialogic and connects people who work toward a world that more clearly recognizes equity and fundamental human equality

every individual's basic human dignity; it also calls us to surface and address the historical and structural forces and factors that oppress and prevent the realization of dignified lives, experienced in diverse ways. Toolbox 1.1 provides a concise visual representation of the contrasts between our understanding of this definition of a *critical global citizenship* and particularly conventional forms of civic engagement and international education. There are exceptions to the patterns suggested in the toolbox, but we offer this table to provoke thinking and conversation about the ways in which standard bureaucratic forms of international education and civic engagement may differ from a deep embrace of critical global citizenship.

This understanding of critical global citizenship is informed through both theory and practice. It is the uniting ideal that holds this book together. Our belief in the dignity of each person led us to this work; that same belief has caused us to make numerous adjustments, adaptations, and structural changes to our own community development and learning principles—and indeed to our language, practices, and personal behaviors. Centering CBGL practice that endeavors to simultaneously serve community partners and student learning, on equal footing, in unfamiliar and unpredictable contexts, is challenging. We turn to one avenue of critical CBGL inquiry in chapter 2 by investigating global citizenship traditions.

Notes

1. In this volume we move away from the terms *GSL* and *international service-learning*, though those terms and the literature associated with them still point toward important theoretical and conceptual roots in this work. Though significant global service-learning work was done responsibly and from a community-driven perspective, through theory and practice insights we understand the importance of moving away from the term *service*, which points to inequity and need as an initial grounding for partnership. In addition to *CBGL*, we have also begun to use the terms *ethical engaged learning* and *FTL*.

2. Future versions of this manual used the term *GSL*.

3. We first shared a very similar definition in Hartman and Kiely (2014b) when describing *GSL*. This definition shifts emphasis slightly and more explicitly recognizes the learning contributions advocated for and/or offered by partners external to campus.

4. For exceptions see Carter (2001), Dower and Williams (2002), and Lewin (2009).

2

SEEKING GLOBAL
CITIZENSHIP

As we begin this chapter, we introduce students who are preparing for their first CBGL experience. They will be part of a three-week development and public health program in Nicaragua. Imagine that you will team-teach this course with a public health faculty member. Though the interactions we describe in this chapter will take place in Nicaragua, the principles and practices we suggest, along with the extent of disruption students often experience, are frequently paralleled in domestic community engagement programs that operate at the intersection of intercultural contact, social class, and human rights. We urge program leaders to be conscious of the ways in which the increasing numbers of excellent domestic intercultural programs (Montague, 2012; Sobania, 2015) may be leveraged to further extend global learning and community capacity building and even serve as an entry point for international immersion experiences (Slimbach, 2016).

Mary is 22 years old. She just completed a 2-year certification in nursing at a community college before transferring to your institution. She is interested in gaining public health insights in a Spanish-speaking country. Mary has limited experience traveling outside the United States and has intermediate skills in Spanish. A White female with a strong Christian faith, Mary has lived her entire life in a relatively isolated affluent neighborhood. She is a U.S. citizen.

Manuel is 20 years old. He is a traditional college student in terms of age and parental socioeconomic status, as both of his parents are successful engineers. He is not average in terms of global experience, however. He was born in the United States when his German father and Bolivian mother worked at the headquarters of a global mining company. Shortly after Manuel's birth, the family moved to Bolivia, where Manuel lived until he was accepted into a strong private high school in New England. He then

31

chose your institution for undergraduate study because he was intrigued by a new certificate program in social entrepreneurship. Manuel is fluent in Spanish and is excelling in his global business major.

Tiana is also 20 years old. She is an African American woman who was raised in an urban community and is a first-generation college student, but she always oriented herself toward international opportunities. During her last year in high school, she applied to and was accepted for a yearlong Rotary exchange program in Peru. She is in the honors program and excels academically. Her Spanish is strong, but she is reluctant to use it conversationally. She is majoring in international studies.

These students are based on students who have participated in our programs. Diversity of student participation in global learning programs is steadily increasing (Institute of International Education, 2015). The teaching and learning practices shared here appear to be broadly powerful across diverse participant populations (Brownell & Swaner, 2009), yet program leaders must be aware of and responsive to their own and others' positionality (Messmore & Davis, 2016; Willis, 2012). Acknowledging and planning for the varieties of student experience and background in inclusive program design has the potential to lead to rich exchanges and significant learning experiences. Researchers and practitioners continue to make progress in this area, highlighting, for instance, how interrogating the "White Savior Complex" relates to opportunities to employ critical race theory during alternative breaks and other community engagement (Messmore & Davis, 2016). Individual and shared understanding of identity, intersectionality, and domestic and international oppressions develops continuously—and all of these content areas should be part of reflection and dialogue on the relationship among self-identity, social interaction, knowledge sharing, and cross-cultural contexts (Hartman & Kiely, 2014b, 2017; Morrison, 2015).

Understanding students' backgrounds is essential for thoughtful engagement of the pedagogical practices we suggest throughout this book. Many of these practices require students to personalize their learning in a way that can be both exciting and uncomfortable. Students should consider their own biographies along with the life stories of the people they meet. They should share and interrogate their personal values, as well as those of other program participants as a precursor to both individual growth and quality team building. And they should be encouraged to interpret their experience to decide how to live their life after the program in what will be an expanded perception of the world.

Just as America's founders saw U.S. universities as central to creating democratic citizens (Hartley, 2011), we see a vital role for universities and community organizations in helping individuals understand their ethical roles and positions in an unmistakably interconnected global economy and, possibly, global community. GSL has emerged as a widely recognized promising practice in this respect (Hartman & Kiely, 2014b; Longo & Saltmarsh, 2011; Whitehead, 2015). Understanding the connection points between CBGL and global community building requires effort to understand the impulses that lead us to CBGL, international volunteerism, or similar programs, as well as critical questioning to develop the rigor of emerging global service sensibilities.

Why Go? Latent Global Citizenship Sensibilities and the Desire to Serve

Interrogating the desire to leave the traditional classroom context, learn, or serve in diverse ways (Westheimer & Kahne, 2004) is an essential step in understanding each participant's assumptions about upcoming experiences, learning, and civic engagement. This is an early instance of the kind of continuous, sequenced reflection we further explain in chapter 3. Diverse and ongoing reflective activities cue participants in to the continuously reflective nature of the experience and ensure that participants who communicate or think differently have multiple ways to assert and consider their motivations.

Throughout the theoretical, experiential, and interpersonal CGBL experience, participants should be asked to write in informal, low-stakes, and individualized forms of reflection such as journals as well as more polished representations of learning to share with other readers. Participants should also be prompted to share their reactions to course experiences in structured group discussions, some of which, as the course proceeds, may very well become highly charged with dissonance and tension. Finally, reflective readings should create integrative links between course experiences and significant concepts and provide the starting points for writing and discussion. At the beginning of the program, participants should reflect on their assumptions regarding service, learning, development, and global citizenship. If the term *global citizenship* seems too theoretical, distant, or problematic, reflection should begin with participants' sense of the dignity or fundamental equality of all persons or discussion of the assertion that "all people are created equal." We suggest participants write an introductory reflective essay responding to some version of the following prompt: "What moves you to participate in this program, course, or community partnership experience?"

The resulting reflective essays might be shared in an online discussion forum, and they can serve to introduce participants to one another. These introductions will typically demonstrate diverse rationales for a similar concern for people elsewhere. Among the students introduced earlier, for example, Mary mentions the importance of her Christian faith and a high school mission trip in developing her desire to engage in service. Manuel shares an interest in getting to know another part of Latin America while, he writes, "giving back" and supporting "their development." Tiana mentions growing up with limited resources, Rotary's calls to service, and a strong sense that supporting public health initiatives in the majority world is "the right thing to do."

Program leaders can respond to these essays individually online, develop a discussion in which participants share these essays and ask one another clarifying questions, or use both vehicles. Whatever method or combinations of methods are chosen, this is an excellent moment to provoke deeper thinking by asking participants to clarify terms that are frequently amorphous and value laden, such as *Christian faith*, *giving back*, or *the right thing*. Additional activities including introductory articles that focus on some of these common assumptions, values, and concepts during the early program orientation may approach the question of motivations and assumptions in a slightly different way, such as is achieved through the expressing global citizenship activity featured in Toolbox 2.1 with facilitator instructions in Toolbox 2.2. This activity opens participants' thinking on their own motivations and assumptions regarding service and development, concepts intertwined with ongoing exploration of global citizenship and community development (Hartman & Kiely, 2017) during CBGL experiences.

The essential feature of this kind of reflection is its invitation to verbalize and externalize assumptions, ideas, and conceptions that can range from ill-formed notions to theoretically rigorous convictions. As we share in chapter 3, these early stages are crucial for establishing a program atmosphere in which participants feel that it is safe to share their convictions and values and to talk about them openly without judgment. This process then gives way to deep discussions in which participants consider and question their own assumptions and those of the other program participants. Ultimately, part of the process of interrogating assumptions involves understanding and identifying the source of one's "grand narratives," those overriding systems of thought that have provided, in more or less coherent ways, a sense of internal meanings participants attribute to their evolving sense of self, others, and the world (Kegan, 2000; Rhoads, 1997). Throughout this book, we describe and explain how the paradigms for student development and adult learning align with recent trends in the theories of global learning and international development to help inform and guide quality CBGL. To reflect on and engage in global citizenship or community-driven development well through CBGL as an academic vehicle is to hone one's capacities for careful listening,

TOOLBOX 2.1
Global Civic Action? Student Instructions

Student Instructions

Global civic activities are those actions undertaken in an attempt to enact global citizenship. Represented in the following checklist are some examples of how people try to apply ideals that relate to common human dignity, shared global community, and single planet sustainability. Place a 1 next to the action that most closely models your sense of ideal global civic activity. Place a 2 next to the action that is the second closest to your ideal global civic activity, and so on. These activities or actions refer to you, as you are currently situated (not some imagined, hypothetical person). The example that is farthest from your own philosophy should receive the highest number (23).

Please mark your answers in the LEFT column only, leaving the RIGHT column BLANK.

_____ _____ Traveling to the U.S.–Mexico border to learn more about the plight of migrants and the work of organizations supporting migrant rights

_____ _____ Giving blood

_____ _____ Tutoring a migrant worker

_____ _____ Adopting an eight-year-old boy

_____ _____ Enrolling in a course that focuses on better understanding global inequity

_____ _____ Chaining yourself to an old-growth tree as loggers enter the forest

_____ _____ Voting

_____ _____ Leaving your car at home and biking to work every day

_____ _____ Becoming a police officer

_____ _____ Giving US$100 to Oxfam International, a global hunger relief organization

_____ _____ Organizing more than 20 friends to attend protests that raise awareness of climate science and reject climate change deniers

(Continues)

TOOLBOX **2.1** *(Continued)*

_____ _____ Choosing professional work that makes a difference internationally

_____ _____ Choosing professional work that makes a difference at home

_____ _____ Conducting participatory research on how to better meet the needs of migrant workers

_____ _____ Engaging in ongoing efforts at conscious consumption, including buying locally, reviewing and buying fair trade or green products, and so on

_____ _____ Writing a letter to a congressional leader to advocate for ensuring quality health care for every U.S. citizen

_____ _____ Developing a microlending project for low-income individuals

_____ _____ Serving on a committee at a religious institution (e.g., church, synagogue, temple)

_____ _____ Organizing your peers to work for affordable housing

_____ _____ Enlisting in the U.S. Armed Forces

_____ _____ Participating in a one-week meditation retreat

_____ _____ Developing and implementing a curriculum for school children that emphasizes human commonalities and peace and social justice leaders while deemphasizing warfare and national patriotism

_____ _____ Communicating with a friend or family member—sharing a story or stories—to help him or her understand an important contemporary justice issue

Note. Adapted from the original *How Do You Define Service?* by Kent Koth and Scott Hamilton (1993). Paper presented at the Washington Campus Compact Conference, Tacoma, Washington. Revised 2003. Global civic adaptations by Eric Hartman (2006) and since.

TOOLBOX **2.2**
Global Civic Action? Facilitator Instructions

Facilitator Instructions

- This activity will take at least 40 minutes.
- Have the students divide into groups of 3.
- In this group, have the students share their rankings from the "Global Civic Action?" handout, and ask them to complete the exercise again but this time ranking them based on group consensus. (They will need to fill out the right-hand column for this.)
- After 15 minutes, bring the group back together. Ask the following questions:
  - What are your observations?
  - What criteria did you use to complete the ranking?
  - What did you observe in the interactive exercise?
  - What were commonalities?
  - What were differences?
  - Would you argue that any of the examples are not service?
  - Does it change your evaluation of an item if it ends with "in a developing country" or "internationally" (e.g., microlending, housing)? How? Why?
  - Is there a universal definition of *good global civic activity?*
  - Did mention of place (domestic, international) influence your ranking? How? Why?
  - If there are so many types of global civic activity, how do individuals and groups working toward global citizenship proceed with a common language?

This activity is designed to engage students' reflective thinking on the questions of global citizenship and civic action. It also serves as a good, early group process to allow participants to start to get to know one another. The kinds of civic action can be changed. Students can even provide their own "top three ways to make a difference" or "things other people think are service but that I do not" in order to create one larger list that will then be ranked. This process relates centrally to the question of whether students are "really doing anything," which will come up as a concern during most CBGL experiences. This activity also introduces participants to consideration of some ways to be of service after the immersion experience, an important topic as the program comes to a close.

respectful engagement, and collaboration across cultures to advance common human dignity and inclusive community.

We include next a review of global citizenship theorizing to support CBGL program leaders' practice in engaging participants in reflection and dialogue on the sources and assumptions of their approaches to global citizenship. As we conclude this chapter, we offer our own conception of a critical global citizenship, based on significant synthesis of intercultural experiences and diverse theoretical traditions. Dialogue on what global citizenship means should be engaged throughout the CBGL program experience. We advise creating a course readings list embedded within continuous reflective practices. The art of instructing a CBGL course is sequencing these readings for a particular group of students so as to create individual and group dialogue relating these texts to program experiences and personal values. In the context of a discussion of global citizenship, the texts addressing this subject will move students from general sources that help name and define global citizenship to sources that highlight and interrogate significant theoretical strands. Following are four brief, accessible texts we recommend to stimulate participants' initial thinking on the topic as it relates to cross-cultural global engagement:

1. *Learning to Read the World Through Other Eyes* (Andreotti & de Souza, 2008)
2. "The Case for Contamination" (Appiah, 2006)
3. "The Reductive Seduction of Other People's Problems" (Martin, 2016)
4. "Seduced by 'The Reductive Seduction of Other People's Problems'" (Starr, 2016)

Each of the preceding texts wrestles with the challenge of global citizenship in different ways. Taken together, and in dialogue with the experiential components of any CBGL program, they expose students to both the challenges and the pathways others engage as aspiring global citizens. These four texts were chosen for their online accessibility, their diversity of approaches, and their brevity. Educators leading courses with significant space for interrogation of global citizenship may wish to engage other brief articles or speeches (Hartman, 2011; Illich, 1968; Schlabach, 2013; Zemach-Bersin, 2008) or one or more of many relevant full-length texts (Carter, 2001; Dower & Williams, 2002; Green & Johnson, 2014; Lewin, 2009; Tiessen & Huish, 2014). New provocative articles, videos, and podcasts on this topic emerge regularly. Readers interested in staying up to date with the most recent texts in this vein should follow globalsl on Facebook or Twitter or join the e-mail list to receive regular updates.

Before we proceed further, it is worth making an explicit point about educating for global citizenship that will animate an educator's experience of the program. Among the radically decentering aspects of CBGL practice is how it compels educators, practitioners, and theorists to join in this dialogue with our students. Just as our students experience the program personally, so should we. As they interrogate their personal biographies, so should we. As we demonstrate throughout this book, our conclusions and convictions arise from grappling with these shared experiences, and our experiences with students inform a continuous interrogation that extends to all parts of our CBGL practice. Thus, although we approach critical global engagement as a central project of CBGL, we begin each new program listening to our students and partners in community organizations while reviewing and reflecting on our guiding assumptions about CBGL practice and global citizenship.

CBGL leaders and global citizenship educators may use the following section to (a) review and/or develop familiarity with multiple rationales for global citizenship to share with students and (b) consider the importance of accepting diverse ways of knowing within the context of these varied rationales.

Locating Global Citizenship Among Theoretical Traditions

Many reviews of global citizenship begin with Diogenes the Cynic who, in the fourth century BCE, proclaimed himself a citizen of the world. Two thousand years later, in a book-length review of millennia of global citizenship and cosmopolitan theorizing, Carter (2001) suggested *cosmopolitanism* indicates a belief in equal human dignity, global community, respect for other cultures, and a desire for peaceful coexistence. The terms *cosmopolitan* and *global citizen* are frequently used interchangeably. *Cosmopolitan* literally translates to suggest an individual who is a citizen of the cosmos rather than a person having any special affiliation with a more localized entity. Although Carter's (2001) definition is easy to memorize and Diogenes's formulation appeals to many individuals, the common assumption in our nation-state–centric world today emphasizes national rather than global citizenry.

We include Toolbox 2.3 toward the end of this chapter to clarify diverse global citizenship approaches and related applications. In addition, it offers challenging questions that may be used to provoke support for a rationale and to consider alternatives. This process may assist educators in encouraging students to recognize multiple legitimate ways of knowing, as detailed further in the chapters on reflection and academic integration. Neither the table nor the text that accompanies it should be considered a substitute for an in-depth reading of a tradition. Instead, the section briefly highlights some of the common themes and differences among the rationales as a method of drawing attention to the opportunity to interrogate and better understand underlying assumptions regarding global citizenship.

Rationales for global citizenship are secular and faith based, essentialist and utilitarian, neoliberal, Kantian, and utilitarian in terms of national security and economic opportunity. There is also an increasingly strong strand of critical, counterhegemonic global citizenship theorizing (Andreotti, 2014; Larkin, 2015). These multiple, and sometimes seemingly opposed, sources of ethical inspiration for global citizenship are important because they emphasize two key aspects of the concept. The first key aspect is the principle that every person is equally worthy of recognition or moral equality (Carter, 2001; Nussbaum, 1992). This is a notion of equality fundamental to democratic theory (Donnelly, 2003; Rorty, 1998; Schwartz, 2008) and prominent in many religious traditions (Glendon, 2001; Herbert, 2002). The goal of global citizenship is to extend that courtesy of equal recognition throughout the human community, though without minimizing meaningful and important differences (Andreotti & de Souza, 2008; Bennett, 1993).

The second key aspect of global citizenship thinking that is highlighted by the diversity of rationales for global citizenship is this: The justification for belief in equal human dignity is less important than agreement on that belief. This is in part because global citizenship thinking embraces *fallibilism*, defined as the notion that our knowledge is inherently imperfect, subject to revision, and open to change (Appiah, 2006). Human rights scholars (Appiah, 2006; Donnelly, 2003; Ignatieff, 2003), global citizenship theorists (Appiah, 2006; Falk, 2000; Nussbaum, 1997), theologians (Friesen, 2000), and philosophers (Rorty, 1998) all recognize this inescapable contingency of knowledge and, even without abandoning the goal or idea of truth, acknowledge the necessarily incomplete understanding of it available to any one among us at any single geographical, cultural, and temporal point.

Put another way, *why* human dignity matters is less important than the agreed-on principle that it does. Human dignity becomes a transcendentally important end in itself (for whatever reason). This emphasis on moral agreement rather than philosophical or theological foundations does not undervalue theory or ethics but recognizes the uncertainty of knowledge and the inherent value in appreciating diverse cultural frameworks.

In this way, global citizenship thinking always contains within it a profound tension. On one hand, cosmopolitanism features an abiding commitment to celebrating diverse truth systems and accepting multiple forms of human flourishing. Yet on the other hand, this celebration of diversity is paradoxically coupled with an insistence on seeking a vast, inclusive human community that celebrates the most essential parts of common human dignity; it assumes a core profundity to that common human experience, a profundity that is not erased by cultural difference. Global citizenship is not relativistic; there is a core actionable and defensible belief in human dignity. Precisely what this belief requires is the subject of numerous ongoing rights and policy debates.

Secular Essentialism

The Universal Declaration of Human Rights may be one of the most well-known explicit approaches to global ethics, and therefore we begin with that secular essentialist approach to global citizenship. Essentialism suggests that human life has certain fundamental, defining features. Nussbaum's (1992) argument for global citizenship is based on an essentialist understanding of the human experience, one that is most fully and concisely articulated in her "Human Functioning and Social Justice: In Defense of Aristotelian Essentialism." The important point for consideration of rationale, however, is not the precise measure or articulation of each component essential to a fully human experience (something that is, of course, highly contested) but rather the understanding that if one believes in the notion of fundamental rights, natural law, or human equality and justice in unbordered ways, then one must logically begin to consider the question of citizenship or equal recognition in a way that is supranational (Nussbaum, 1997).

This rationale is often intuitively appealing to undergraduates. Across numerous institutional and cultural contexts, we have found that U.S. and international students often affirm, for example, the essentialist belief that "all [people] are created equal." We have also discovered that an invigorating and challenging way to begin a CBGL course or program is with discussion of that statement, interrogation of why it is believed, consideration of how it affects contemporary reality, and exploration of what its limits are as belief, practice, and policy.

Faith-Based Essentialism

In addition to the potential persuasive power of drawing on the values of rights-based liberalism central to many expressions of democratic idealism, students often hail from religious traditions with core ethics that suggest not only a fundamental global equality but also an unbordered obligation. In addition, several institutions (e.g., Notre Dame University, Seattle University, Providence College, Brandeis University, Elizabethtown

College, Messiah College, and Goshen College) have embraced their respective Catholic, Jewish, and Protestant traditions to emphasize callings couched in social justice teachings, efforts at discipleship focused on service to others, or peacemaking (Earlham College, Guilford College, and Haverford College feature historic Quaker affiliations). These and other religious-essentialist frameworks provide students with additional and/or different rationales for global ethics and participation rooted in their core beliefs.

At Providence College in Rhode Island, for example, Hartman cotaught a seminar with a Catholic theologian titled "The Secular and the Sacred in Pursuit of Human Rights and Human Dignity." This course exposed students to the historical and contemporary manifestations of Catholic social thought and rights theory—ideally prompting them to sharpen analytical understanding and personal reflection relating to two broad, interrelated worldviews that likely had significant impact on their personal beliefs, perceptions, and experiences. As will be developed more completely in chapter 4 on reflection, challenge and support are often fundamental to working with students as they consider new application of latent or previously unquestioned values.

Familiarity with different religious traditions' approaches to universal values may help educators demonstrate to students that many of the students' long-standing support systems are still in place, if only from a different, more global perspective. Notably, meeting students where they are is often consistent with the second principle of global citizenship: accepting multiple legitimate pathways to understanding common human dignity. Educators should be empathetic listeners for the strands of human dignity present somewhere in most students' understandings of the world. In a divisive national political environment (in the United States), dichotomous pairings are too frequently accepted as settled: liberal–conservative, secular–religious, inclusive–provincial, urban–rural. These are false dichotomies—global citizenship thinking should transcend national debates and move individuals toward robust consideration of the higher principles of various theoretical, religious, and ideological frameworks. Such work of deconstructing settled dichotomies frequently must begin with an educator willing to see the value in each of the perspectives brought to the classroom conversation.

Expertise is not necessary, but an ability to point students toward related resources is helpful to demonstrate a commitment to honoring and respecting multiple journeys toward celebration of shared dignity. Some knowledge of liberation theology (Gutierrez, 1988) or an opportunity to complete a report on Paul Farmer's (2003) efforts might therefore be helpful for students coming from a Catholic tradition, or the history of Christian Peacemaker Teams (2015) or familiarity with faith-based groups' efforts in the Jubilee 2000 campaign may be clarifying and inspiring for students of many backgrounds. Muslims may be interested in the Aga Khan Development Network (2007) and its cooperation with the One Campaign (2016), whereas Jewish students may find grounding and supportive networks in American Jewish World Service (2016). In all cases here, the educator is acting not as an expert but as a curious cosmopolitan, asking to learn more about how specific traditions understand the notions of common human dignity and respectful difference.

For educators there are at least two reasons to draw from these varied philosophical approaches to ethics and their practical value for students engaging in CBGL. First, this practice supports the assumption of human dignity by encouraging students to draw on their own expertise while simultaneously encouraging further understanding of aspects of other traditions. Second, it challenges students by implicitly or explicitly recognizing the diversity of approaches to what are often popularly considered fundamental truths, thus highlighting the contingency of knowledge and creating opportunity for reflection on the notion of decision-making within relativism, which will be discussed further later in this chapter. This engaged, personalized reflective practice is therefore moving continuously between the firmly held truth of global citizenship (celebrating human dignity through diverse commitments) and its challenging paradox (the harder one looks at the question of truly global citizenship, the more adept one must be at recognizing and learning from multiple truth systems).

Engaging students in this conversation breaks the façade of disinterested consideration and makes explicit the relationships among moral aspirations and empirical reality. This can serve as a "callout," as when individuals who believe deeply in common human dignity realize they have not thought seriously about the people in the supply chains relating to their life. This kind of explicit contrast between purported belief and daily experience frequently serves as a jolt that opens new questioning. It also provides opportunity to authentically engage the historical interaction between human rights, development, and religion. This may include the prominent role of progressive believers and churches in abolitionist and civil rights movements, as well as the argument that the social contract has its roots in medieval Catholic thought suggesting legitimacy of rulers depended on their service to the common good (Herbert, 2002). Yet educators and students must also—for all universalizing efforts, whether communism, Christianity, or capitalism—openly and honestly reflect on the often reprehensible histories of horrors perpetrated in the name of "universal" ideologies.

Application 1: Integrating Biography, Experience, and Text

Mary, the student with whom we began the chapter, initially has difficulty buying food and communicating with vendors in the local market. Though she has tested for intermediate Spanish language skills, she has difficulty with the local accent. Over the next week, her localized Spanish listening skills improve significantly, and she becomes more adept at communicating. She also begins to adjust to housing conditions that are much more basic than what she is accustomed to (no clean water for drinking or taking showers). As the first few days pass, Mary has an opportunity to observe community health practitioners and local doctors.

Mary meets pregnant women with few resources who have traveled hours, primarily by walking many miles, to reach the local hospital in the hope that their babies can be delivered there. After giving birth, the mothers rest together with their new babies in a single cinder block room with eight twin beds and no air conditioning. One of the mothers, Isabel, invites Mary in to see her new baby. They enjoy moments of awe and reverie together watching the child stretch its arms and legs, yawn, and learn how to breastfeed.

The following day, three things happen in rapid succession: First, Mary bumps into Isabel carrying her baby down the street on their way home; they exchange warm goodbyes and hopes of reconnecting. Second, a woman's screaming pain during a difficult childbirth is audible throughout Mary's shift at the hospital; the child doesn't make it. Third, as a matter of chance, the topic of discussion in class that evening is comparative maternal and child mortality rates and related policy decisions. A key part of the course is developing student understanding of the social determinants of health, which affect longevity to a much greater extent than clinical care (Schroeder, 2007). At the beginning of class, Mary is unengaged. Halfway through, she bursts out in anger and tears, asking why they've been brought here to "serve" when they really can only observe, when policy structures are so important, and when the situation seems so hopeless.

Following Mary's display of raw emotion, the class conversation shifts. The students have been growing into a strong team, and several of them reach out to comfort and hug Mary right away. You choose to honor this as a teachable moment, leading the class through careful and caring reflection on Mary's concerns and letting the content of the class follow this important conversation. The interrogation of global citizenship has made you aware of the importance of faith and public health for Mary. Because you are aware of the dominance of Catholicism and the roots of liberation theology in Latin America, you share the story of Paul Farmer. Farmer is a public health leader who was inspired by the liberation theology insight that "people of faith must make a preferential option for the poor" (Farmer, 2003, p. 1; Farmer, Gutiérrez, Griffin, & Weiss Block, 2013). You share this example, and you also offer that both you and your coleader struggle with how to act justly in global context. You each share your stories and struggles, your perspectives on the actions you can take, and a deeper analysis of the complexity of factors that influence issues affecting people for which you have no solution.

The conversation shifts to a discussion of what duty we all have, as individuals, to attempt to understand others and, perhaps, act to support progress toward greater social justice. The conversation does not end with a neat and tidy resolution. You make clear that part of the course and, indeed, the life-long global citizenship journey is to continue to explore different strategies, frameworks, and personal commitments that individuals choose to advance that effort. We are, after all, all growing into our abilities to understand and direct our global civic selves.

The example and theoretical tradition help Mary locate her cosmopolitan desires in a tradition and community that is familiar. This sense of familiarity combines with her ability, through program readings (Schlabach, 2013), to see how others have struggled and grown in similar ways. Each of these components offers subtle support to Mary amid the many challenges she faces, through both the experiential components of the program and the readings that cause her to rethink her understanding of service (Andreotti & de Souza, 2008; Freire, 2000; Illich, 1968; Talwalker, 2012). Mary's journey continues after the immersive period of the program concludes, as is discussed in chapter 9.

Utilitarianism

Utilitarianism is a popular theoretical framework in the United States, with its own appeal and rationale in terms of global citizenship. It is typically understood as suggesting that the greatest good should be sought for the greatest number. *Good* is often measured in terms of happiness or, as is the case with Singer's (2002) analysis, through a combination of life expectancy and quality-of-life indicators. There are strains of utilitarianism in Singer's (2002) *One World*, which encourages residents of developed countries to consider donating financial resources to address global poverty, taking greater steps to protect the environment, and the plight of others around the world. Singer (2002) worked to persuade readers through sharing information about positive possibilities in globalization and skillful use of hypotheticals, as demonstrated next.

In terms of fairness, Singer (2002) simply provoked readers to consider John Rawls's "veil of ignorance" in global context. Familiar to political science and philosophy students, the veil of ignorance suggests that to determine what would be a just society, individuals need only imagine that they would be born into that society without previous knowledge of their rank, race, gender, or other background factors. If the individual imagining the society were to do so with the notion of later entering it from behind a veil of ignorance regarding his or her own status, Rawls's reasoning suggests the society would be a just one. Singer (2002) chastised Rawls for confining the veil of ignorance exercise to national societies and then provoked readers to imagine global society within the context of a veil of ignorance. Certainly place of birth takes on unjustifiably important meaning (Singer, 2002). As inequality continues to increase in the United States, Singer's formulations are all too appropriate for domestic application as well. There is a 13-year gap, for instance, between the U.S. county with the lowest life expectancy (McDowell County, West Virginia, 70.1 years) and the county with the highest life expectancy (Marin County, California, 83.3 years) (Measure of America, 2009).

Despite the stunning inequalities existing in the world, Singer (2002) was careful to point out that some crucial measures of well-being have shown gains. Average life expectancy between 1962 and 1997, for example, increased from 55 years to 66.6 years. Importantly, the biggest gains in life expectancy occurred in developing nations. The Food and Agriculture Organization suggested that even as the global population increased, the number of people undernourished fell from 960 million in 1969–1971 to 790 million in 1995–1997 (Singer, 2002). Singer used these data to suggest wealthy people in the world, wherever they are located, ought to be more deliberate about sharing wealth and addressing pressing needs because their actions, he argued, can make a difference.

In two separate instances in the book, Singer (2002) provoked the reader to consider whether, in a given situation, he or she would make the required effort to save the life of an innocent child. In the first situation, the costs are decidedly minimal, whereas in the second situation, the costs are roughly equivalent to an upper-middle-class retirement savings in the United States. Both hypotheticals force the reader to consider the ethical dimensions of costs in close, personal terms:

> I asked the reader to imagine that on my way to give a lecture, I pass a shallow pond. As I do so, I see a small child fall into it and realize that she is in danger of drowning. I could easily wade in and pull her out, but that would get my shoes and trousers wet and muddy. I would need to go home and change, I'd have to cancel the lecture, and my shoes might never recover. Nevertheless, it would be grotesque to allow such minor considerations to outweigh the good of saving a child's life. Saving the child is what I ought to

do, and if I walk on to the lecture, then no matter how clean, dry, and punctual I may be, I have done something seriously wrong. (Singer, 2002, p. 156)

Singer (2002) then compared his unwillingness to interrupt his travels to a lecture with individuals' unwillingness—despite clear opportunities to do so—to take small steps to save lives, efficiently and inexpensively, on a global scale. The question at the core of each hypothetical is as follows: What is the value of the life of an innocent child? Singer (2002) never answered that question in terms of dollars, but he did propose that conservative estimates that include graft, corruption, and other transaction costs suggest that a US$200 donation to international development organizations is enough to save a life. Singer (2002) was careful to point out that the estimate includes accounting for the many problems that do exist in international aid and that his estimate is not for food for a month, immunizations, or something of that nature but rather estimated costs for the complete act of saving a life. Hypotheticals are often highly effective for working through philosophical questions with students, and Singer (2002) is particularly adept at illustrating applicable scenarios, one of which has been animated and set to music on YouTube as part of The Life You Can Save campaign (The Life You Can Save, 2010).

For Singer (2002), the global economic system currently does not function in terms of justice; wealth distribution is too uneven, accompanied by related inequities in health, opportunity, and life expectancy. Nonetheless, the idea of global citizenship through the ideology of neoliberalism suggests open markets and free access to capital as central to promoting equity and building bridges between disparate cultures. For neoliberals, the equity is in maximizing freedom of individual choice through limited government and the opportunity to do business in a global market. At times, this reasoning leads to cosmopolitan justifications for evading taxes, as proponents suggest libertarian approaches to economics and social organization are clearly the only fair possibilities in a global economy (Schattle, 2005). In more restrained moments, however, this notion is at the core of some classic articulations of capitalism (Smith, 1776/1993), as well as contemporary accounts of indirect routes toward universal economic and political freedom (Friedman, 1982).

Application 2: Integrating Biography, Experience, and Text

In another example of application, Manuel comes to the course with strong support for microfinance initiatives and the expansion of markets throughout Latin America. Having grown up in the United States and enjoyed the privileges of economic abundance, he feels strongly that every person should experience such opportunities. And he also believes that there is a fundamental fairness to market expansion; he sees markets as expanding the structures of equality around the world. Yet his rural Nicaraguan experiences unsettle him too. He is quieter about his concerns than Mary was, but he journals about questions regarding the efficacy of microfinance interventions that sometimes seem to support the development of hundreds of the same kind of one-person shop, shops that sell phone cards, Coke products, bottled water, and a few very limited dried and canned goods. He is even more worried about what he continues to hear from farmers and leaders in the community where the course takes place. They tell him that it is impossible to compete with the U.S. farm subsidy system (Wahlberg, 2004). His journal reflects his sense of concern with market fairness. He writes, "If each American farmer receives thousands of dollars in direct and indirect farm subsidies, how can anyone expect farmers here to compete?"

Manuel's interest in policy, market structures, and subsidy systems causes you to encourage him to begin to think about focusing his course work and reflections on the relationships between major nongovernmental organizations and government efforts to support equity and opportunity within the global food system and what he is experiencing and learning on the ground. You encourage him to begin further academic inquiry on this topic by looking at Oxfam's work on Food Policy (Oxfam, 2016), investigating the Massachusetts Institute of Technology's (2016) Poverty Action Lab studies specific to food systems and/or microenterprise, and reviewing the U.S. Agency for International Development's (2016) approach.

As Manuel quickly learns in respect to his embrace of neoliberal cosmopolitanism, there are strengths and weaknesses to each of these theoretical traditions. That is a central concern and understanding of educating for global citizenship: Students and cosmopolitans must develop the facility to consider and criticize multiple ways of knowing.

Kantian Categorical Imperative

The Kantian categorical imperative offers another formulation for consideration of ethics in global context (Kant, 1785/2012). In three separate but related formulations, Kant (1785/2012) suggested individuals should undertake only those actions that they could will to be maxims. The *categorical imperative* is useful in the global context because it does not require empirical knowledge of all situational possibilities. Rather, it suggests that the individual undertake the mental exercise of considering his or her actions writ large (Kant, 1785/2012). Particularly with respect to global resource use and environmental impacts, this rendering has clear applications and additional opportunities for challenging questions. Would the successful individual in the neoliberal paradigm will that everyone has enough opportunity for resource consumption so as to own and commute in a Humvee? If so, how long would resources last? What would be the pollution effects?

More challenging applications of the Kantian categorical imperative might consider whether every person could or should consume a Western, meat-centric diet or engage with personal transportation (e.g., car use) in a manner that is typical in the United States. These types of mental exercises arguably challenge students to see the limits of their own contexts while highlighting some of the strengths of "developing" communities. They also create opportunities to consider notions of sustainable consumption and production patterns as articulated within the global sustainable development goals (United Nations, 2016). Finally, such inquiry may lead to engagement with global civil society efforts to combat global warming through both personal and political choices (350.org, 2016).

Particularistic Approaches

Although the arguments reviewed thus far reflect worldviews that include some explicit concern for others, there is another set of rationales for global citizenship that are utilitarian in the second sense of the word; that is, there is a particularistic, even selfish usefulness in global ethics that transcends any intrinsic value. To avoid confusion, we refer to this set of utilitarian arguments as *particularistic approaches*, because their rationales all relate to the benefits conferred to a particular individual or group. Particularistic arguments include the recognition that peace is less costly than war and more helpful in creating stable markets for profit, advocacy of global peace to ensure local security, recognition that economic freedom allows individuals more opportunity to buy goods from more established economies and therefore allows greater profits for businesses, and even a cynical embrace of the value of soft power in convincing the less powerful that current hegemonic structures are legitimate.

Application 3: Integrating Biography, Experience, and Text

Tiana proves to be a particularly observant student. She is not merely aware of the environment around her and learning from people in this small Nicaraguan community, she also listens carefully to other students' insights and seems remarkably attuned to her peers' personal growth. As the in-country portion of the program nears its end, she offers the following reflection in her journal:

> We were talking about ethical frameworks in class, and I think I get the idea of the Kantian categorical imperative (I think it's an especially fancy golden rule). I know there are some environmental practices at home I need to work on (honestly, I drive everywhere—like across a mall parking lot). But I guess I'm just less and less convinced that there's "an answer" when it comes to global ethical questions.
>
> Mary's commitment to Catholicism, and the way it makes her focus on seeing God in others, inspires me. But I don't have the faith she has and, more importantly, I think seeing the value in others is only a small part of what global citizens need to figure out. Once you believe in common human dignity, which so many of the course readings emphasize (and I certainly believe in it)—once you believe in that, the real question becomes, so what? How, in an extremely unequal world, do we make any real progress on honoring our shared dignity?
>
> In terms of working at that "how" question, Manuel inspires me too. He came into all of this thinking he had a solution—microfinance. But he's bumped into some real issues on the ground—it seems like public infrastructure is pretty important for scaling businesses, and other issues (Would *everyone* eventually become a business owner?).
>
> But I feel like in some way the how and the why questions can learn from one another. What I mean by this is—in class we've talked a lot about how people can have different "whys" behind the assumption of common human dignity. There are many different paths to the light.
>
> I feel like when we look at good examples of community development, the lesson is the same: There are many different paths to the light. If a community wishes to focus on environmental sustainability, it may be a community of small shareholder farms. That might not look like development to some people, but it could absolutely achieve environmental sustainability, human longevity, and happiness. Alternatively, there are many positives in the Western model: access to higher education, bureaucratized economies, access to stuff that pretty much makes life easier and more comfortable. But I also get that it's a really limited view of the world, and possibly not sustainable for people elsewhere (if you assume that material possessions are an important part of our model).
>
> So, I guess I'm saying, on the one hand, I'm confused and seeing that there's more to learn than I've ever imagined before. And then on the other hand, I feel like I'm seeing development happen in a true diversity of ways, both in course texts and in this community—where sometimes public health workers seem very helpful and other times traditional life ways are getting women to do a lot of things that probably support longevity, like

encouraging them to work in their little farms, consume the food they grow, and be one with their natural environment. (I know that's not exactly how it's been expressed to us, and I might be romanticizing it, but that's what I'm seeing right now anyway.)

I believe so firmly in common human dignity, especially around women's rights, so I get that I'm really attached to that part of my worldview. But I also think that part of the key for making progress on global citizenship is going to be to hold on to the "how" about as loosely as the "why." What matters most are the outcomes for people and communities, and a lot of that will be situational rather than according to a singular theory of development. It's overwhelming. I'm spinning—and learning.

As Tiana's reflection suggests, comparing and contrasting approaches and the logical difficulties within them is central to the practice of cosmopolitan thinking and to the process of educating for global citizenship.

Postmodern, Postcolonial, and Critical Approaches to Global Citizenship

Many of the approaches suggested earlier (essentialism, utilitarianism, Kantian thought) are connected with an account of reality rooted in enlightenment thinking, positivism, and modernism. Critical and postmodern thinking has also added to the discussion. These positions will be particularly significant for helping students engage with multiple perspectives and enacting this cosmopolitan thinking as they reflect on the experiences of the course.

Postmodern writers are often deeply critical of modernity, yet they recognize possibilities in specific opportunities with social movements (Yappa, 1996). They must, despite their dissatisfaction with the enlightenment project, make judgments based on available information in order to take ethical stands and make normative choices (Yappa, 1996). There is a great deal of writing in development that has roots in or connections with discourse theory and postmodernism (Escobar, 1994; Esteva & Prakesh, 1997; Rahnema & Bawtree, 1997). Because global citizenship involves questions of what experiences and opportunities people ought to have (to support actual experiences of human dignity), the problem of defining *development* is always nearby.

Esteva and Prakesh (1997), as well as Escobar (1994), called for locally developed knowledge and initiative to lead development on a global scale. Their arguments fit well within the articulation of the fourth generation of development thinking identified by Korten (1990) and others, which is characterized by loosely defined, self-managing volunteer networks of people and organizations. The fourth generation is community driven, with communication among communities, governments, international nongovernmental organizations, and others allowing for improvements and enhanced insights locally (Korten, 1990). This fourth generation of development thinking parallels the understanding and skills we are encouraging in global citizens: the capacity to know oneself and one's values; the ability to see the beauty and insights coming from other peoples and places; and the skills to work among each, cocreating realities more beautiful than those that existed before (Korten, 1990). Toolbox 2.3 provides a summary and application examples of the global citizenship theoretical frameworks reviewed previously.

Scholars of global community–campus partnerships have recently drawn on critical thinking (Andreotti, 2006; Hartman & Kiely, 2014a) and postcolonial thinking (Andreotti, 2011; Andreotti & de Souza, 2008; Bruce, 2016; Thiessen & Huish, 2014), suggesting reconsideration of global epistemologies as central to the work of social justice (Larkin, 2015) and the need for an ontological project at the core of learning and service partnerships, an ontological project that supports critical inquiry into and through our core assumptions (McMillan & Stanton, 2014). The Diné (Navajo) example that began chapter 1, for instance, challenges students to let go of existing conceptions of how they will perform "service," consider creation stories from another culture, learn an unfamiliar history, and then reengage the questions of service and purpose. This experience typically sparks new insights into how one might be of service and how one might conceptualize one's place among other people and the natural world.

A critical examination of the multiple, complex, and partial lenses for understanding and enacting global citizenship is essential for troubling the grand narratives of enlightenment thinking and modernist development. Dispositions of criticality and cultural humility informed by a postcolonial perspective (Andreotti, 2006; Burbules & Berk, 1999) celebrate the potential in careful listening, understanding, and collaboration born of cross-cultural contact approached with deep respect for historically marginalized individuals, communities, and epistemologies (Andreotti & de Souza, 2008; Balusubramaniam, Hartman, McMillan, & Paris, 2018; Larsen, 2015). Andreotti (2006) summarized the way in which a critical global citizenship education provides significant activities and reflective processes to engage multiple ways of being and knowing:

TOOLBOX 2.3

Engaging Diverse Rationales for Global Citizenship

Approach	Example(s)	Application	Challenging Reflective Question(s)	Example(s) of Integration
Secular essentialism suggests a secularly derived notion that human life has certain fundamental features.	UN Declaration of Human Rights	Educating others about rights; advocating for rights	How do we reconcile the frequent emphasis on individual rights with the additional emphasis on communal rights?	Drawing on personal faith as a reason to promote a secular expression of human rights
Faith-based essentialism suggests a religious basis for the notion that human life has certain fundamental features.	World Vision ("a Christian humanitarian organization dedicated to working with children, families, and their communities worldwide to reach their full potential"; see www.worldvisionusprograms.org/about_us.php)	Following faith-based ethics to work with organizations such as World Vision, which is "serving the poor in nearly 100 countries" (wvi.org/map/where-we-work), facilitating child sponsorship, and organizing fund-raisers	How do our ethics around fundamental human equality relate to discrete faith associations?	Being part of the legacy of liberation theology by cooperating with Catholic and other faith institutions to promote better secular government treatment of individuals as holders of human rights

(Continues)

Toolbox 2.3 (*Continued*)

Approach	Example(s)	Application	Challenging Reflective Question(s)	Example(s) of Integration
Utilitarianism suggests that the greatest good should be sought for the greatest number.	Several of the arguments advanced in Peter Singer's (2002) *One World*; many classic theoretical conceptions of liberal economics (now *neoliberalism*)	Supporting policies thought to raise incomes and life expectancies globally	Is fundamental human equality sufficiently respected in an approach that may ignore individuals and/or marginalized communities in pursuit of the greatest good for the greatest number?	Recognizing broad development indicators such as access to education while integrating an essentialist approach by putting a new and tighter focus on each individual rights holder and whether he or she is indeed a recipient of the right in question
The *Kantian categorical imperative* suggests that individuals should undertake only those actions that they could will as maxims.	Integrated in much environmentalism; associations with fair trade	Consuming resources and buying products with the categorical imperative as a filtering question	Is it possible to apply this ethic in a lived experience? Does global justice ever demand a breach of this ethic?	Leveraging global civil society (fair trade, reducing consumption) while adhering to other efforts when necessary

Particularistic approaches suggest self-interested or groupcentric rationales for promoting global ethics because that outcome will serve the local group or individual well.	Promotion of others' rights in an effort to build national soft power and enhance national security; promotion of peace and trade in order to expand one's business	Exchange programs with explicit focus on sharing national values; investment in emerging markets; funding international students' visits and educations	If a fundamental commitment is basic human equality, shouldn't the focus be other oriented rather than self-reverential?	Earnestly promoting global ethics while drawing on support made possible only by recognizing the particularistic local benefits
Skeptical postmodernism suggests reality is relative and fragmented, with no possibility for global thinking.	Esteva and Prakash (1997) argued that global thinking and global ethics were fundamentally beyond human capabilities	Creating the possibilities for communities to develop (or not) as they wish, without any outside interference	Aren't there individuals in these communities who may wish for (fundamental?) rights and disagree with the local perspective?	Cooperating with communities to share other perspectives while respecting practices deemed not to be rights violations
Affirmative postmodernism and critical traditions suggest deep criticism of modernity while allowing for the possibility of meaningful and valid social movements.	Arturo Escobar (1994) critiqued 50 years of development history while allowing for the possibility of progress through listening to local communities	Locally driven development efforts such as The Glocal Forum that connects communities and their resources and experiences worldwide	Aren't the communities driving these efforts often articulating an interest in fundamental human rights? Shouldn't that focus our collective efforts?	Drawing on local experiences and expertise to promote broadly agreed-on human rights, such as often occurs through global efforts

In this sense, critical literacy is not about "unveiling" the "truth" for the learners, but about providing the space for them to reflect on their context and their own and others' epistemological and ontological assumptions: how we came to think/be/feel/act the way we do and the implications of our systems of belief in local/global terms in relation to power, social relationships and the distribution of labour and resources. (p. 49)

This especially strong orientation toward learning from all partners is promising for CBGL for two distinct, interrelated reasons. The first is that engaging in other civilizational approaches to rights, community, or right action is entirely consistent with the intellectual work of becoming a global citizen. The second, and equally vital, reason this is so important is that the history of community development makes abundantly clear that only co-owned and locally created initiatives will truly flourish (Chambers, 1997; Korten, 1990). Outsiders may be catalysts (Bergdall, 2003) or particularly helpful sidekicks (Two Dollar Challenge, 2016), but they should never drive issue identification, analysis, or solution creation.

Community members must be drivers in all of this work, as will be further developed in chapter 4. Comparing and contrasting rights thinking with the African Ubuntu philosophy (I am because we are) (Larkin, 2015), the Haitian *resipwosite* understanding of reciprocal partnership (Murphy, 2015), or the Andean Quechua conception of *ayni* (reciprocity) (Porter, 2000) walks students through civilizational logics and intellectual assumptions even as they experience a diversity of influences on the ground.

A Journey Toward Critical Global Citizenship

The preceding review of primary strands of global citizenship theorizing is intended to support program leaders in curricular and cocurricular contexts, across disciplines and program sites, in their efforts to advance global citizenship consideration. As we shared in chapter 1, our definition of *global citizenship* draws on several of these strands and our own experiences in university–community engagement around the world. As we continue to grow in our thinking and experience, it is possible that our definition will shift as well. Consistent with a commitment to critical reflection and cultural humility, the ideal of global citizenship itself is tentative and open to change (Andreotti, 2006; Hartman & Kiely, 2014a). It draws on these many diverse influences and also allows us to move forward.

For us, global citizenship is a commitment to fundamental human dignity, couched in a critically reflective understanding of historic and contemporary systems of oppression, along with acknowledgment of positionality within those systems; it connects with values, reflection, and action. A critical global citizenship calls us all to humble, careful, and continuous effort to build a world that better acknowledges every individual's basic human dignity (Hartman & Kiely, 2014a).

In any democratic discourse, one should substantiate one's arguments. It is in this context that participants' consideration of multiple rationales for global citizenship enhances other learning goals, such as critical reflection. Toolbox 2.3 provides clear examples through which students' understanding of global citizenship may be challenged and supported, encouraging deeper and more nuanced thinking about global citizenship and its application. We have already suggested, through Mary's example in this chapter, how the global citizenship journey itself may support participants in times of challenge during a CBGL program experience. This may be the case at many points throughout the CBGL experience, particularly as participants return to their life beyond the course or program. The next chapter on reflection offers additional examples of assignments and applications relating to global citizenship thinking, and more assignments and reflective activities are also regularly added to the globalsl website (Campus Compact, 2017a).

3

ADVANCING REFLECTION
AND CRITICAL REFLECTION

We begin this chapter with two stories of powerful CBGL experiences.

I was the only one of my American friends who participated in a service-learning study abroad experience. While my peers were touring historical cities and partying until dawn, I was living in one of the dirtiest city slums of Ecuador and supervising children who were routinely beaten, sexually assaulted, or forced to work the streets all night long. My friends returned with a taste for Spanish wine, while I returned frustrated, confused about social injustices, and 15 pounds thinner after giving my dinner to street children all semester.

When I arrived back to my family in upstate New York, my dumb-founded parents watched helplessly as I refused to enter an overcrowded grocery store, nauseated by the rows of shiny, boxed, endless options and spoiled, cantankerous children who screamed and begged for yet another treat.

I would lie awake at night, eyes wide open, staring at the glowing plastic stars on my ceiling, tucked under plush, pink, warm covers, my room lined with stuffed animals and storybooks, as I pictured the six-year-old children who had called me "mama" wandering the streets under a brutally less for-giving sky until dawn. I felt like I had been yanked out of my universe, experienced another world, and then plopped right back where I had left off and nobody else had missed a beat. I looked the same, everyone expected me to be the same, and nobody else seemed to have changed, but I couldn't even remember who I was before, and suddenly, the people with whom I had felt closest seemed unrecognizable and out of reach. (Lang, 2013)

The next story is told within the broader narrative of a thesis on alternative spring break programming:

For another student who identified as African American, this feeling of "otherness" was a critical moment of her ASB [alternative spring break] experience. Prior to departure to the Pine Ridge reservation, she anticipated being "a person the community members could empathize or identify with because of similar forms of historical discrimination." However, upon her return, she shared the following reflection:

> I was surprised at the reaction I received. When I was working in the elementary school, this was the first time many had seen an African American and [they] called me "freaky looking." This used to happen to me when I was little and this experience kind of brought me back to that. The kids didn't identify with me like I expected. Even at the pow-wow recognition ceremony, the comments made by the host made me feel uncomfortable. At times it seemed like I was being exploited because of my skin color. I really felt like an outsider and that I didn't belong.

> When asked, this participant reported how this was the first in-depth reflection of her feelings of "otherness" she experienced while on the trip. "I didn't bring it up during evening reflections because I didn't want to seem like a distraction. Although we were there to experience different things, I didn't want it to be all about me." (Wendel, 2013)

These anecdotes are representative, not exceptional. In such challenging, unpredictable, and diverse environments, this chapter elaborates on how reflective tools can support CBGL participants' personal, spiritual, political, social, emotional, intercultural, moral, and academic development during programs. It shares how reflective activities can be designed to invite participation and grow trust among participants, simultaneously engaging participants' emotional experience and related academic learning. It charts strategies for navigating the relationship among reflection, intercultural learning, academic content, and healthy return to a student's home community. Fundamentally, it answers the question "Why insist on reflection?" and provides program leaders with techniques to move beyond giving participants vague (though often eagerly embraced) spaces "to reflect" and move toward systematic encouragement of multiple forms of both structured and unstructured reflective learning experiences.

Engaging in Reflection to Advance Learning

This chapter begins by indicating why reflection is foundational and defining precisely what is meant by *reflection* in experiential learning. It moves on to summarize major contributions to reflective practice in CBGL while integrating the insights we have gained through practice. We then turn to sustained consideration of the notion of "critical" reflection, which we distinguish from reflection. We demonstrate how some contributors to the reflection literature have been primarily concerned with systematic learning progress on specified academic goals, whereas others have been much more consciously oriented toward understanding hegemonic structures, power, positionality, and privilege as social phenomenon inside and outside of the course environment (Brookfield, 2000, 2009; Freire, 2000; Kiely, 2002, 2004, 2005, 2015; Mezirow, 1995). Each process has an important place.

This chapter describes what are understood as effective practices in CBGL reflection. Those practices are filtered through experience to offer additional insights and practical applied tips. Finally, the chapter discusses the special role of criticality in CBGL. Notably, the challenging and real stories shared at the beginning of this chapter not only require leadership and pedagogical skills in respect to carefully designed reflection but also necessitate insights that relate to intercultural learning, power and privilege, and critical global citizenship. This chapter first explores the expectation-setting and reflective practices that will support program leaders' abilities to systematically approach those topics. Some reflective activities, such as the fist-to-five activity described in Toolbox 3.1, are not centrally academic exercises. Nonetheless, activities that gauge group energy and cause group members to consider one another's experiences can be useful in learning outside of the classroom, particularly when schedules and ending times may be somewhat unpredictable.

Reflective activity may indeed serve many different goals, including but not limited to supporting students in processing high-intensity dissonance experiences, setting group behavioral norms and expectations, and developing an environment of trust as a precursor for reflective activities that probe personal identity and assumptions. With the exception of Toolbox 3.1, the first portion of this chapter concerns itself primarily with reflection as a tool to advance disciplinary, global citizenship, and intercultural learning. The second portion of this chapter focuses on critical reflection and its role within CBGL. Chapter 7 offers several further reflection tips, tools, and strategies relating to group norms, trust, and processing high-intensity dissonance moments.

Reflection and Its Rationales

Reflection is central to service-learning done well (Ash & Clayton, 2009; Eyler & Giles, 1999; Eyler, Giles, & Schmiede, 1996). Without reflection, service-learning "all too easily leads to reinforced stereotypes, simplistic solutions to complex problems, and inaccurate generalization from limited data" (Whitney & Clayton, 2011, p. 150). It advances intercultural understanding

TOOLBOX **3.1**
Fist-to-Five

Fist-to-five is typically not an activity that is central to planned and targeted academic learning, yet it is an effective ritual for gauging group opinions and emotions and setting the climate for open, active, participatory, non-judgmental reflection and dialogue. Establishing this kind of ritual has many salutary benefits, and among them is the regular assertion of a space in which individuals are prompted to share the kinds of concerns that may start longer, important conversations rooted in students' experience and reflective processing. It's a bridge between experience and the possibility of longer discussion. The exercise provides a sense of how the group is feeling and makes everyone aware of each other. The topic can be emotional, intellectual, or even simply logistical. To implement, leaders ask participants to respond to a question by holding up fingers. The activity is described in the following table with sample prompts for each stage.

Step	Example Prompts
Define a question.	"How tired are you right now?"
Define the response.	"Hold up your fist if you're more exhausted than you've ever been in your life and are basically asleep with your eyes open. Hold up five fingers if you are wide awake and as ready to go as a fresh cup of coffee. Or hold up any number of fingers in between." (Humor goes a long way in getting the group to play along.)
Encourage people to respond quickly and all at once.	"One, two, three, go!"
Ask everyone to look around the room and assess the temperature of the group.	"Okay, so it looks like the majority of the group is exhausted. Let's all note the folks who are showing fists right now and be sensitive to them. Also, let's make tonight's discussion a short one. Amber, you seem to have the most energy, so would you be up for kicking off our discussion tonight?"
Remind everyone that they can lead a fist-to-five whenever they want to gauge the group.	

Give the group ownership over fist-to-five. Once people get the hang of it, they will be tempted to throw out fist-to-five throughout the day. Remind them to be sensitive to the "fists" in the group and to draw strength from the "fives." Use this as a tool for team building, airing out problems, and just generally checking in.

Good Uses of Fist-to-Five
1. Making decisions and voting in direct, democratic, and participatory ways
2. Determining emotional feelings and energy levels
3. Checking understanding (e.g., of an academic concept)
4. Managing plans and logistics
5. Sharing opinions

and cross-cultural communication skills (McAllister, Whiteford, Hill, Thomas, & Fitzgerald, 2006). And it is the key component in deliberately fostering a global perspective (Braskamp, Braskamp, & Merrill, 2009). It is, in short, the foundation for learning deeply about self, others, values, and academic content (Eyler & Giles, 1999; Rhoads, 1997). Drawing on decades of research in international and intercultural education, Vande Berg, Paige, and Hemming Lou (2012) stated,

> Most students do not, then, meaningfully develop either through simple exposure to the environment or through having educators take steps to increase the amount of that exposure through "immersing" them. Instead, students learn and develop effectively and appropriately when educators intervene more intentionally through well-designed training programs that continue throughout the study abroad experience. . . . The data show that students learn and develop considerably more when educators prepare them to become more self-reflective, culturally self-aware, and aware of "how they know what they know." (p. 21)

Reflection is symbolized in the hyphen that connects service to learning (Eyler & Giles, 1999; Jacoby, 2015). According to Hatcher and Bringle (1997), reflection is "the intentional consideration of an experience in the light of particular learning objectives" (p. 153). Reflection that is systematic, structured, and intentional should occur before, during, and after the service experience (Eyler & Giles, 1999). CBGL practitioners should incorporate into their course design diverse reflection strategies at different stages of the students' service-learning experience. For example, prior to engaging in the service experience, time should be spent providing novice students with opportunities to practice the art of reflection (Jacoby, 2015; Kiely & Kiely, 2006). Most students are not familiar with the concept of reflection, and providing students with a framework for engaging in different methods of reflection enables students to develop their reflective abilities (Collier & Williams, 2005). Once such framework that we discuss later in this chapter is Ash and Clayton's (2009) DEAL model.

Whitney and Clayton (2011), like several others in the service-learning literature (Bringle & Hatcher, 1999; Eyler & Giles, 1999), discussed the role of reflection in terms of advancing learning goals and improving student mastery of content, while also pointing toward the possibility that reflection will lead to consideration of outcomes, deeper understanding of learning processes, clarification of values, and even understanding of "the role of power and hegemony as constraints on civic agency" (Whitney & Clayton, 2011, p. 151). Drawing on several decades of research, practice, and empirical insight, Whitney and Clayton (2011) suggested critical reflection is "a process of metacognition that functions to improve the quality of thought and of action and the relationship between them" (p. 150).

Applying Reflection Models in CBGL

Robust forms of reflection are systematic and educationally meaningful. Reflection must be "purposeful and strategic," and it must "begin with the end in mind" (Whitney & Clayton, 2011, p. 153). It is a deliberate learning process that simultaneously engages cognitive learning, ethics, and application (Baxter Magolda, 2003) in ways that challenge students to move beyond current content understanding, self-understanding, and critical thinking capability.

Drawing from reflective traditions in experiential learning (Dewey, 1916; Kolb, 1984), and after decades of focus on reflective practice applied to service-learning, Clayton and colleagues have developed the DEAL model (Ash & Clayton, 2009; Whitney & Clayton, 2011) for critical reflection. The DEAL model suggests the following three essential steps for systematic critical reflection: "Description of experiences in an objective and detailed manner, Examination of those experiences in light of specific learning objectives (in the case of service-learning, at least in the categories of academic enhancement, civic learning, and personal growth), and Articulation of Learning" (Whitney & Clayton, 2011, p. 156).

The DEAL model's growing status in the service-learning field is due to its application of learning theory insights to reflective practice; its integration of assessment; and its empirical validation as a process that enhances student critical thinking and objective learning (Ash & Clayton, 2009). It has been validated by multiple independent researchers using blind evaluations of student progress on objective content mastery and critical thinking skills at multiple points throughout evaluated semesters (Jameson, Clayton, & Bringle, 2008; McGuire et al., 2007).

We will consider several other key contributions to understanding how reflection works for CBGL learners, but we begin with example reflective questions to stimulate thinking about reflection design in the context of a sandwich model CBGL program. (A CBGL sandwich model involves academic preparation and processing before and after a travel experience including intercultural immersion. Sandwich models, along with several other immersive CBGL program structure possibilities, are discussed in chapter 6.) Toolbox 3.2 demonstrates reflective prompts specific to CBGL in terms of how they relate to both the DEAL model and the pre-, during, and postimmersion experience typical of sandwich programs. It is important to note, in addition, that local community engagement and even facilitated intercultural dialogue on campus can be productively disruptive in ways that parallel the disruption and questioning that is common during an immersion experience.

The DEAL model is helpful for structuring reflection and, as demonstrated previously, is applicable before, during, and after immersive learning experiences that may occur in a sandwich model program. With any program, involving community engagement near or far, throughout the semester or during breaks, the DEAL model may be paired with a time line of learning and engagement similar to what is expressed in Toolbox 3.2. The reflective process is further informed through considering learning design principles (see chapter 7), understanding student development (Baxter-Magolda, 2003; Perry, 1981), and embracing different learning styles and strengths (Ash & Clayton, 2009).

Learning design principles are useful when considering ways in which course content can be enhanced through reflection with any type of service (Collier & Williams, 2005). Course content and service type may vary considerably. It is possible to enhance academic learning through professional experience, physical labor, or unconventional forms of service such as listening and learning at the request of community partners. These experiences may also enhance prosocial development, group cohesion, or personal and professional development. What matters is the systematic relationship between specified learning goals (further discussed in chapter 7), experience, and targeted reflection questions.

Sample Intercultural Learning Prompts Before, During, and After Intercultural Experiences Using the DEAL Model

	Before	During	After
Describe	Complete the identity pie activity to represent what "makes you, you" in terms of your biography and cultural background. (Activity is available in chapter 4.)	Describe an event that made you think about culture in a new way today, or carefully describe an intercultural interaction you had today.	Have conversations with six friends or family members about your experience, and describe the perceptions they have about the place you visited.
Examine	How did sharing identity pies and having a discussion about identity relate to the assigned readings on culture?	What do your observations in public spaces demonstrate about varying communication patterns and cultural assumptions?	How has your academic and experiential interrogation of culture affected your ability to see the biases and assumptions of your home culture?
Articulate Learning	What have you learned about yourself as a cultural being through our preparation for travel and service?	How does our experience here in the community affect your understanding of yourself and others as cultural beings?	How can you apply the insights you've developed about culture and intercultural communication to improve your capacities for listening and communicating?

Toolbox 3.3 demonstrates how reflection questions provide a link between experience and targeted discipline-specific learning.

What is difficult to capture in a chart such as the one offered in Toolbox 3.3 is the extent to which reflective practice brings course concepts to *life*. Through combining best practices in systematic preparation with careful attention to the need for dynamism and flexibility, several colleagues

Employing Reflection Questions to Link Experience With Targeted Learning

Course	Site and Service Description	Literature	Learning Objective	Reflection Question(s)
Development Economics	Assist with physical labor supporting the construction of a community's first library and Internet center in rural Ghana	Introductory texts on development economics	Identify and analyze dominant approaches to development	How has your experience with the challenges of physical labor and project management in a developing country affected your evaluation of dominant approaches to development?
Engineering: Professional Experience	Design and implement support for community water systems throughout Honduras	Engineering texts; significant literature on high-performing teams	Demonstrate increased understanding of personal role in and contribution to dynamic teams	How have the challenges of implementing water systems in cross-cultural teams in developing communities affected your understanding of the role you inhabit on a high-performing team?
History of the Holocaust	Engage in some direct physical service through restoration of Jewish graveyards near Auschwitz; learn about the Holocaust	Historical texts and several pieces on the challenge of remembrance	Communicate historical issues to a broader public	How will you communicate the visceral experience of being at Auschwitz, hearing from survivors, and being at one of the most notorious sites of the Holocaust to friends and family members?

(Continues)

TOOLBOX 3.3 (*Continued*)

Course	Site and Service Description	Literature	Learning Objective	Reflection Question(s)
Nationalism and Literature	Support youth reconciliation programming at an interfaith summer camp in Northern Ireland	Works of fiction from multiple Northern Irish perspectives	Analyze the role of story in defining and redefining *identity*	How have the texts we've examined presented multiple Northern Irish realities? How do you see these disparate realities reflected in the worldviews of community members with whom we've worked?
Community Development	Gather data to support a local women's rights organization's grant application in rural Tanzania	Texts on development, community-based research methods, and rural Tanzania	Demonstrate ability to engage in community-based research and continuously refine methodology	What assumptions about the research process have changed as you've engaged with community partners? How have you altered your approach?

have achieved deep learning experiences with students that went well beyond the initial course design.

A faculty member directing a program in rural Bolivia explained to students that "lack of redundancy" was a characteristic of developing countries. The students were able—just as would have been the case on campus—to conceptualize that lack of redundancy may mean unreliable transportation systems, access to water, inconsistent electricity service, or inconsistent stock in stores. Yet when a hammer actually did break on a construction site—causing a significant issue for the workers because it was one of the few hammers available nearby—students saw the effect of this concept quite clearly. The faculty member integrated the experience with students' reflective discussion and journaling that evening, asking how experiencing lack of redundancy related to and affected their interpretation of the development theories they studied. Furthermore, the discussion turned to whether it is legitimate to theorize about development from afar without engaging with, seeing, or experiencing the depth of challenges faced in rural communities in developing countries.

Also in Bolivia, a different faculty member was engaged in a conversation with a community partner about human rights, when the community partner said many of her friends felt that human rights might be useful elsewhere, but in Bolivia they protected only criminals. This utterance triggered a long discussion with students and community members that illustrated the contingent and culturally contextualized nature of human rights—one of the goals of the course. It also highlighted the power and positionality of the community partner in Bolivian society. Although a similar discussion could have taken place in a classroom on campus, leveraging the community partner's comment into a conversation harnessed the energy of the moment into an engaging, personally connected, and educationally rich discussion.

In Ghana, students and a faculty member were learning about the local community through an informal tour provided by a community partner. Knowing that microfinance was a very popular idea, the community partner took care to introduce the group to a farmer involved in a microfinance project. The farmer shared that he was part of a microfinance program that permitted him to grow "the strategic crop" for the region. Curious about the limited frame placed on the farmer, the faculty member asked a few follow-up questions and quickly learned the "microfinance program" was actually a corporation's program designed to ensure coca production from smallholder farms. This unanticipated learning moment led to rich discussion on precisely what microfinance is, as well as how corporate programs that cooperate with smallholder farms can be both beneficial and limiting for rural communities.

The previous examples illustrate how faculty members leveraged particular experiential moments, often drawing from and engaging in dialogue with local community members' experience and knowledge, to deepen students' thinking about course concepts and delve into the complexity of theory in practice. This kind of effort should occur systematically throughout a course experience and also dynamically when the opportunity presents itself. To systematically advance reflective questioning, we find it helpful to consider learning objectives in the context of anticipated academic and experiential content throughout the experience, as illustrated in Toolbox 3.3 on disciplinary content and in Toolbox 3.4 in respect to several common thematic areas in CBGL. Importantly, we have not included a disciplinary content example in the four learning areas considered in the following list. We have instead focused on reflective questioning, texts, and exercises that provide opportunities for staggered exploration of the core CBGL content areas of global citizenship and civic action, service and development, intercultural learning, power, positionality, and privilege. Some of the following examples refer to specific texts, exercises, or experiences. Depending on faculty members' leadership decisions and the unpredictable nature of local contexts and conditions, these reflective questions can complement academic reading. In addition, best practices in reflection suggest that questions should be "connected, contextualized, continuous, and challenging" (Eyler et al., 1996).

The four Cs suggest that reflection must be

1. connected to academic assignments that continuously build knowledge and sophistication of analysis;
2. contextualized in the community experience and broader social issues;
3. continuous by happening before, during, and after a service experience; and
4. challenging in terms of pushing students to reflect and question evermore deeply (Eyler & Giles, 1999).

Toolbox 3.4 demonstrates how the four Cs can be integrated through continuous reflection on CBGL. It also demonstrates how questions may be explicitly connected to specific texts and contextualized through learning from the experience, as is the case when students are asked to revisit their understandings of culture after working with host community members. In terms of challenging students through reflection, like many best practices in education, that goal is often best achieved by working with each student individually. Toolbox 3.5 employs the DEAL framework in light of pre-, during, and

Learning Goals, Experience, and Reflection Before, During, and After CBGL Experience

Content Area	Learning Objective	Before	During	After
Global citizenship and civic action	Describe and begin to implement personal commitment to human dignity	After reading the introduction to Nussbaum's (2002) *For Love of Country?* how would you describe your own commitment to the notion of human dignity?	Consider the Global Civic Action Guide (on the globalsl website) and indicate if you can imagine being involved with any of those organizations. If not, how might you advance your commitments?	Develop and deliver a community presentation describing your CBGL experience, why it mattered to you, and ways in which you might continue to stay involved with the related issues.
Power and privilege	Demonstrate understanding of positionality and its effects	Complete the identity pie exercise (Toolbox 3.2).	After you examine your initial identity pie, ask: How has your time in the community affected your understanding of your home and host cultures, specifically in respect to power and privilege?	How does your positionality give you special "voice" to possibly advocate for or influence particular kinds of policies and attention to social issues?
Service and development	Articulate personal philosophy of service	Why are you coming on this trip?	Complete the "Global Civic Action?" activity (Toolbox 2.1).	How has this experience affected your understanding of service? How might you continue to serve?
Intercultural understanding	Exhibit increased understanding of culture and ability to communicate across cultures	Develop a "stereotype list" with peers (Toolbox 3.5).	Revisit, critique, and consider stereotype list in light of experiences.	Develop a friendly "elevator speech" response for trusted friends who label community partners with stereotypes.

TOOLBOX **3.5**
Focusing on Intercultural Understanding and Comprehension of One's Own Positionality

	Before	During	After
Describe	As a group, develop a "stereotype list" of ideas you believe you or others hold about the community or country where you will be working and cooperating.	Revisit, critique, and consider the stereotype list in light of experiences.	Develop an "elevator speech" response for friends and family who may label community partners with stereotypes.
Examine	Which stereotypes are negative? Positive?	Which of your ideas have been challenged and how? Which have been confirmed and how?	What have you learned about your culture through this activity?
Articulate learning	How do you benefit from these stereotypes? How do these ideas connect to dominant group privilege?	How has confronting your stereotypes through experiential learning helped you to become more culturally competent?	How can you learn from the reactions to your speech to further develop your capacities to support more intercultural understanding?

postimmersion opportunities to demonstrate how one theme may be continuously revisited to encourage student learning and reflection in a specific area. In this case, we offer further elaboration on the development of intercultural understanding and appreciation for the dynamic nature of one's own positionality in specific CBGL contexts.

Theorists have suggested there is a pattern or set of stages of university students' cognitive development in which the final stage tends to be characterized by a meta-awareness of one's own learning process and an ability to make decisions and reach judgments in the context of continuously changing knowledge (Baxter-Magolda, 2003; Chickering, 1969; Kegan, 1982, 1994; Perry, 1981). These cognitive developmental theories can provide a helpful reflective framework for cooperating with students in their struggles as they work to understand new ideas as well as accept new understandings of knowledge, its foundations, and its evolving character. Applications of this theoretical insight on cognitive development are extensive. We explore these practices later in the section on critical reflection, but we first consider several specific implications for academic learning in terms of both course content mastery and skill development.

Perry (1970, 1981) suggested that college students move through a patterned progresion of thinking stages from dualistic to relativistic thinking and finally to making a commitment to a particular perspective and potential action in light of continuously developing knowledge. They begin with dualistic thinking, which posits a right and a wrong and a deference to their teachers as the arbiters of correct and false knowledge, before moving into a relativistic space in which students begin to open their mind to the possibility of multiple valid perspectives on a particular concept, idea, topic, or problem. Following a relativistic phase, according to Perry (1970, 1981), students embrace the need to make a commitment to particular judgments while recognizing the knowledge is both grounded in and evolving with the context (Fitch, Steinke, & Hudson, 2013). The trajectory he suggested is consistent with the kind of development of critical thinking sought by liberal educators, that thinking should embrace a diversity of ideas and recognize multiple legitimate ways of knowing (Association of American Colleges & Universities, 1998), while maintaining the ability to lead ethically and effectively.

This process can be nurtured through application of targeted reflection questions specific to disciplinary content areas. When students demonstrate dualistic thinking, faculty members should ask a question that encourages further nuance. When their answers are nuanced but relativistic, faculty members' individualized journal responses should encourage them to consider the implications of decisions for individual human lives that take place in a specific political, cultural, and social context. In other words, faculty members should demonstrate that commitments to ideas (or lack thereof) have implications for people's lives under particular contextual conditions. Both in the United States and abroad, CBGL frequently demonstrates that most people experience contexts that are strikingly complex, dynamic, and unpredictable, in which a shift in policy may have profound implications for individual lives and families. Toolbox 3.6 suggests this kind of dynamic in relation to indigenous health care policy.

Thus far we have considered how reflection can be systematically developed to describe, examine, and articulate learning before, during, and after immersion; how specific course content and learning goals should relate to reflection questions; and how ongoing reflection during course experiences should respond to students individually, calibrating to their degree of nuance in thinking. Responding to students where they are as individuals can be

TOOLBOX **3.6**

Individualized Reflection to Develop Critical Thinking Skills

Reflection Question	Student Response	Faculty Response
We have reviewed several articles relating to indigenous health care, self-determination, and childhood vaccinations. On the basis of these articles and your experiences speaking with community members and observing in local health clinics, what do you think is the best policy for the local community?	*Dualistic response:* Every child should have access to vaccinations. That is clearly the policy most strongly correlated with longer lives.	You make a good point about longevity, but the Indigenous Tribal People's Convention was clearly developed because many indigenous community worldviews consider some things (e.g., relationship with the divine) more important than longevity. How would you address this perspective?
	Relativistic response: It is impossible to say. There are good arguments on both sides. For example, longevity wins the day on one hand, whereas on the other hand, self-determination should arguably be held as a preeminent right for all peoples.	You make good points, but you must nonetheless take a position. That is what human rights lawyers, policymakers, and advocates or abstainers must do every day. We make decisions whether we expressly advocate for particular policies or simply go along with what others have decided. So weighing the best arguments, current evidence, and context, put yourself in the position of a human rights judge. Would you side for required childhood vaccinations or complete community autonomy on health-care decisions? Why?

achieved through individualized journal responses and interpersonal reflective questioning during class discussion. We will now consider the role of different kinds of learning strengths and styles.

Educators should design activities that provide a variety of opportunities for reflective processing and expression (see Eyler et al., 1996). Different types of reflective spaces for students comfortable expressing themselves individually, interpersonally, in teams, or through creative outputs are demonstrated next. These categories and related types of reflective activities are organized in Toolbox 3.7. Some of the activities are self-evident, whereas others are described in greater detail throughout this book, including the comfort zone

TOOLBOX 3.7
Diverse Opportunities for Reflection

Individual/ Semiprivate Writing	Public Writing	Interpersonal With Class	Interpersonal/Experiential With Community	Creative
Journal, reflective essays, thank-you letters to the community, explanatory letters to friends and family, letter to legislator, research paper	Editorial, conference poster or presentation, posts to social media, reflective blog, or creation of online petition	Facilitated discussion, identity pie (Toolbox 4.1), presentations, elevator speech development, group journal, and structured feedback	Comfort zone activity (Toolbox 4.4), seven strangers exercise (Toolbox 7.6), ethnography, listening exercises, elevator speeches, presentations, asset-based mapping	Photo essay assignment, development of website, multimedia reflective blog, development of product for the community, newsletter, video, publication, grant proposal, radio segment

activity (Toolbox 4.4), the group journal (chapter 7), and the seven strangers activity (Toolbox 7.6).

Critical Reflection

The preceding section clarified what is meant by reflection in CBGL, best practices for reflective planning using the DEAL model, awareness of the flow of a sandwich course (described more comprehensively in the program models section in chapter 6), backward design (further discussed in chapter 7), and student development theory. We now turn to highlighting what we believe (along with other adult learning scholars such as Brookfield, 1995, 2000, 2009; Freire, 2000; Kiely, 2004, 2005, 2015; Mezirow, 1995) are important differences between reflection and critical reflection. As Brookfield (2009) stated, "This conflating of the terms 'reflection' and 'critical reflection' implies that adding the qualifier 'critical' somehow makes the kind of reflection happening deeper and more profound" (p. 294).

Brookfield (2009) clarified that reflection is not inherently critical. He described at least four intellectual traditions underpinning the concept and use of critical reflection, each of which brings a set of assumptions, practices, and implications for how reflection is used (Kiely, 2015). Brookfield (2009), whose writing on critical reflection draws heavily from Marxist thought, Gramsci, and the Frankfurt tradition of critical social theory, contended,

> Critical reflection turns the spotlight squarely onto issues of power and control. It assumes the minutiae of practice have embedded within them the struggles between unequal interests and groups that exist in the wider world. For reflection to be considered critical then, it must have as its explicit focus uncovering and challenging the power dynamics that frame practice and . . . hegemonic assumptions (those assumptions we embrace as being in our best interests when in fact they are working against us). (p. 298)

For CBGL educators and practitioners, the use of critical reflection from a critical theory tradition indicates engaging in a learning process that recognizes and critiques ideology (political, economic, social, and cultural), uncovers hegemonic assumptions, and examines relations of power with the goal of becoming critically aware of how each distorts our worldview. It also involves exploring ways to act and challenge the status quo to achieve a more just and equitable set of social, political, economic, and cultural relations (Brookfield, 2009). That is, the work of CBGL is bound up with the effort to critically examine the distortions of our own and others' taken-for-granted assumptions in order to imagine and re-create a world that better respects every person's basic dignity (Hartman & Kiely, 2014a). It is aligned with critical service-learning (Kiely, 2005; Mitchell, 2008) in the Freirean tradition (Deans, 1999) and engages ongoing analysis and critique of multiple forms of structural violence (Galtung, 1969). Critically reflective practice can help us move beyond hegemonic structures and discourses that prevent us from enacting mutual respect and equal treatment around the world, while our commitments remain to this value of equity and basic moral equality among all people.

Especially because CBGL may be pioneering, path breaking, or perhaps even radical, a faculty member cannot plan for all of the insights and outcomes that may result from it. This is the case for any course that is community engaged and thereby includes unpredictable interactions with others. That community engagement requires ongoing adjustment and flexible planning is made clear in the service-learning literature (Eyler & Giles, 1999; Jacoby, 2015; Sandmann, Kiely, & Grenier, 2009), but we are suggesting something that goes one step further. One cannot plan precisely for outcomes when CBGL is part of the development of critical consciousness or conscientization (Freire, 2000), transformational learning (Edwards, 2008; Kiely, 2004), movement building (Swords & Kiely, 2010), or doing the pioneering work of global citizens creating an as-yet-unimagined tomorrow (Falk, 2000). This is the case in two different ways.

First, critically reflective practice and the movement-building work of service-learning that explicitly and intentionally challenges long-standing institutional arrangements, power relations, and dominant cultural norms that serve to oppress rather than empower necessarily involves creating new pathways and possibilities (Swords & Kiely, 2010). Students as civic actors and cocollaborators in community development may imagine and implement an unplanned possibility. For example, several community initiatives and advocacy campaigns have grown from youthful idealism into full-fledged nonprofit organizations, social sector initiatives, and movements (see amizade.org, www.engagegrassroots.org, www.wateraid.org/us/water-for-waslala, www.teachforamerica.org). This cannot be a precisely targeted learning outcome but may be a more likely result with the infusion of critically reflective practice, a practice that highlights the distance between ideal and real social structures. Second, our understandings of humility, continuously developing knowledge, and history lead us to embrace the notion that ongoing criticality (Burbules & Berk, 1999) is important for everyone to develop as a life habit. As Freire (2000) recognized, this permanent position of criticality is itself an unsettled outcome. It is continuously shifting, asking, wondering, sometimes acting, and always returning again to question. It is never finished.

Kiely's (2002, 2004, 2005, 2015) work questions current conceptions of reflection in the experiential and service-learning literature (Eyler & Giles, 1999; Kolb, 1984) and demonstrates the shortcomings of many programs that claim to advance transformational learning. Although the terms *critical reflection* and *transformational learning* are often employed without robust attention to their theoretical roots, Kiely conducted a longitudinal study of a CBGL program that engaged students in critically reflective practice before, during, and after their CBGL experience. His research demonstrates the value of critical reflection for students' perspective transformation in CBGL and its connection to individual and social action. However, as his study indicated, students who engage in critical reflection often experience perspective transformation or profound shifts in their worldview that are personal, ethical, political, cultural, intellectual, and spiritual (Kiely, 2002, 2004). Such shifts, while illuminating distorted and sometimes harmful assumptions about one's self, culture, consumption habits, ways of knowing, institutional structures, and the sources and solutions to persistent problems in the community, can also lead students to disengage. They may feel frustrated, particularly with status quo thinking that neglects to consider the complex structural factors that affect social problems, and experience difficulty communicating the meaning of their CBGL experience to friends, family, coworkers, and others. Indeed, the student and scholar featured in the story that began this chapter identified strongly with Kiely's insights.

Kiely (2004) referred to the challenges students have returning home in communicating, sharing, and sometimes reconciling their worldview shift with those who haven't experienced a shift in perspective as the *chameleon complex*. Having experienced a deep shift in how they see and understand the world, students have begun to question and challenge current social and cultural norms that they find harmful and oppressive. They are often unable to share and connect with their peers and family and instead hide their true colors while feeling frustrated and conflicted about how to negotiate and maintain stable and meaningful relationships. They struggle to share their sense of how they have changed and who they are becoming with the people around them. Because of the potential for students to experience the chameleon complex upon return and long after participating in CBGL, it is crucial that faculty incorporate numerous reflection assignments and exercises for students to hone their skills in reflection and critical reflection. Ongoing reflective activity supports students' capacities to move through disruption and confusion toward transformative action. Such reflective activity may support their capacities to respond to one of the greatest challenges in the CBGL learning cycle: negotiating one's newfound insights and identity with loved ones and friends after the experience. This theme of understanding the Chameleon Complex and therefore channeling students' insights and energies following a CBGL experience is further explored in chapter 9.

Critical reflection as it is understood in the critical theory tradition, therefore, differs from much of the dominant cognitive developmental, technical-rational, and constructivist reflection traditions in service-learning in terms of its intentionality regarding interrogation of taken-for-granted assumptions and common sense wisdom; its examination of ideology and hegemony; its embrace of alternative perspectives; and its explicit questioning of power and self-interest in relation to harmful practice, systemic oppression, marginalized communities, and the development of critical consciousness (Freire, 2000; Kiely, 2002, 2004, 2005, 2015; Mezirow, 1991, 1995). This reflective orientation thereby moves well beyond learning that focuses on students' personal growth, objective content mastery, and disciplinary skill development toward becoming part of a larger, ongoing movement challenging dominant norms and existing structures, policies, and institutions that have historically benefited certain groups' interests over others (Kiely, 2015; Swords & Kiely, 2010). Brookfield (2009), for example, proclaimed that the focus of critical reflection is "always on analyzing commonly held ideas and practices for the extent to which they perpetuate economic inequity, deny compassion, foster a culture of silence and prevent people from realizing a sense of common connectedness" (p. 298).

To set up reflection in service-learning as concerned purely with learning goals within disciplinary fields is unfair. We recognize that service-learning scholars who have written about reflection (Ash & Clayton, 2009; Eyler & Giles, 1999) are interested in advancing transformational learning and that they often include reflective activities that advance that goal. Yet our suggestion here is that an embrace of critical reflection, which clearly represents a values orientation toward philosophical and intellectual traditions that focus on ideology critique, questioning of hegemonic assumptions, and concern for the marginalized, is more likely to lead to individual and social transformation beyond the focus of the course, as documented by Kiely (2004, 2005).

Engaging in critical reflection, to a much greater extent than is the case with structured reflective practice for specific learning goals, requires the faculty member to decenter himself or herself as an authority figure (Freire, 2000; Weiler, 1991). This means faculty need to share control over how knowledge is constructed and how decisions are made over the content and process of the service-learning course and community work. In addition, faculty need to engage in dialogue with multiple and diverse stakeholders in order to create a democratic learning environment and civic space.

Faculty members and teachers may find this process disorienting, as it often "breaks the wall" of authority and expertise created by the traditional academic model. Critical reflection asks a lot of our participants in terms of questioning assumptions, critiquing dominant and oppressive norms and structures, sharing feelings, and taking concrete action steps. The end goal of critical reflection is a lifelong commitment to continuously considering the legitimacy of habits and social structures and being willing to make ongoing adjustments and realignments to create a better, more just world. CBGL educators and practitioners should model and demonstrate how they have approached these challenges in their own lives (Brookfield, 1995, 2000; Kiely, 2015) and remind students in a very real and inspiring way that our lives are spiritual and political statements. Students also model faculty behavior in this and other aspects of CBGL, so honest sharing about personal struggles to live justly and well is powerful and important. In reflection, authority and expertise are not nearly as valuable as integrity and commitment.

CBGL educators and practitioners may also find themselves as the object of questions from participants and community members—interrogated and challenged by those with a critical consciousness. By practicing critical reflection themselves, CBGL program leaders can respond, think deeply, and even alter their own perspectives and actions as necessary. Brookfield (2009) recognized the challenge of power and privilege within our own practice, writing "better to acknowledge publicly our position of power" and to engage with others "in deconstructing that power, and to model a critical analysis of our own source of authority" (p. 301). Without practicing the critical thinking and reflection required of participants, CBGL program leaders risk perpetuating problems and then becoming defensive about them.

Tilley-Lubbs (2009) provided an excellent example of CBGL program leader reflection on the privilege and hierarchy issues she created via an intercultural service-learning course model that positioned students as "haves" and community members as "have-nots." When she began the work, her "only concerns focused on responding to perceived community needs and providing an opportunity for everyone to meet" (p. 62). She wrote, bravely, that she nonetheless "enacted historian Wise's (1980) words, 'An ironic situation occurs when the consequences of an act are diametrically opposed to the original intention,' and, 'when the fundamental cause of the disparity lies in the actor himself, and his original purpose'" (p. 62). Tilley-Lubbs's reflections led her to develop service-learning practice more consistent with her ideals than the charity approach she had inadvertently embraced. Relationships with students and community partners (see chapter 5) can benefit from Tilley-Lubbs's insights:

> "Service-learning is a way of building relationships; not hierarchical relationships that are top-down, helper–helpee, but nonhierarchical relationships in the sense that each partner has something to gain and each has something to give" (Jackson & Smothers, 1998, p. 113). Additionally, I acknowledge that the "served control the service provided" thus making them "better able to serve and be served by their own actions" (Sigmon, 1979, p. 3). . . . I seek creative ways to involve students with families in empathic relationships that foster attitudes of concern for social justice and equity not based on deficit notions but rather on a realization of their responsibility to help people meet their basic needs. . . . The bottom line is the imperatives of involving the women in the process of praxis to transform charity into collaboration. (Tilley-Lubbs, 2009, p. 65)

As we emphasize throughout this book, the skills and practices of CBGL are profoundly interdependent. One cannot, for example, engage community-driven partnerships thoughtfully without considerable critical reflection and cultural humility, the topic of our next chapter.

4

POWER, SELF AS A CULTURAL BEING, CULTURAL HUMILITY, AND INTERCULTURAL COMMUNICATION

At Kansas State University, international students who have requested opportunities to further connect with their new campus community are paired with students in a course on leadership across cultures, most of whom have domestic origins. Throughout the semester, they have formal and informal opportunities to meet one another. After receiving introductory orientations to collecting oral histories and cooperating across cultures respectfully, students in the leadership course are tasked with interviewing the international students. They collect the stories, are coached through an editing and revision process, and celebrate and thank their interviewees as part of an initiative to demonstrate the diversity in the Kansas State University community (Your Fellow Americans, 2015). At the culminating event, an invited local state representative issues a declaration of welcome, then watches the students celebrate one another. Near the end, a domestic student shares her learning experience, pausing to say that she made a change through the experience—she is certain she will speak up now if she hears anyone associate Muslims with terrorism.

In a different CBGL experience in Bolivia, during the U.S. war with Iraq, a visiting U.S. faculty member asked the local site director if they could arrange a Spanish–English exchange with students from the Cochabamba public university. Conversation began slowly, over *salteñas* and sodas, but the Bolivian students soon began asking pointed yet polite questions about the U.S. invasion. In quick succession, the visiting students learned that the

Bolivian young people believed there must be a draft for young U.S. men, the Bolivians learned that there was no such draft, and the U.S. students saw the extent to which their country is often viewed as a case of imperialist power projection. This was all achieved in a respectful manner, followed by one question about why none of the young men on the program were fighting. As each individual shared his or her story, John, one of the U.S. students, mentioned that he was a pacifist. A Bolivian professor, who had remained quiet throughout the exchange, spoke up to say she had never before met a U.S. citizen who was a pacifist; in fact, she hadn't believed they existed.

In Tanzania, as further developed in chapter 5, a group of students cooperated with Hartman and a local women's rights nongovernmental organization (NGO) to support data gathering as part of the development of a grant application. During that process, Hartman and a few students had the opportunity to accompany Juma Massissi, the NGO director, on a visit to a village where a woman had requested legal representation. Hartman later recalled,

> We entered the front room of the home of a village elder. It was a dark contrast to the bright sunlight outside, and it took my eyes some time to adjust. The homeowner sat in a chair against one wall; I squeezed in and stood against another wall while two of my students sat in chairs near me. One took notes on a laptop; the other observed. Across the room from us Juma stood next to a small corner table upon which the husband and three of his male friends and family members sat, their feet dangling near the floor. The woman who brought the complaint—the first wife—sat on the floor on the other side of Juma. Two more of my students and scores of community members peered in on the proceedings through the small door and only source of light in the room.
>
> The dialogue proceeded primarily in Swahili. I only understood parts of that, and my students understood even less. Swahili and English are both national languages in Tanzania, but in the rural spaces English only goes so far. Despite our limited linguistic understanding, the placement of bodies and their language spoke volumes. As I mentioned the woman complainant had arranged herself on the floor, her knees tucked underneath her, bare feet sticking out from below a long dress. The men sat above her, imperiously. The husband, as he made his case, grew increasingly animated, voice rising, eyes dilating, him pointing repeatedly at his first wife as his anger filled the room.
>
> It was this body language and vitriolic tenor that set off my student. At some point, I took my eyes off of the dialogue and saw that she was shaking, her jaw clenched, tears streaming down her face.
>
> She caught my eyes and cut a whisper between us. "This is so wrong," she insisted. I told her to try to stay calm. That it wasn't our place to speak at the moment. (Hartman, 2014b)

Each of the intercultural experiences mentioned in the opening of this chapter involves varying degrees of preparatory learning, intentional program elements, challenge and support, mutual interest in engagement, and carefully facilitated reflection. This chapter provides a review of the literature that informs our understanding of intercultural learning, distills the related insights into relevant program activities, and considers the ways in which deliberate choices regarding the program experience may influence learning outcomes.

When we refer to *intercultural learning*, we call attention to the development of three interrelated capacities: the capacity to understand oneself as a cultural being, the capacity to develop an orientation of cultural humility, and the capacity to communicate and behave appropriately in varied cultural contexts. These three capacities have distinct roots in various scholarly traditions (Bennett, 1993; Deardorff, 2006; Kiely, 2002, 2011), though in practice they are intertwined and interdependent.

A distinguishing feature of our approach to intercultural learning is that it draws from both constructivist and critical theory traditions to consider the ways in which power, privilege, and positionality intersect with intercultural learning and the development of reciprocal community–campus partnerships (Bennett, 1993, 2012; Deardorff, 2006; Gallardo, 2014; Gorski, 2008; Kiely, 2002; Savicki, 2008). Because CBGL is often about confronting injustice, intercultural learning is engaged simultaneously with critical analysis of cultural norms and rituals that may serve to legitimize ongoing structural violence (Collier, 2014; Gorski, 2008; Kiely, 2002; Sorrells & Nakagawa, 2008). Thus, a constructivist paradigm, which in study abroad emphasizes the importance of meaning-making and the cocreation of perceived reality to facilitate cross-cultural understanding and communication, becomes, within the critical paradigm, the deconstruction and reconstruction of that reality toward more just relationships (Gallardo, 2014; Kiely, 2015; Ross, 2010; Sorrells & Nakagawa, 2008). Put another way, although previous conceptions of intercultural competence frequently emphasized increasing appreciation for diverse perspectives, often including cultural adaptation and the growing embrace of relativism as desired outcomes (Bennett, 1993), cultural humility highlights the profound role that contingency plays in shaping our lives, both in terms of the arbitrariness of many cultural assumptions and through the realization that oppressive systems can be reimagined, reformed, and reshaped (Gallardo, 2014; Kiely, 2002; Lasker, 2016; Ross, 2010; Tervalon & Murray-García, 1998). The theoretical development of these areas of practice is explained next, along with relevant teaching tools and discussion of the intercultural learning process throughout a CBGL experience.

Defining *Intercultural Competence* in the Field of International Education

For many years the study abroad student learning literature specified one major outcome of interest: intercultural competence (Bennett, 1993; Dinges & Baldwin, 1996; Kim, 1991, 2001; Lambert, 1994). Deardorff's (2006) Delphi study with 23 prominent intercultural experts led to a near consensus that *intercultural competence* is "the ability to communicate effectively and appropriately in intercultural situations based on one's intercultural knowledge, skills, and attitudes" (p. 249). This definition affirmed the work of numerous other scholars in the fields of intercultural communication and learning who emphasize communication and the development of specific knowledge, skills, and attitudes as central to adapting, interacting, and functioning well in another culture (Bennett, 2012; Hoff, 2008; Kim, 2001; Ward, Bochner, & Furnam, 2001).

One of Deardorff's (2006) own key findings was that the definition of *intercultural competence* was in a state of evolution. Indeed, that theme of moving definitions, conceptualizations, and even worldviews was picked up by Vande Berg, Paige, and Hemming Lou (2012), as they claimed that the field of "study abroad has evolved through three significantly different accounts of the nature of knowing and learning" (p. 10). According to this view (Vande Berg et al., 2012), the field began first with a positivist worldview, in which study abroad exposed students to "a world that is stable, unchanging, and profoundly material" (p. 15). This positivist paradigm included an implicit assumption that some human societies were superior to others. In the 1970s, many leaders in the field began to embrace the second, relativist paradigm, which values sensitivity to and appreciation of diverse cultural norms, values, and perspectives and suggests equality among cultures (Bennett, 1993; Vande Berg et al., 2012). In addition, this phase in study abroad thinking included a presumption that more immersion necessarily leads to better learning (Vande Berg et al., 2012).

Third and currently, the constructivist paradigm suggests "a learner individually creates and together with other members of his or her cultural groups cocreates the world even as he or she perceives and experiences it" (Vande Berg et al., 2012, p. 18). A central assumption in this paradigm—based on data from numerous institutions, programs, evaluations, and research projects—is that "most students learn to learn effectively abroad only when an educator intervenes, strategically and intentionally" (p. 19).

Bennett (2012) demonstrated the implications of the constructivist understanding of intercultural learning. First, he defined *intercultural learning* as "the acquisition of generalizable (transferrable) intercultural competence;

that is, competence that can be applied to dealing with cross-cultural contact in general, not just skills useful for dealing with a particular other culture" (p. 91). This definition itself signifies some significant movement for the study abroad field, from a space where acceptance or understanding in a different culture may have been viewed as a success (the relativist paradigm) to a place where one must possess enough self-knowledge and contextual awareness to move respectfully and with humility among multiple cultures. This necessity of self-knowledge calls attention to the importance of understanding oneself as a cultural being.

Bennett (2012) pointed out, "For a praxis of intercultural relations, the minimum conceptual requirement is a self-reflexive definition of culture" (p. 101). Bennett is calling attention to the insight that any definition of *culture* is in some way a product of culture. He is also recognizing that advancing intercultural learning fundamentally encourages a self-reflexive act. Supporting student understanding of a self-reflexive definition of *culture*, however, is no small undertaking, particularly if one agrees with the claim that many U.S. students "are—with fine irony—culturally conditioned to dismiss the very notion of cultural difference" (Engle & Engle, 2012, p. 300). What is clear to us through experience working with students from a variety of countries and cultural and religious backgrounds is that there are too few structured, safe, and carefully facilitated opportunities for students to reflect on their identities and the sources of the assumptions that inform who they are and what they value and believe. This intersection of deeper understanding of culture as a cocreated reality and the challenge of working with students who may be conditioned to see themselves as independent of culture (Vande Berg et al., 2011) integrates with recent insights in GSL (Kiely, 2004, 2005; Kiely & Nielsen, 2003; Locklin, 2010) and related developments in medicine (Tervalon & Murray-García, 1998) and social work (Richards-Desai & Lewis, 2017) to inform our approach to intercultural learning. That approach—cultural humility—simultaneously encourages listening, sensitivity, humility, and appropriate action to question and transform oppressive systems.

Recognizing the Intercultural Learning Process

Study abroad and service-learning educators have drawn from a number of learning process models to better facilitate students' intercultural learning experiences (Kiely, 2011). Theories that have informed the intercultural, study abroad, and CBGL fields include Allport's (1954) contact theory, Bennett's (1993) developmental model of intercultural sensitivity, Kolb's (1984) experiential learning model, Festinger's (1957) theory of cognitive dissonance, Kim's (2001) model for intercultural transformation, Mezirow's (1991) transformational learning theory, culture shock and U curve models (Lysgaard, 1955; Oberg, 1960), W curve models (Gullahorn & Gullahorn, 1963), reentry or reverse culture shock models (Austen, 1986; Martin, 1993; Pusch, 2004), Paige's (1993) intensity factors, and Ward and colleagues' (2001) "ABC" model of acculturation (Kiely, 2011).

Common to the development and use of these processes is a set of assumptions about what happens when students travel outside their home culture and spend time studying, working, and/or performing service in unfamiliar places (Kiely, 2011). The affective, cognitive, visceral, and behavioral dimensions of this intercultural process are typically described as a process of *adaptation, adjustment,* or *acculturation* (Savicki, 2008; Ward et al., 2001) and comes with the following set of commonly held assumptions:

- Crossing a border into another country or community puts students in unfamiliar cultural contexts, interactions, and situations with people, places, and events.
- These new and often unfamiliar intercultural experiences can be jarring, disruptive, dissonant, and disorienting (commonly referred to as *culture shock*).
- This dissonance leads to an adjustment process with distinct stages, transitions, and/or learning processes.
- The identification of the patterns, elements, and dimensions of this process through thoughtful and intentional observation, reflection, and dialogue will help in supporting students as they make sense of and learn from their intercultural experience particularly in terms of how they adjust to, adapt, communicate, and function more effectively in new, unfamiliar settings, situations, and/or cross-cultural contexts over time.
- CBGL contributions to this area of research have made clear that it is important to consider how students continue to learn from intercultural experience and integrate critical approaches to global citizenship into their personal, professional, and academic life following a course or program (Hartman, 2008, 2014a; Hartman & Kiely, 2014b; Kiely, 2004, 2005, 2011; Slimbach, 2010; further discussed in chapter 9).

This literature demonstrates that an essential starting point is recognizing that all individuals have spent their entire lives adapting, adjusting, and acculturating and have become socialized into a particular way of thinking and acting—albeit always evolving (Bennett, 2012). Students have already constructed a cultural identity or worldview (albeit still evolving) that is made up of life experiences, feelings, values, expectations, personality traits, and sense of self, along with diverse sets of skills, knowledge, attitudes, and behaviors—all of which will have varying degrees of influence on their intercultural learning experience during and after participating in a CBGL course or program (Kiely, 2002, 2005).

Self as a Cultural Being: Frames of Reference

In the process of developing a transformative model for service-learning (Kiely, 2005) and deepened insights regarding the importance and challenges of post-immersion reflection, Kiely (2002, 2004) integrated significant insights from the adult learning literature (Brookfield, 1995, 2000; Mezirow, 1991; Mezirow & Associates, 2000; Taylor, 1994, 1998) with current understandings in the study abroad (Bennett, 1993; Kim, 2001; Laubscher, 1994; Martin, 1986, 1993; Paige, 1993) and civic engagement fields (Eyler & Giles, 1999) to explore how transformational learning might enhance students' knowledge and ability to engaged in individual and social action as a result of CBGL experiences. Kiely's (2004, 2005, 2015) research supports our capacities to critically reflect on the complexity of the relational nature of CBGL programs at the intersections of identity, culture, experience, agency, structure, worldview, and transformational learning while providing opportunities to step into the inquiry systematically.

One must begin with systematic inquiry regarding the ways in which previous experience and socialization influence one's perception and interpretation of experiences with CBGL and how these experiences affect one's worldview. Mezirow and Associates (2000) suggested that one's meaning structure or frame of reference, which serves as a filter for giving meaning to experience, contains a number of different dimensions:

- Sociolinguistic (cultural canon, ideologies, social norms, customs, "language games," secondary socialization)
- Moral-ethical (conscience, moral norms)
- Epistemic (learning styles, sensory preferences, focus on wholes or parts or on the concrete or abstract)
- Philosophical (religious doctrine, philosophy, transcendental worldview)
- Psychological (self-concept, personality traits or types, repressed parental prohibitions that continue to dictate ways of feeling and acting in adulthood, emotional response patterns, images, fantasies, dreams)
- Aesthetic (values, tastes, attitudes, standards, and judgments about beauty and the insight and authenticity of aesthetic expressions, such as the sublime, the ugly, the tragic, the humorous, the "drab," and others)

Each of these frames of reference acts to construct a worldview with a set of assumptions, often taken for granted, that shapes and informs our values, beliefs, and daily habits (Mezirow & Associates, 2000). The value of deliberately facilitated intercultural learning is that it draws our consciousness to becoming more aware of our unique biography and worldview, and it helps us see how these dimensions of our evolving selves serve as lenses that filter our experience of culture through interactions with peers, faculty, community members, and practitioners (Kiely, 2005). It is essential then to incorporate intercultural activities into CBGL programs to prepare students to meaningfully and thoughtfully engage with and learn from diverse stakeholders with whom they interact. See Toolbox 4.1, "Identity Pie," for an example of an introductory reflective activity that will support participants' capacities to construct and develop awareness of the meanings they attribute to the diverse individual and contextual dimensions of their evolving identity and frames of reference, while exploring the diversity of such frames, including misperceptions, stereotypes, and shared meanings, within the larger group of peers (Brislin, 1993; Cafferella & Merriam, 2000; Kim, 2001; Lebedko, 2014; McIntosh, 1989; Sparrow, 2000; Watt, 2007).

Burleson (2015) and Andreotti and de Souza (2008) also developed excellent free online resources that support opening participants' awareness of their everyday cultural assumptions. In an efficient text developed through her training in sociocultural psychology and through ongoing collaboration with a nonprofit network in Pine Ridge, South Dakota, Burleson (2015) provided a set of exploratory prompts designed to surface one's cultural assumptions:

- Is your day governed by what time it is?
- Do you consider yourself an individual more than a group member?
- Do you consider speed an indicator of greater intelligence?
- Do you adore youth over elderhood? (p. 3)

These kinds of questions do not stand alone but should be thoughtfully embedded through the learning arc of an experience. Early questions like those provided, along with activities like the identity pie, give sustained attention to surfacing and critically reflecting on one's assumptions and exploring the ways in which reality is experienced uniquely everywhere as a cocreated, cultural product. The different values, beliefs, and assumptions that make up one's frames of reference act "like a 'double edged sword' whereby they give meaning (validation) to our experiences, but at the same time skew our reality" (Taylor, 1998, p. 7). The construction of a worldview or frame of reference, as Mezirow (1991; Mezirow & Associates, 2000) suggested, simultaneously justifies, explains, and distorts the meanings we attach to experience.

TOOLBOX **4.1**
Identity Pie

The primary purpose of this activity is to assist participants in becoming more aware of their identity and worldview, the different aspects of the culture they identify with, and, importantly, how culture and other social, political, and spiritual elements of their worldview affect their beliefs, values, behaviors, and sense of self. In a comfortable and safe way, the activity should help students better understand their identity, as well as dominant (and marginalized) norms and beliefs of their home culture. In addition, the activity may lead to exploration of dominant (and marginalized) norms and beliefs of the culture they will be engaged with through their CBGL course or program. It can also be repeated in conjunction with community partners onsite.

The exercise should begin a journey into uncovering visible and invisible aspects of culture. It can proceed to examining more complex and contested cultural, political, religious, and social dimensions of identity and may move to the marginalization and harm some people experience as members of a marginalized or oppressed identity in a context. It should highlight how culture defines who we are, how we understand ourselves and others, and the misperceptions we might have about our own or others' cultural identity and assumptions (i.e., stereotypes). Because this exercise focuses on the social construction of identity along with the socially structured dimension of power relations, it is a learning process that merges both the constructivist and the critical paradigms.

Instructions for students:

- Write down 5 to 10 aspects of your individual culture and identity.
- Provide examples of visible and invisible aspects of culture and identity for inspiration.
- Represent how the attributes you've listed constitute your "identity pie."
- Larger slices of the pie represent more dominant aspects of your identity.
- A caveat: It is not necessary that you use the pie as a metaphor for drawing, but you do need to draw the things that you feel compose your cultural identity. The pie can assist with describing elements of your identity that have greater or lesser significance by varying slice size.
- Be prepared to share your drawing with a partner and/or the group.

(Continues)

TOOLBOX 4.1 *(Continued)*

Instructions for facilitators, all connected to exploration of self as a cultural being:

- Once the students have had some time to think about their identity pies and write down elements that make their identity, ask for a volunteer to share an item that he or she wrote down. (To facilitate discussion in reticent groups, you may wish to give the students time to share their pies with a partner before the group discussion or model how you define yourself culturally. There is always the option not to share or to share only certain items that participants are comfortable sharing.)
- For each item, ask for clarification about the meaning of the item to the individual and the role it plays in the individual's life (e.g., what does it mean to be a Christian, a southerner, a woman, an African American, a brother, a feminist, a global citizen, a liberal, etc.?).
- Interrogate the ways in which dominant identities are frequently less visible. For example, students who carry privileged identities are often less likely to list those identities (White, male, U.S. citizen, traditional college age) in contrast with students whose nonprivileged identity markers may have more obviously shaped their experiences of dominant culture.
- Alternatively, identify and consider dominant cultural values, assumptions, and norms—visible and invisible—as they relate to the ways in which participants describe their cultures and identities (e.g., if an individual identifies herself as a southerner, ask what it means to be a northerner or how it feels to identify as a Muslim or an African American in the United States or other countries). This discussion might lead to consideration of power relations among individuals and groups, levels of access, or certain rights or privileges given to specific groups. The facilitator will need to be particularly sensitive to individual and group comfort levels and remind participants to speak from their own experiences and perceptions rather than make broader claims about what culture is or how others experience it.
- In the United States, introduce some strong cultural forces that are frequently harder to see but nonetheless shape U.S. identities. For example, how does continuous experience in a capitalist economy influence your worldview? Has anyone lived outside of a U.S.-style political-economic structure for any length of time? How did it affect your assumptions, whether in relation to time, health care, or something else?

- Conclude the activity by brainstorming how one might respond when confronted with values, norms, meanings, and assumptions that differ from one's own or how those aspects of one's identity influence relations of power, access to resources, and agency.
- Consider approaches to community-building that support and appreciate diverse identities.
- Return to the multiple meanings, experiences, and complex relationships that are associated with culture and identity later in the program experience (e.g., after experiencing a particularly powerful or confusing cross-cultural encounter).

Crossing Borders: Unfamiliar Frames of Reference

The frame of reference that students and faculty bring to experiences will influence how they navigate all border crossings, including, but not limited to, social, spiritual, economic, linguistic, cultural, political, historical, religious, racial, ethnic, epistemological, and ideological borders (Camacho, 2004; R. Jones, Robbins, & LePeau, 2011; Kiely, 2002, 2005). Kiely's (2002, 2005) transformative service-learning model provides a useful approach for CBGL educators to design programs with *context and border crossing* in mind. Kiely's longitudinal research indicates that there are at least four key contextual elements that influence students' CBGL experience: (a) personal, (b) structural, (c) programmatic, and (d) historical. Each of these factors plays an important, tangible role in students' learning experience before, during, and after program participation. It is important to consider each dimension as part of the CBGL programming prior to students' departure.

Next we provide an example of how historical and structural elements may influence students' perceptions of appropriate development practice or service. This example is offered in the hope that deep, probing inquiry during preparatory activities and course work may illuminate the distortions of development discourse (Escobar, 1994) and the ways in which power and injustice flow throughout everyday language, through consideration of assumptions regarding service and development (Hartman, 2017b).

After demonstrating that child development and global health development leaders have launched global campaigns to end orphanage volunteering and clinical activities by uncredentialed volunteers, Hartman drew on a framing of power analysis (Dugan, Turman, & Torrez, 2015; Liu, 2013) to suggest eight prompts that illuminate how these activities remain popular despite the advice of those experts (and the agreement of the authors that such activities are harmful). Toolbox 4.2 provides an example of a power analysis using these prompts.

TOOLBOX **4.2**

Power Analysis: Global Service and Development Discourses

Prompts	Global Volunteering, Service, and Development Discourses
What is power?	The capacity to act or to have agency. The chance to be born into a socially constructed reality where one's presumed helpfulness is always latent. The opportunity to be rewarded for unreflectively acting in ways consistent with a dominant discourse based on past inequities, active discrimination, and stereotypes. The capacity to (re)create categories of *needy* and *helpful*.
Who has it?	Organizational staff members, faculty and staff, prospective and current volunteers who are privileged (in comparison to vulnerable populations) in terms of one or a combination of the following: socioeconomic class, race, nationality, educational opportunities.
How does it operate?	Power operates through dominant discourse. The power of framing is reiterated through mass media when wealthy development novices and celebrities embark on medical missions and orphanage trips. It is also reasserted when funds spent on volunteering programs funnel back to the media and publicity is leveraged to sell future programs. It is solidified through countless well-intentioned but misguided social advocacy and philanthropic campaigns that construct distant others as helpless and needy. It persists because of schooling systems and sociocultural assumptions that do not work to systematically advance understanding of global health and global development.
How does it flow?	
What part of it is visible?	International volunteers have the resources to fly to a host community. They cross borders, navigate, and act, supported by various forms of capital—social, economic, political, and linguistic. Through social media and technology access, and particularly in relation to personal networks, they possess power to frame the story of their volunteering experience—its rationale and successes.
What part of it is not?	Significant parts of these structures are almost entirely invisible in terms of dominant cultural assumptions and discourse.
Why do some people have it?	Unearned privilege, frequently intertwined with colonial and White supremacists' histories.
Why is that compounded?	The dominant narrative serves many organizations' bottom lines and many students' professional development desires. The people harmed by it are frequently silenced, and the harms are often not immediately obvious.

Note. Adapted from "Community-Engaged Scholarship, Knowledge, and Dominant Discourse: A Cautionary Tale From the Global Development Sector," by E. Hartman, 2017a, *Journal of Leadership Studies*, *11*(1), p. 63.

It draws on the critical reflection tradition that requires participants to reflect on harmful consequences that result from unequal relations of power (Brookfield, 2000; Kiely, 2015; Mezirow, 1991) and consideration of discourse analysis within international development (Escobar, 1994). Hence, the analysis focuses on surfacing the power of dominant discourse in reproducing hegemonic assumptions regarding ethical action in the field of global development.

Even when the relationship between assumptions regarding service and appropriate behavior is not as problematic as the situation detailed earlier, a number of CBGL studies (Hartman, 2008; Kiely, 2004; Porter, 2000) have found that it is somewhat common for program participants to reevaluate and transform their understanding of service and development throughout CBGL experiences. Many students who participate in the Navajo Nation program case that began chapter 1, for example, leave with a quite different understanding of service and an expanded sense of ways of knowing and being. This transformed perspective shifts the lens in which students interpret their CBGL experience, often noting the knowledge and assets of community members and injustices of which they were previously unaware. In addition, and importantly, this shift in worldview influences how students interpret and struggle to integrate their learning postprogram, particularly in respect to challenging and resisting unjust dimensions of the status quo and majority thinking (i.e., norms, values, policies) as they now perceive them (Kiely, 2004; Mangis, 2011).

Critical Reflection, Cultural Humility, and Professional Practice

We have emphasized the importance of lifelong learning and critical self-reflection. This is the first component of cultural humility, and it intersects with our emphasis on critical global citizenship (Hartman & Kiely, 2014a) and critical reflection in that we understand this self-reflective process as intertwined with a fallibilistic approach to knowledge and assumptions (Appiah, 2006). Fallibilism holds that absolute certainty is impossible, that "our knowledge is imperfect, provisional, subject to revision in the face of new evidence" (Appiah, 2006). To act and think with cultural humility is to hold one's knowledge, beliefs, and assumptions tentatively.

The concept of cultural humility grew from critique of the application of cultural competence in the medical field. The seminal piece advancing this idea (Tervalon & Murray-García, 1998) argued that competence suggests an achieved, settled state, whereas developing one's cultural capacities must be an ongoing process. This development of cultural humility requires the ability to respectfully listen and observe while continuously reminding oneself that one's own assumptions and expectations are culturally contingent.

The second component of cultural humility is the importance of recognizing one's positionality and learning how to navigate culturally embedded power imbalances in terms of crossing borders of race, class, gender, nationality, and other dimensions of power and privilege in CBGL contexts (Kiely, 2005, 2015; Mitchell, 2008; Yoder Clark & Nugent, 2011), such as the power of discourse framing exhibited in Toolbox 4.2. At first glance this combination of valuing self-questioning (component 1) and challenging systems (component 2) may seem to be fundamentally contradictory. Yet we contend that these values may be held together in ethically grounded ways, indeed that they are complementary tensions within collaborative human systems. Parker Palmer (2016) wrote,

> If I were asked for two words to summarize the habits of the heart citizens need to help democracy survive and thrive, I'd choose *chutzpah* and *humility*. By chutzpah, I mean knowing that I have a voice that needs to be heard and the right to speak it. By humility, I mean accepting the fact that my truth is always partial—and may not be true at all—so I need to listen with openness and respect, especially to "the other."

The third component of cultural humility includes striving for institutional accountability, advocating for organizational, institutional, and systems change to redress observed power imbalances (Chavez, 2012; Gallardo, 2014; Gorski, 2008; Kiely, 2015; McIntosh, 1989; Sorrells, 2013; Tervalon & Murray-García, 1998). Similar to and drawing from critical reflection's emphasis on questioning hegemonic assumptions (see chapter 3), cultural humility looks squarely at relations of power and indicates the importance of challenging power imbalances and reimagining institutional structures to redress inequities (Kiely, 2015). Though it originated in the context of medical care, more recently, the fields of social work (Richards-Desai & Lewis, 2017), psychology (Gallardo, 2014), physical therapy (Hilliard, 2011), and intercultural communication (Gorski, 2008; Sorrells, 2013; Sorrells & Nakagawa, 2008) have embraced critical approaches to cultural humility. It makes sense that fields that aim to be respectful of cultural difference while advancing specific commitments to health, social justice, and human flourishing would embrace cultural humility. It is an orientation that simultaneously indicates deep respect for others and critical self-reflection while advancing a robust sense of the continued importance of assessing right and wrong in respect to power imbalances and institutional equity. In sum, cultural humility is a commitment to critical self-reflection and lifelong reevaluation of assumptions, increasing one's capacities for appropriate behaviors and actions in varying cultural contexts. This capacity for appropriate, culturally relevant action is coupled with awareness of one's positionality within systems of power and aligned in service of collaboratively reconsidering and reconstructing assumptions and systems to enact a deeper and broader embrace of shared dignity, redressing historic inequities.

The Flow: Before, During, and After Intercultural Experiences

Continuous and careful support in the process of "crossing borders" in CBGL contexts provides significant opportunities for intercultural learning (Kiely, 2004, 2005); that is, educators should design CBGL programs so that students have multiple and diverse opportunities before, during, and after participation to critically examine their assumptions, the assumptions of others, and the sources and solutions to social problems, as well as opportunities to develop the skills, attitudes, and behaviors to affect positive individual and social change (Eyler & Giles, 1999; Hartman, 2014b; Rhoads, 1997).

We reengage one of our earlier toolboxes, Toolbox 3.2, to illustrate pre-, during, and postimmersion reflection on intercultural learning using the DEAL model. As Vande Berg and colleagues (2012) suggested, the primary finding of the most recent scholarship on intercultural learning is that "deep learning involves faculty and students coconstructing knowledge, with teachers helping students become more self-aware and able to shift frames of reference" (p. 414). This process is fundamentally dependent on specified learning goals and a well-prepared faculty or peer mentor (Vande Berg et al., 2012). Specific examples of particular disciplinary goals are further developed later.

Preparatory Inquiry: Personalizing

Personalizing is another key learning process identified in Kiely's (2002, 2005) study. Because facilitated engagement across perceived difference can lead to profound, unexpected intercultural learning moments, it is important to prepare for and recognize the ways in which each individual student responds to his or her CBGL experience in individually unique yet culturally patterned ways. Deliberate program decisions offer opportunities for sharing personal biography (Toolbox 4.1) and connecting with others' stories through activities such as the seven strangers (Toolbox 7.6), the comfort zone activity (Toolbox 4.4), or the collection of oral histories (Haubert & Williams, 2015; further discussed in chapter 5).

Program Factors That Support Connecting

The depth and effectiveness of the learning processes described previously are dependent on the quality of the connections and interactions students have with learning partners and how prepared students are to develop relationships and engage in meaningful collaboration (Kiely, 2002, 2005). Connecting involves learning how to create, nurture, and develop deeper relationships with student peers; the instructor; and, importantly, community partners (Kiely, 2002, 2005). See Toolbox 4.3 for activities that support connecting.

For students to learn through relationship building, they must learn to develop cultural humility and empathic relationships with community members. Connecting means actively listening, becoming an astute observer, developing an understanding through multiple perspectives, and engaging in meaningful dialogue with community members.

The seven strangers assignment (Toolbox 7.6) offers one example of an assignment that cultivates connections. The comfort zone activity (Toolbox 4.4) develops related capacities, though in each case the facilitator must take great care in introducing the processes and calling participants' attention to the ways in which one must be respectful, honest, and open throughout such learning experiences. The oral histories at the center of Haubert and Williams's (2015) academic and community partnership design create a deliberate, sustained space for the cultivation of relationships. Through assignments and through program design decisions, such as ensuring local students participate in courses, creating cross-cultural teams, and ensuring that locally rooted students are learning from and working collaboratively with community partners (see chapter 5), connections should be systematically cultivated.

TOOLBOX **4.3**
Connecting

Learning Process	Meaning
Connecting	Building relationships through informal and formal social interaction and participant observation; sensing, sharing, feeling, caring, participating, observing, relating, listening, comforting, empathizing, intuiting, creating, and doing (i.e., shared learning experiences, cooperative projects and service, shared meals, interviewing, developing oral histories, copreparing shared meals, skits, homestays, dancing, singing, stories, and conversations)

TOOLBOX **4.4**
The Learning Is Outside Your Comfort Zone

The goal of this assignment is to have participants practice moving beyond their comfort zones in regard to political ideology, social class, race, gender, ethnicity, or culture and reflect on the experience as a way to prepare for their GSL experience. Another goal is to begin a conversation about privilege, segregation, and boundaries; this conversation can connect to course material, group dynamics, and shared experiences. This assignment has been used regularly in a number of contexts but consistently at a racially and socioeconomically diverse institution. The boundary-crossing challenge has been relevant and engaged with integrity for students representing multiple and diverse identities.

Instructions for Participants

Visit with a group in your local area that you have not interacted with because it feels uncomfortable. This can be an event, an organization, or a restaurant or social venue. Examples might include a Catholic church, a gay bar, an African American Baptist church, a Chinese New Year celebration, a primarily White suburban shopping complex, the Islamic Center, a non-profit organization that serves a population new to you, or a political group you disagree with. Choose an environment in which you'll be able to talk to people and in which they will be likely to want to share with you. Take this seriously and cross a real boundary for *you*. Be thoughtful and safe about your choice and have it approved by the instructor.

Enter this environment in a spirit of openness. While in this new environment, please engage in a minimum of three conversations with people in that environment. The goal with these conversations is to go beyond basic scripts. Ask open-ended questions that generate meaningful responses and conversations from those around you. Practice listening skills. Do not lie about the reason you are in this environment (e.g., pretending to want to join their religion)—tell people that you are there to learn and grow.

You may complete this assignment in pairs with another person. Be aware of how the person you conduct the assignment with may be affecting your experience and reflect on that. (Consider questions such as, Did their presence hinder or help your ability to converse? How do you believe their identity affected the way you were perceived? What insights did they share that surprised you?)

(Continues)

TOOLBOX 4.4 *(Continued)*

After completing the assignment, reflect on your experience:

- Briefly describe the environment you visited and the cultural boundary you crossed. What did you feel like while in the new environment? What was most challenging? What was easy?
- Note any stereotypes you hold about the place or group that you visited. Were they challenged or confirmed by your experience? Did you uncover any of your implicit biases? How will awareness of your implicit biases help you to be more culturally humble?
- Through your conversations, did you gain insight into the multidimensional, contextual experiences of the people you met? How does intersectionality play out among the people you met or in the community you visited?
- Connect your experience to a concept we've discussed in class or course readings. Cite appropriately.
- How will your learning from this experience translate on your CBGL course? How might you experience diversity among the group or in the culture you are visiting? What goals do you have for yourself in terms of boundary crossing while on this journey?

Example Boundary-Crossing Choices

The following is an expanded list, but you may wish to restrict the list in a manner that is sensitive to your participant population and local context depending on the goals of your course content, the level of diversity your participants are familiar with, and the options in your community.

Choice	Examples	Facilitator Notes
Religious services and groups	Church, mosque, synagogue, temple, atheist club, pagan celebration	These are often friendly to outsiders and have regular meetings so are easy to schedule.
Restaurants and bars	Gay bar, drag show, Ethiopian restaurant, fast food, soul food, Indian food	These are easy to access, yet having meaningful conversations in these environments can be difficult. If exercise is part of preparation for an immersion experience, this is a good choice for a student who is concerned about food in the community you will be visiting.

Events	Chinese New Year, Turkish festival, gay pride parade, Hindu dance performance, African drumming concert	These provide unique experiences but may be hard to find depending on the community your participants live in.
Nonprofit organizations	Services for people with disabilities or at-risk youth, elderly, military	Often the best way to connect to these organizations is to offer to volunteer
Self-help groups	Alcoholics Anonymous, Narcotics Anonymous, Overeaters Anonymous	Someone must check with the group to determine if it's open to the public. Also, participants need to be clear that they are there to learn (don't pretend to be a part of the group). An area of exploration can be to challenge one's stereotypes about the socioeconomic status, race and ethnicity, gender, and other attributes of participants.
Neighbor-hoods and communities	Latino neighborhood, White suburban neighborhood, African American neighborhood	Wandering around a neighborhood is not a good choice, but finding a destination event, restaurant, or organization to visit and exploring the community along the way can work well.
Political events, rallies, protests	Visiting the offices or campaign headquarters of a politician, attending a rally or protest (Tea Party rally, Black Lives Matter, women's march)	These are often accessible to anyone, but in regard to protests, participants should be thoughtful about their safety and risks.

Intentionally Staggering Dissonance, Challenge, Support, and Learning

In the study abroad and intercultural learning literature, a heavily referenced and often monolithic concept used to describe the difficulties students have when they come into contact with people, places, situations, and events in an unfamiliar cultural context is *culture shock* (Kiely, 2005; Ward et al., 2001). Often, the lack of familiarity with aspects of a different culture can be "shocking" or "disorienting" and sometimes cause students to experience feelings of frustration, anxiety, confusion, denial, fear, and/or insecurity (Ward et al., 2001). More recent research has attempted to unpack the culture shock monolith and identify and examine the specific ways in which students grapple with and learn from the multiple types of dissonance they experience in different CBGL contexts (Doerr, 2011; Hermann, 2011; Kiely, 2002, 2005; Locklin, 2010).

For example, Kiely (2002, 2005) found that students experience different types of dissonance with various levels of intensity, from language barriers that prevent one from using transportation or buying food at the local market to the sight of children searching for food in a pile of garbage. The first two examples are low-intensity forms of dissonance, which can be addressed through instrumental learning (improved language skills). However, the last example is a form of high-intensity dissonance that cannot be immediately reconciled through instrumental forms of learning (i.e., learning how to speak a language or read a bus schedule) and may continue to affect participants after the program ends. The student profiled in the Tanzania program that began the chapter, for example, was clearly experiencing high-intensity dissonance as she shook and cried through the experience; there was no set of rules or textbook formula for learning how to respond to that complex situation or the cultural systems that legitimize it. Adapting to high-intensity dissonance related to experiences of structural issues like lack of access to education, health care, employment, and housing cannot be solved through individual forms of instrumental learning such as skill and knowledge development alone. Rather, thoughtful engagement of structural issues requires learning to understand how community members, policymakers, and clients understand and approach specific challenges. This may lead to learning how to contribute to efforts to change existing cultural and institutional norms and policies; such an effort will likely require a resolute commitment to advancing social and structural change over significant periods of time (Kiely, 2005). Supporting students' continuous learning following experiences of high-intensity dissonance is further discussed in chapter 9.

There are a variety of practical ways educators can assist students in processing and learning from both high- and low-intensity dissonance before, during, and after the CBGL program. The three vignettes at the beginning of the chapter illustrate several different approaches to this challenge, with the domestic example providing comparatively low-intensity points of entry. The kinds of carefully facilitated campus conversations have been shown to advance students' intercultural skills (Savicki, 2008). In addition, having students reflect on and respond to scenarios that describe high- and low-intensity dissonance and/or engage in role-play activities that allow them to act out dissonant situations can be effective instructional strategies (Kahn, 2011; Kiely, 2002, 2004, 2005; Mangis, 2011; Yoder Clark & Nugent, 2011). Preparing and nurturing an environment of trust from the outset is extremely important as part of preparing a community of learners that will turn toward one another and their course or program leadership for support during destabilizing experiences. The group agreement process (Toolbox 7.4), fist-to-five activity (Toolbox 3.1), and other rituals of broad participation and sharing take on added significance as building blocks of trust that support the group as they respond to critical events and experiences.

In immersive or geographically proximate community engagement, ensure students have an opportunity to become accustomed to a new environment over time. For example, in a program in rural Nicaragua, Kiely and Nielsen (2003) were careful not to structure activities in remote areas of the region with extremely resource-poor communities the first few days of the program. By spending time acclimating to the new language, housing, and environment while limiting activities to less demanding situations, the students were able to develop and adjust their cognitive, emotional, and physical responses to the context incrementally and prepare for higher levels of dissonance that occur in clinical and service settings later in the program (Kiely & Nielsen, 2003). Another important component in preparing for and learning from dissonance is to build in time to connect and build relationships with community members and establish structured rituals for engaging in reflection (individually or as a group) at different times during the day (see chapter 3).

Harnessing Intercultural Learning to Achieve Specific Disciplinary Outcomes

Intercultural learning can be conceived of in broad terms, or it can be focused more specifically. In both social work and engineering, professional standards require the kinds of competencies that support intercultural skill development. The Council on Social Work Education (CSWE) provided competencies for social workers, including the following:

Social workers understand how diversity and difference characterize and shape the human experience and are critical to the formation of identity. The dimensions of diversity are understood as the intersectionality of multiple factors including but not limited to age, class, color, culture, disability and ability, ethnicity, gender, gender identity and expression, immigration status, marital status, political ideology, race, religion/spirituality, sex, sexual orientation, and tribal sovereign status. (CSWE, 2015, Competency 2)

Social workers also understand the forms and mechanisms of oppression and discrimination and recognize the extent to which a culture's structures and values, including social, economic, political, and cultural exclusions, may oppress, marginalize, alienate, or create privilege and power" (CSWE, 2015, Competency 2).

These standards are useful as guiding principles for CBGL practitioners. Toolbox 4.5 suggests systematic ways in which such specific and challenging outcomes could be achieved.

The field of engineering also has clear standards in respect to the "ability to function on multidisciplinary teams" (ABET, 2012, p. 3) and "the broad education necessary to understand the impact of engineering solutions in a global, economic, environmental, and societal context" (ABET, 2012, p. 3). Numerous outcomes, instructional methods, and assessment strategies can also be developed for these standards. We share examples in Toolbox 4.6.

Recognizing and Challenging Culturally Embedded Power Imbalances

In addition to grappling with various forms of dissonance, when students learn from community-based mentors and peers, cooperate in applied projects, and begin to develop deeper relationships with community partners, these experiences sometimes cause students to feel moral outrage toward certain policies, structures, institutions, and those who are complicit in causing the oppression of others (Kiely, 2002, 2005). In other words, as they gain a deeper cognitive, emotional, and visceral understanding of how community members experience oppression, they begin to "take it personally"—in terms of their role and connection to the problems and issues they see and feel their community partners struggling with. As was the case for students who worked with the women's rights organization in rural Tanzania, or the student whose experiences in Ecuador began chapter 3, these experiences generate a range of individualized emotional responses including anger, frustration, confusion, and sadness, as well as empathy, compassion, and love.

TOOLBOX 4.5
Achieving Social Work Standards

Learning Outcomes	Instructional Methods and Service Activities	Assessment
Upon completion of this course, students will be able to do the following:	*What instructional strategies or service activities will foster this outcome?*	*What evidence measures do I plan to use to assess the achievement of this learning outcome?*
• Contrast U.S. and host community understanding of social diversity and oppression with respect to age, class, color, culture, disability and ability, ethnicity, gender identity and expression, immigration status, marital status, political ideology, race, religion/spirituality, sex, sexual orientation, and tribal sovereign status	• Texts describing social diversity in both contexts; dialogue with LGBTQ and women's rights advocacy groups in host community; class lecture and discussion	• Report comparing existence of social and political rights in host and home country, highlighting the ways in which cultural and political structures advance or negate those rights
• Develop an approach (i.e., program, policy brief, technology, educational activities, and/or social media tools) to help address, prevent, and eliminate the domination of, exploitation of, and discrimination against any person, group, or class on the basis of age, class, color, culture, disability and ability, ethnicity, gender identity and expression, immigration status, marital status, political ideology, race, religion/spirituality, sex, sexual orientation, and tribal sovereign status	• Provide primer on video development and editing; show students examples of excellent student-produced advocacy videos; engage in extended dialogue with host country rights groups about their desires for an advocacy video, its message, and its intended style	• Develop and deliver advocacy video supporting host country rights groups

TOOLBOX 4.6
Achieving Engineering Standards

Learning Outcomes	Instructional Methods and Service Activities	Assessment
Upon completion of this course, students will be able to do the following: • Describe their own strengths, weaknesses, and strategies for improvement in respect to working on multidisciplinary and multicultural teams • Analyze the impact of the CBGL program's engineering solutions in a global, economic, environmental, and societal context	*What instructional strategies or service activities will foster this outcome?* • Text and lecture describing the characteristics of high-functioning multidisciplinary and multicultural teams, including characteristics of contributing individuals • Provide examples of professional and academic reports focusing on the interaction between engineering solutions and global, economic, environmental, and societal context; discuss best practices in class	*What evidence measures do I plan to use to assess the achievement of this learning outcome?* • Personal inventory on strengths checklist; journal entry reflecting on strategies for improvement; individual discussion with team leader or mentor; observation • Write a concise report according to professional standards describing the impact of the program solution in the four requested contexts; present to project or community leaders

These emotions instill a greater sense of responsibility and a commitment to finding ways to alleviate and transform oppressive conditions (Kiely, 2002, 2005), a commitment consistent with cultural humility (Gallardo, 2014; Tervalon & Murray-García, 1998) and movement building in CBGL (Swords & Kiely, 2010). Understanding and navigating such commitments is the subject of our final chapter on returning home and participating in ongoing transformation.

Dissonance, discomfort, and reimagination in the name of global citizenship are not experiences to be navigated alone, however. Community members and community partners whose primary roles are outside the classroom are often key interpreters, allies, and mentors in understanding and changing assumptions and systems. Community-driven learning, service, and partnership are the subjects of our next chapter.

5

COMMUNITY-DRIVEN
PARTNERSHIPS

Your students put this experience on their résumés when they go home. What will our young people say on their résumés? Hung out with White people for a few weeks?

—Matthias Brown, Association of Clubs, Petersfield, Jamaica

Richard Kiely, who cofounded a CBGL health program between a community college and various community members living in Puerto Cabezas, Nicaragua, was abruptly presented with a challenge in 1994, two years into the program. While he and the students were in Puerto Cabezas, he arranged for the director of a local NGO to give a presentation on his role and the NGO's activities. The director began his presentation by saying he had one "important question." As the group gathered around him, he said, "Before I begin, I'd like to know what your approach to community development is." Dead silence. "Well, then," the director admonished, "you really should have a firm grasp of your approach to community development." He continued, "How will you know if a particular approach has been effective, if you're not sure what it is you are doing?" Kiely realized that he and his coleader hadn't explicitly discussed approaches to community development and capacity building with their students or community partners. Not surprisingly, they approached their practice from their disciplinary backgrounds in political science, history, public health, counseling, and nursing, along with their experiential knowledge and background navigating cross-cultural contexts. However, neither faculty member had a robust theoretical grounding informing the program's approach to community development or theory of change. They had not intentionally incorporated reflection activities into the community development theory underpinning the CBGL program, though their approach to partnership building was implicit and intentional in terms of their participatory approaches to relationships and planning with key community partners (Kiely & Nielsen, 2003). This experience, on reflection, led the faculty to more purposefully engage in dialogue with students and their partners on their collective understanding of community development and capacity building and also review other models and theories in international and community development in a variety of fields of study that became more intentionally incorporated into course work, preparation, and planning.

Kiely shares that story here in the same spirit that Tilley-Lubbs's (2009) reflections closed chapter 3. CBGL program design is inherently less familiar and less predictable than fulfilling traditional faculty teaching and research roles within one's area of expertise. CBGL is a much more complex endeavor with a higher level of unpredictability. In addition, on occasion, given that we are working in real time with multiple stakeholders who bring unique experiential lenses to CBGL work, we have all realized incorrect assumptions, insufficient information, or quite simply personal error in planning and implementing CBGL activities. We take these experiential lessons—so long as they come in the context of deliberate partnerships guided by cultural humility and a participatory mind-set that values shared power and leadership—as learning experiences that point the way toward better reflection, dialogue, partnership, and collaboration. As the field matures, we all enter with more information and knowledge about what works best under what conditions.

Our definition of *CBGL* explicitly indicates it is both a learning methodology and a community-driven approach to learning and development. This is counter to service-learning's roots in educational institutions, where the focus on student learning has frequently dominated and has even been excessive (Cruz & Giles, 2000; Jacoby & Associates, 2003; Larsen, 2015; Stoecker & Tryon, 2009; Stoecker, 2016). The demands, however, of simultaneously balancing institutional, student, and community goals are extraordinary, even if those goals are often complementary and can be synergistic.

It is essential to attend to the community side of these complementary goals for a number of ethical and practical reasons. First and foremost, community-engaged initiatives purport to serve a greater public good. If we cannot address who, why, and how we serve, we cannot be held accountable for what we suggest. Second, how we collaborate and partner with community members outside of academic institutions has strong implications for how students experience and understand diverse lenses for learning, service, community development, intercultural communication, and even ethics. Third, CBGL, as an educational and community-driven intervention, requires substantial resources and time commitment from all participants. It therefore should be undertaken only if it clearly supports mutual learning and community development.

For us to serve communities well, we require some comprehension of the meaning of service, just as supporting community development requires some understanding of that process and set of practices. We explore these issues before offering consideration of what constitutes "community" and reviewing the implications of the community–campus partnership literature for CBGL. We close with FTL principles that were developed to support a strategy for nurturing relationships, communicating with partners, and considering economic implications of partnership decisions. Taken together, these topics point the way toward chapter 6, which specifies how partnership principles, student learning goals, and institutional resources practically affect program planning and partnership development decisions. We begin with reflective exploration of what constitutes community.

What Is Community?

As Green and Haines (2002) pointed out, "Community is one of the simplest concepts in the social sciences, yet it frequently lacks definition" (p. 3). Green and Haines, who prefer a place-based conception, defined *community* "as including three elements: 1) territory or place, 2) social organizations or institutions that provide regular interaction among residents, and 3) social interaction on matters concerning a common interest" (p. 4). In the broadest sense of the definition, *community* entails two or more people who maintain a relationship based on a common or shared place, institution, purpose, activity, interest, identity, culture, language, value, or belief system.

In the service-learning and community engagement literatures, *community partner* has often been used as a signifier of "off-campus partner organization" (Bringle & Hatcher, 1996; Jacoby & Associates, 2003). This formulation suggests a disconnected higher education institution that is not part of a broader fabric of relationships and is not embedded in larger systems that are intertwined with real social issues and challenges (Reeb & Folger, 2013). Campuses frequently benefit from numerous privileges, including having the power of discourse-framing, serving as an intentionally organized space for learning, and acting as the arbiter of what counts as legitimate knowledge, relative economic wealth, and comparative physical safety. Yet campuses are also multilayered organizations, part of complex "psycho-ecological systems," which implicates them in contributing to and addressing profound social and environmental challenges (Reeb & Folger, 2013, p. 395). This relational complexity is coupled with the reality that community and campus stakeholders hold very different perspectives on the benefits and challenges that come with CBGL partnerships (Gazley, Littlepage, & Bennett, 2012). Furthermore, campus stakeholders (students, staff, and faculty) have multiple memberships in communities that permeate campus borders to varying degrees.

The importance of campus in and of community is a theme throughout Benford's (2015) chapter contribution to *Bridging Scholarship and Activism: Reflections From the Frontlines of Collaborative Research*. Whether he was in Austin, Texas; Lincoln, Nebraska; Carbondale, Illinois; or Tampa, Florida, it was through immersion and cooperation with community and campus people and organizations that Benford leveraged "his privileged positions within the academy and as a White male . . . to affect progressive social change" (p. 31). Benford's stories raise an important point that has begun to emerge more clearly in the community engagement literature; academic engagement and activism are often "with" and "of" community rather than "for" some separate entity (Hansen & Clayton, 2014). The community–campus dichotomy is false or at least overstated (Clayton, Bringle, Senor, Huq, & Morrison, 2010). The cases reviewed by Benford (creating gun-free zones on campus, challenging intercollegiate athletics, and even advancing renters' rights in the community) highlight the extent to which institutions are of the community as much as they may also be apart from the community.

In a community-driven approach to CBGL, careful, cooperative coplanning ensures shared meaning and goals throughout program preparation, delivery, and evaluation. Coplanning with diverse stakeholders drawing from the knowledge and assets they bring to the planning table (Cervero & Wilson, 2006; Kretzmann & McKnight, 1993; Sandmann, Kiely, & Grenier, 2009) should include partner organization staff and off-campus community members, as well as involve students, faculty, and staff who reside in a specific geographic location or are allied with a specific interest (Clayton et al., 2010). In CBGL, community is further formed by the community members' shared interest in addressing a specific issue that has been collaboratively identified. In this sense, community that forms in CBGL is often place based (i.e., located in a geographic region) and interest oriented (i.e., shaped by a common interest to engage in service work to address a specific issue).

The experience mentioned in chapter 4, in rural Kayanga, Tanzania, can be further developed here to illustrate the challenge and nuance of serving community goals. Working in the context of an established relationship between a third-party provider (further discussed in chapter 6) and the Women's Emancipation and Development Agency (WOMEDA), a local women's rights organization, Hartman was pleased to hear a direct, specific, and actionable request from the director, Juma Massissi. "Can you do evaluation?" was Massissi's first question. Soon it became clear that the U.S. Agency for International Development (USAID) had indicated its interest in funding women's rights work in this remote part of northwest Tanzania, at the edge of the energy grid. But organizations applying for funding needed to demonstrate their abilities to evaluate their services. Massissi was worried: "We've never done evaluation."

Compelled by a specific request from a community organization, Hartman coordinated his students and WOMEDA staff members, cooperated with Massissi to arrange interviews, and ultimately worked with this large group to complete a qualitative and quantitative evaluation. At some point in Hartman's efforts to do what he could to meet this request, it occurred to him that this particular intervention—promoting women's rights—was not clearly supported throughout the community. Certainly, WOMEDA was indigenous to the area, locally led, and locally staffed, but if Tanzanians in and around Kayanga were polled, would they support women's rights? That was much more difficult to determine. There were clearly many local, vocal, and powerful resistors. Ultimately, for Hartman, his students, and the community partners, common membership in the issue-oriented community of human rights and women's rights supporters compelled them to work together. It was essential, given Hartman's support of the community-driven assumptions discussed throughout this chapter, that several members of that issue-oriented community were also members of the geographical community of Kayanga. Massissi and Hartman were members of distant and distinct geographic communities, but their shared membership in the values community that believes in the importance of human rights and women's rights brought them into cooperative relationship and led them to connect their respective organizational networks.

To make matters more complicated, communities have dynamic, evolving membership and are rarely, if ever, fixed or static for any length of time. In addition, in CBGL programs, smaller communities can form around a more specific set of interests or commonalities. For example, in a previous program, a small subgroup of U.S. students formed a partnership with a local school in Nicaragua and decided to partner with a local NGO that provides education to homeless children. In another instance, a small group of students worked with an agency that supports undocumented immigrants along the U.S.–Mexico border and then returned home to develop a website to raise awareness and educate a wider group of people about the conditions undocumented immigrants face, immigration policy, and comprehensive immigration reform. It is imperative that all individuals who have taken a leadership role in the CBGL planning process reflect on who is participating in the planning process and who has a stake in the CBGL program and in what ways. A faculty member may decide to design a CBGL course with students and agency staff in the host community in mind, but other faculty, agency representatives, or community-based individuals may wish to participate and have a stake in the CBGL program.

Hence, although we recognize the importance of considering community in an intentional and conscious manner, we also concede that any conception of community is a moving target, always in motion—as it should be. We say this because part of the goal of a community-driven approach to CBGL is to continuously find ways to build community, foster inclusiveness, and expand the network of stakeholders and potential partners who might bring new and/or additional knowledge, skills, and resources to bear on a specific challenge. This vital question—Who are your partners and stakeholders?—is further discussed in chapter 6, along with stakeholder mapping as an important dimension of defining community and community building in CBGL. As off-campus and on-campus stakeholders are identified, FTL queries (further discussed in the following sections) may provide helpful exercises in shared, reflective meaning making and planning.

CBGL grows from intentional program planning that highlights service, learning, and partnership as a relational process (Clayton et al., 2010; Enos & Morton, 2003; Hartman, 2015a; Jacoby and Associates, 2003; Swords & Kiely, 2010; Sandmann et al., 2009). Before further discussion of these relationships, however, we consider a few of the primary understandings of service and community development that are relevant for CBGL.

Integrating Service, Community Development, and Community Partnership

Service-learning movement pioneer Nadinne Cruz suggested, "Service is a process of integrating intention with action in the context of a movement toward a just relationship" (Morton, 1995, p. 31). Scholar-practitioners following in Cruz's footsteps have worked to understand the relationship between approaches to service, community partnerships, and justice (Cruz & Giles, 2000; d'Arlach, Sánchez, & Feuer, 2009; Jacoby and Associates, 1993, 2003; Larsen, 2015; Reardon & Forester, 2016; Reynolds, 2014; Sandy & Holland, 2006; Stoecker, 2016; Stoecker, Tryon, & Loving, 2011; Strand, Marullo, Cutforth, Stoecker, & Donohue, 2003; Worrall, 2007) while the international development literature has had a separate and somewhat parallel discussion on the stages of development thinking (Korten, 1990; Li, 2007). It is important for CBGL leaders to familiarize themselves with these discussions regarding the implications of development approaches (Chambers, 1997; Escobar, 1994; Esteva & Prakash, 1997; Korten, 1990) and partnership principles (Bringle & Hatcher, 1996; Community Campus Partnerships for Health, 2013; Gelmon, Holland, Driscoll, Spring, & Kerrigan, 2001; Hartman, Paris, & Blache-Cohen, 2014; Jacoby & Associates, 2003; Jones, 2003; Stoecker & Tryon, 2009; Strand et al., 2003) because partnership processes will strongly influence targeted and tangential student learning outcomes, as well as community impact.

Full partnership between a university and a distant community requires considerable commitment of institutional resources (Nolting, Donohue, Matherly, & Tillman, 2013; Reardon & Forester, 2016). As the entirety of partnership responsibilities become clear, leaders may become more interested in cooperating with NGOs and community organizations that facilitate universities' connections to communities around the world. This option is further discussed in chapter 6, but even if leaders ultimately choose this route, it is important to be familiar with community development principles to better evaluate and cooperate with such organizations.

Asserting "attend deeply to partnerships" as one of five key recommendations in CBGL, Crabtree (2008) suggested, "The literature on university–community partnerships, derived primarily from domestic service-learning contexts, can be instructive" (p. 55), and there are a number of excellent reviews (see Bringle & Clayton, 2013; Bringle & Hatcher, 1996; Clayton et al., 2010; Enos & Morton, 2003; Jacoby and Associates, 2003; Strand et al., 2003) of partnership approaches, principles, concepts, and examples. However, although we draw from the insights of those models and principles in our own local CBGL work, we have experienced extraordinary structural differences between distant and immersive partnerships and local and nonimmersive partnerships that significantly limit the applicability and transformative potential of much of that research (Bringle, Hatcher, & Jones, 2011; Reardon & Forester, 2016; Tiessen & Huish, 2014). Fortunately, however, research is emerging that is specific to CBGL community partnership outcomes and community satisfaction, suggesting largely positive perceptions and impacts in communities with strong, lasting partnerships (Hartman & Chaire, 2014; Irie, Daniel, Cheplick, & Phillips, 2010; Kiely & Nielsen, 2003; Larsen, 2015; Reynolds, 2014).

In terms of relevant domestic conceptual models, Morton (1995) laid the groundwork for considerable thinking in service-learning with his articulation of charity, project, and social change models of service. In advancing this typology, which is shared in Toolbox 5.1, Morton (1995) suggested that this should not be understood as a continuum from charity to social change, as later became the implicit suggestion in much service-learning work.

TOOLBOX 5.1

Charity, Project, and Social Change

	Charity	Project	Social Change
Description	Direct, immediate relief; often connected to individual relationships	Defining problems and solutions and implementing well-conceived plans for their resolution; often group or organization based	Social system is the focus of change; people affected by the changes are involved in making that change
Strengths	Hebrew word for charity is *tsedakah*, which means anger at injustice provoking one to remedy that injustice; this and other spiritually based service bears witness to the worth of others	No solutions are ultimate; focus on reasonable approaches to measurable action; best practice includes participation of those served; builds existing efforts	"We organize people around their values . . . family, dignity, justice, and hope. And we need to protect what we value" (Morton, 1995, p. 28). Strong ownership of community, hope, future
Weaknesses	Does not address root causes; power remains with the servants	"Expertise" frequently located outside community; may focus excessively on management or financial objectives; may miss root causes	Often does not address immediate needs[a]
Time	Unconcerned with time; direct giving may be single instance, episodic, or perennial; present orientation	Time bound, specific, potentially ongoing	Future oriented, imaginative

a This has been added by the authors and is not explicit in Morton (1995).

Rather, service-learning practitioners should recognize different kinds of strengths in these different approaches, honoring the particular depths, strengths, and weaknesses that may come with each. Morton (1995) made this suggestion through student surveys and dialogue, as well as interaction with strong examples of charity and project models of service in the communities where he has lived and worked.

In its robust articulation, charity is "spiritually based service, outside of time and space, that bears witness to the worth of other persons" (Morton, 1995, p. 26). The project-based approach suggests that "no solutions are ultimate, and that thoughtful, reasonable approaches to measured action—doing something—is the appropriate response to community needs" (p. 27). Social change, in a powerful articulation, "places one squarely in the stream of history leading up to and through the world as it is" (p. 28). As you approach CBGL, do you imagine your students volunteering in centers that provide meals to individuals who are hungry (charity), developing curriculum and delivering life-skills lessons to support individuals who are seeking new employment (project), or cooperating with local advocacy groups to advance national policy that guarantees affordable housing and living wages (advocacy, project)? Perhaps your response shifts depending on the community and the geopolitics of the movement. Part of that insight is expressed in David Korten's (1990) rendering of the evolution of community and international development thinking, which provides a useful parallel to Morton's service-learning-specific work.

Korten (1990) drew on a development practitioner's assertion that "it is impossible to be a true development agency without a theory that directs action to the underlying causes of underdevelopment" (p. 113). Is the university, department, or program, if it is partnering directly with a community, taking on the role of a development organization? If the institution is partnering with a community development organization, how does that organization express its development theory and strategy? Korten's historical understanding of the development thinking of NGOs suggests four generations of staged development, each with NGO roles and strategies and a specific problem focus, level and type of participation, duration, and underlying theory for how change occurs (Toolbox 5.2). Each generation brings both strengths and limitations in how to foster community development. For example, "Generation One: Relief and Welfare" is still appropriate for acute disaster relief operations.

NGOs that follow a first-generation model of community development focus on these "relief and welfare" activities (Korten, 1990, p. 117). Under this approach, NGOs work within a deficit model of development, responding to shortages in food, health, safety, housing, water, and so on, often resulting

TOOLBOX 5.2

Korten's Four Generations of Development Thinking

	1: Relief and Welfare	2: Community Development	3: Sustainable Systems Development	4: People's Movements
Description	The NGO assumes logistics management orientation to address shortage	The NGO works with the community in a project management effort to catalyze local resources and stimulate self-help	Broad coalitions mobilize regional, national, and international movement to reform institutional and policy constraints	Loose networks activate and educate to coalesce self-managing networks in service of people-centered development on a global scale
Strengths	Addresses immediate need	Local mobilization and ownership	Addresses root issues	Powerful people's movements—environment, human rights, women's movement—succeed and move on social energy more than money
Weaknesses and Challenges	Does not investigate, educate about, or address root causes	Does not address structural constraints on community	Involves (typically) challenging power holders; long process	Challenge to nurture people's movements and avoid bureaucratizing (thereby inadvertently squashing) the movement
Time	Immediate	Project life	10 to 20 years	Indefinite future

from a natural disaster, war, or conflicts that lead to large displacement of communities. The limitation of a relief and welfare approach is that it is usually a short-term strategy to respond to the immediate needs of individuals and families and addresses only the symptoms of a much larger problem. It does not address the underlying source causing the individual symptoms and/or needs. To overcome the potential for long-standing dependency relationships between the NGO and the community, this approach needs to move from relief efforts to a community development approach aimed at developing deeper, longer-term relationships with community members and organizations with a focus on recovery and reconstruction (Korten, 1990).

Second-generation development approaches therefore focus on longer term community development, and NGOs are more apt to work closely with local organizations to assist them in becoming more self-reliant (Korten, 1990). The role of the NGO shifts from a "doer" for the community to a mobilizer who works with community leaders to organize people, identify resources, build relationships, seek collaborative opportunities, and assist with project design, development, and coordination. Second-generation approaches work under the assumption that if "you give an individual a fish, it feeds her for a day, but if you teach someone to fish, it feeds her for a lifetime."

Third-generation approaches focus on "sustainable systems development" aimed primarily at changing institutional and policy dimensions of local problems (Korten, 1990). Because policy and institutional change takes much longer to achieve, this approach requires a much greater time commitment, and the focus expands beyond local communities to regional, national, and international networks. Third-generation approaches entail significant research on policy, advocacy with policymakers, consciousness raising, and education about the flaws and inadequacies in existing policies or institutions, as well as efforts to design and implement more satisfying alternatives (Korten, 1990). NGOs that focus on third-generation strategies work under the assumption that teaching people to fish doesn't necessarily feed them for a lifetime if existing policies or institutions prohibit or limit access to water and other resources. The Jubilee 2000 debt relief and forgiveness campaign aimed at countries with massive debt is an example of work within the third-generation development approach.

Unfortunately, policy and institutional changes at the national and international levels often cannot be solved by community-based NGOs. It takes a large number of people to develop an awareness of a harmful or flawed policy and/or institution, achieve some consensus on what alternatives are needed, and maintain some ongoing level of organization and mobilization in order to realize profound change. Korten (1990) argued that social movements are needed: fourth-generation approaches to development. A social movement is a widespread voluntary action aimed at substantive change in existing institutions and/or policies that are harmful yet routinely taken for granted. This notion of harmful yet accepted institutions and policies relates clearly to the practice of critical reflection we shared and discussed in chapter 3. Examples of fourth-generation voluntary social movements include the civil rights movement, the feminist movement, and the environmental movement (Korten, 1990). These movements can simultaneously be said to have realized profound change and to be ongoing, committed struggles for improving communities and the environment across national borders. When you are planning and designing an approach to CBGL with partners, it is important to consider a number of key questions: What is the level of participation of diverse community stakeholders? What program model will be most effective? And what knowledge, resources, experience, and assets might each stakeholder contribute to the CBGL partnership effort (Clayton et al., 2010; Cruz & Giles, 2000; Jacoby & Associates, 2003; Kiely & Nielsen, 2003; Strand et al., 2003; Swords & Kiely, 2010; Worrall, 2007)? Korten's four-generation framework is summarized in Toolbox 5.2.

Two additional insights are essential as you consider how your institution or program will approach CBGL. First, as we alluded to previously, many of the insights in the domestic service-learning literature do not carry to contexts in which students and faculty engage partnerships that are geographically distant, even if they are still in the same country, because of the structural constraints against continuous interaction (Kiely & Nielsen, 2003; Reardon & Forester, 2016). Second, community-based approaches to development, advocacy, and people's movements are fundamentally dependent on deep and meaningful relationships (Enos & Morton, 2003; Hartman & Chaire, 2014; Swords & Kiely, 2010). Each of these insights is explored in turn in the following.

As discussed in Hartman and Chaire (2014), CBGL relationships frequently involve merely annual in-person interactions, punctuated with e-mail exchanges and phone calls during the remainder of the year. This limited personal interaction, often necessary because of funding constraints and the academic calendar, lessens the relevance of much of the domestic service-learning literature, which has focused on specific individual relationships and presumptions of timelines that do not apply to most CBGL work. Hartman and Chaire (2014) explained,

> The structure of distant partnerships, often mitigated by a third party provider, is significantly different from local campus–community partnerships. Clayton et al. (2010), for example, summarize Enos and Morton's (2003) conceptualization of partnerships as follows:

Transactional relationships are instrumental and often designed to complete short-term tasks. Persons come together on the basis of an exchange, each offering something that the other desires. Both benefit from the exchange, and no long-term change is expected. This is distinct from transformational relationships wherein both persons grow and change because of deeper and more sustainable commitments. In a transformational relationship, persons come together in a more open-ended process of indefinite but longer-term duration and bring a receptiveness—if not an overt intention—to explore emergent possibilities, revisit and revise their own goals and identities, and develop systems they work within beyond the status quo.

In a CBGL partnership, a third party provider is often in a long-term, possibly transformational partnership with community organizations, while universities engage with those partnerships on a single or sometimes continual basis over many years. Alternatively, universities may have direct relationships with community organizations, but they rarely have the capacity to offer continuous presence in that relationship. (pp. 17–18)

It is more logistically challenging in international partnerships to nurture continuous, deep relationships between faculty and students on the one side and community members and community organization staff on the other. In many cases, however, an intermediary organization, or one specific individual or small group within the university, will maintain the ongoing, deep relationship, while individual faculty members and students move in and out of the relationship (Hartman, 2015a; Hartman & Chaire, 2014). Sometimes this will lead students and new faculty members to develop lasting, transformative relationships with community members (Clayton et al., 2010; Enos & Morton, 2003; Kiely & Nielsen, 2003). But the overarching structure of geographically distant CBGL programs may reinforce a structure of short-term relationships that are often specific to particular projects or components of larger projects. This realization about the structural differences between CBGL relationships and most domestic service-learning relationships is even more important when considered in light of the centrality of relationships to community-engaged interventions.

Community Engagement, Relationships, and Trust

As Stanton and Wagner (2006) and others have argued, graduate school and faculty expectations often socialize individuals *away* from community. This assertion is important, as it highlights just how different the behavioral expectations of community partnership may be from typical academic community norms. Individuals working to coplan with community, coresearch with community, engage in participatory budgeting and discussion processes, or simply cooperate with community must work to be in solidarity with community members (Hartman, 2015a; Hartman, Sanchez, Shakya, & Whitney, 2016; Jacquez, Ward, & Goguen, 2016; Nigro, 2017; Stoecker, 2016; Stoecker & Tryon, 2009; Strand et al., 2003). Writing specifically on participatory research methodologies, Wheatley and Hartman (2013) suggested that such community-engaged methodologies require "a radical departure from accepted standards and common expectations" (p. 157).

The centrality of deep relationships and continuous connection comes through clearly in Kiely and Nielsen's (2003) threefold framework for developing GSL partnerships. They indicated that quality GSL partnerships depend on three important dimensions of relationships: "1) the level of *collaboration*, 2) the depth of *connections*, and 3) the willingness to make a *commitment* to developing and maintaining a long-term partnership" (Kiely & Nielsen, 2003, p. 40). This section discusses the most important factors that are involved in supporting the relationships at the core of CBGL partnerships.

Collaboration

CBGL planners must develop and manage partnerships with a collaborative mind-set (Kiely & Nielsen, 2003; Longo & Gibson, 2016). Identifying appropriate community members and organizations to work with to design and manage high-quality programs means understanding potential partners' needs, interests, motivations, values, beliefs, and roles in the community. It also means valuing and appreciating the knowledge, experience, assets, and resources they bring to the CBGL relationship. Community partners often act as historians, teachers, translators, cultural mediators, power brokers, business negotiators, logistical facilitators, safety providers, and information providers (Kiely & Nielsen, 2003; Nigro, 2017; Sandmann et al., 2009).

Kiely and Nielsen's (2003) description of how they initiated a program (now in its 23rd year) with community partners in Puerto Cabezas, Nicaragua, is useful for understanding how important collaboration is to the success and sustainability of CBGL programs. One key dimension of collaboration was spending quality time visiting with potential Nicaraguan partners to learn about health problems and issues. This included visiting existing programs organized to promote specific health interventions and listening carefully to their goals, objectives, and expectations for a possible partnership prior to developing service-learning courses and program components. Another key dimension of collaboration was locating key stakeholders such as local community connectors who are well respected and who can speak multiple languages and communicate effectively with community members with diverse socioeconomic, cultural, political, and social backgrounds. Local community connectors have cultivated trusting, often lifelong, relationships and built extensive civic and professional networks. They can connect visiting students and faculty with their social networks; assist with service project coordination; translate norms, customs, and values; and assist with health, safety, transportation, housing, and food.

On the basis of the previous descriptions and our research on CBGL programs (Kiely, Hartman, & Nielsen, 2005), it is clear that one of the initial considerations for administrators and faculty who are thinking about developing a distant GSL partnership without the support of a third-party provider (see chapter 6) is not only to conduct a site visit prior to designing and implementing a CBGL program overseas but also to go into the planning process with a collaborative mind-set. If you choose to work with a third-party provider, it is important to evaluate its community partnership practices through the lenses of collaboration, connection, and commitment. Without a high level of participation of the host community partners, the quality of the relationship and level of commitment is likely to suffer. Greater involvement of host community partners from the onset of the program also ensures they have significant ownership of the CBGL program and remain committed to cocreated learning and/or development goals.

Community Connections

CBGL activities provide students with numerous opportunities to directly connect with diverse members of the community (Jacoby & Associates, 2003; Kiely, 2002; Kiely & Nielsen, 2003). If partners are distant, it is important for CBGL program administrators and faculty to design activities in consultation with their community partners in order to enhance intercultural connections through previsit Skype or Google Hangout meetings, deliberate precourse connections through usage of social media, thoughtful orientation activities on-site, shared community-driven service work, meals, daily site visits, and recreational events. Lillehaugen (2016) chronicles creative use of Twitter as a platform for international interaction during the academic year, supporting indigenous language learning and preservation. Careful planning of such specifically targeted activities can substantially increase the possibility for numerous and diverse connections during any program, well beyond collaborative service work. Working hands-on with diverse members of the host community allows students to develop deeper connections with community members that depend on a high level of trust and respect and that reflect shared concerns around solving important social problems affecting the local community. As discussed in chapter 4, the deliberate, programmatic cultivation of opportunities for interpersonal relationship building has implications not only for the importance of the service partnership but also for intercultural learning and even later global civic engagement. See Toolbox 4.3 ("Connecting") for more suggestions.

Haubert and Williams (2015) suggested that community-engaged research, including the collection of oral histories and the development of focus groups relating to community development background and possibilities, should be undertaken not only for assessment purposes but also for its relationship building potential both inside and outside of the host community. In 2007, they began working in Rocha, Nicaragua, where some residents had never before seen U.S. citizens. Collecting oral histories helped them learn that because of Rocha's specific experiences, "community gardening and economic cooperatives smacked of Sandinista politics and . . . turned off the residents" (p. 183). Their insistence on triangulating their data through oral histories, community meetings, and surveys did raise some tensions between them, as Winthrop University researchers and practitioners, and the local mayor. Yet they feel this deliberate decision was important, as they have now "gained the trust of both" the residents and the mayor, "while also demonstrating to community members that their voices are valued" (p. 184).

The depth of this relationship with the community; its continuous maintenance over six years; and the multiple, continuously expanding interconnections between the university and the community suggest that Haubert and Williams (2015) engaged in reciprocal and even transformative (Clayton et al., 2010) relationships with community members through their partnership. Their emphasis on community-engaged research as a central component of partnership and relationship building follows from their assertion that

> an in-depth understanding of the unique culture and history of the community is a necessary, if not always sufficient, condition for successful service-learning partnerships because it helps in achieving what Max Weber called *verstehen*, or deep understanding of the participant's worldview. (Haubert & Williams, 2015, p. 186)

Whatever the service experience chosen by community and campus partners, these coplanners and coeducators should have clear dialogue with one another and with program participants about the strengths, limitations, and ideal outcome with each approach.

Amizade's programs in Bolivia, Jamaica, Northern Ireland, Tanzania, the United States, and elsewhere have included a variety of ongoing service projects, including relearning histories; building schools and community centers; supporting conflict mediation under the supervision of locally situated and skilled mediators; developing web pages and writing grants; and providing social services, educational materials, and other important community resources. The diversity of student connections also extends and deepens faculty connections. Faculty members must be deliberate in nurturing these relationships outside the program by Skyping, e-mailing, sending cards, and otherwise continuing communication. By interacting with the community through cooperative work, students often develop fairly significant relationships with members of the host community.

Importantly, CBGL programs often place students in situations where they will experience firsthand the resource-limited conditions that many people confront daily (Kiely & Nielsen, 2003). Because many university students from the United States and other locations in the Global North have not directly witnessed the acute resource limitations that characterize some communities in the Global South, their service-learning experiences often become a powerfully emotional and visceral medium through which lifelong partnerships are developed. As discussed in chapter 4, programming decisions that facilitate personalizing and connecting "often lead students to feel a greater sense of empathy and solidarity. The depth and variety of service work allows partnerships to grow and flourish based on trust and shared concerns that transcend cultural, ethnic and national boundaries" (Kiely & Nielsen, 2003, p. 41). Multiple, deliberate connections between CBGL participants and the host community play an important role in ensuring the quality of the relationships that evolve, the different kinds of learning that occur over time, and the ongoing civic commitment that students engage in after participation in the program.

Commitment

When developing CBGL partnerships, administrators and faculty must also consider the long-term feasibility and sustainability of the program on the campus side. If CBGL programs were designed to satisfy the course requirements of the academic institution only, the program would not be based on collaborative partnership. Collaborative partnerships are based on trust, reciprocity, and cooperative effort to satisfy mutual interests (Jacoby and Associates, 2003; Jacquez et al., 2016; Longo & Gibson, 2016). CBGL programs, although constructed in part to meet a specific set of learning goals and objectives in a particular academic program or course, should also be structured to allocate resources and generate and apply knowledge that addresses important community-identified challenges. These problems tend to be complex and often require participation and resources extending beyond one or two semesters. Therefore, it is essential that CBGL program planners understand the commitments and desires of all partnership stakeholders (Kiely & Nielsen, 2003).

If possible, goals and objectives should be specified in advance (and adjusted if need be) and should be measurable by different formative and summative evaluation instruments. It is rare when a CBGL program is able to accomplish the goals and objectives of service projects in one semester. We specify "if possible" because of the insights developed through a large-scale community engagement program that has supported the development and delivery of clean water systems for more than 50,000 people in Honduras (Fleischman, 2017). The program director, Cornell University engineer Monroe Weber-Shirk, suggested that the relationship proceeded through a covenant rather than a clearly articulated memorandum of understanding (Weber-Shirk, 2012).

A covenant suggests a deliberate, deep commitment with open communication and opportunity for readjustment. Weber-Shirk (2012) said a covenant worked where formal contracts would not have, because he and his Honduran codirector had the idea that they wanted to cooperate to improve clean water access, but they were entirely uncertain about what they would be able to achieve together. They did not feel that they could have promised commitments in contractual terms. They trusted in one another enough, however, to begin.

Whether through covenants or memoranda of understanding, addressing issues like access to appropriate health care, employment, food, and shelter requires long-term relationship building, resource development, and community capacity building. The processes and partnerships involved can be broken into discrete, manageable units. In developing the Haiti compact, for example, Piacitelli, Barwick, Doerr, Porter, and Sumka (2013) drew on a work plan development process established by Northwestern University's Global Engagement Summer Institute. Through that process, "students and hosts establish goals and objectives they will achieve together during their alternative break, determine what resources are needed to achieve those goals, and decide on final measures of success" (Piacitelli et al., 2013, p. 104).

CBGL program partners should take great care in establishing the appropriate level of commitment by allocating the time, resources, and technical support needed to address important community problems and ensure that CBGL programs do not cause more harm than good. The Puerto Cabezas, Nicaragua, CBGL program has managed to maintain a positive CBGL partnership for over 20 years in spite of the necessarily brief involvement of students and after both cofounding faculty leaders retired or left the institution

(Kiely & Nielsen, 2003). The transfer of responsibility for program coordination to other faculty, continued institutional support, and strong relational trust with community partners were essential ingredients to enable continuity and exemplified deep commitment to the sustainability of the long-term partnership.

It is clear that strong relationships between partners provide the foundation for the success of CBGL programs. The most important dimensions of CBGL partnerships are (a) a collaborative mind-set that values host community participation and local knowledge and assets, (b) nurturing of reciprocal relationships with diverse stakeholders, and (c) a serious commitment to managing and sustaining a long-term partnership that supports resource development, knowledge generation, and community capacity building (Hartman, Paris, & Blache-Cohen, 2016; Jacoby & Associates, 2003; Jacquez et al., 2016; Kiely & Nielsen, 2003; Longo & Gibson, 2016). These three fundamental aspects of partnerships will help foster relationships that meet the needs and interests of participants who have a stake in the success of the CBGL program.

We have written to this point about the conceptual frameworks through which service and development are understood and the relationships that are central to CBGL community partnership. We now turn to better understanding the economic transactions that occur in concert with CBGL programming, along with demonstrating how those transactions can be leveraged as ends in themselves.

Economic Inequities and the Development of FTL

CBGL programs require considerable sums of money. Tens of thousands of dollars are spent on transportation, food, lodging, and employment for a single, short-term, immersive program. Perhaps more important, CBGL programs take place within highly commoditized education and travel sectors, where students are frequently positioned as consumers, and universities often contract with private companies for education abroad or travel services. In this context, FTL developed through a community-driven, globally networked articulation and operationalization that began with the interests of a rural Jamaican community interested in advancing development through community tourism (Hartman, 2015a; Hartman et al., 2014).

FTL addresses three issues. First, the language of "fair trade" calls attention to the economic exchanges that are taking place as part of the process, and it appeals to deliberate and conscious equity efforts in the immediate project time frame. The implications are numerous. For example, some study abroad and volunteering programs purchase physical space in host communities, capturing all of the local accommodations fees, whereas others deliberately cooperate with community development networks to facilitate shared opportunities for a broad network of host community families to benefit economically and culturally through hosting. In the case of Petersfield, Jamaica, the host family network has agreed that a portion of all accommodation fees will be reserved for a community development project account, thereby ensuring reinvestment in parks, summer camps, and other shared goods (Hartman, 2015a). This has resulted in hundreds of thousands of dollars of reinvestment in the community, through individual family budgets and shared public infrastructure and public goods investments. To be consistent with the commitment to support community development, program leaders must make every effort to purchase accommodations, transportation, meals, and other services through local providers.

Second, FTL moves beyond lofty ideals toward specific standards of practice. As Crabtree (2008) recognized in her review of international service-learning several years ago, "we need more than an ethos of reciprocity as a guide; we need to learn the . . . on-the-ground strategies that are more likely to *produce* mutuality" (p. 26, emphasis in original). Numerous institutions and organizations, including Amizade, Dartmouth College, the University of Dayton, the Foundation for Sustainable Development, Haverford College, Northwestern University, Water for Waslala, and many more, have employed FTL principles, rubrics, and queries to guide conversation through stakeholder networks, encouraging shared meaning making, critical review, and commitment to ethical practice.

Third, FTL calls attention to organizations that have made transparent and verifiable commitments to careful, ethically grounded community development principles. It differentiates these organizations for their willingness to commit to community-driven values, financial transparency, and programming decisions that support redistributive equity beyond what the marketplace will bear. The spaces in which this work takes place are inseparable from the highly commoditized education, study abroad, and voluntourism sectors. Those large sectors and their marketing departments reach out to and influence the same students who may enroll in ethical programs or courses.

Unscrupulous volunteer program companies and organizations cater to consumers who consider themselves compassionate but who come to these experiences with years of having digested harmful stereotypes about the developing world.

In very practical terms, this means that organizations that systematically invest in communities are competing with corporations with marketing departments larger than the community-based organizations themselves. These marketing departments sell the perception of doing good to people who understand themselves as good. It's not that hard a sell; it is typically supplemented with glossy photos, opportunities to go to beautiful places, and the clear allure of adventure. (Hartman, 2015a)

Numerous standards for community partnership or criteria for what constitutes quality partnership have emerged in respect to community-engaged research (Reardon, 1994; Strand et al., 2003), the integration of service and learning (Porter Honnet & Poulsen, 1989; Sigmon, 1979), community–university partnerships (Community Campus Partnerships for Health, 2013), service-learning partnerships (Jacoby & Associates, 2003), asset-based community development (Kretzmann & McKnight, 1993), campus–community partnership benchmarks (Torres, 2000), and international volunteerism (Comhlámh, 2012; The International Ecotourism Society, 2011). Each of these frameworks has something important to contribute, and they have all influenced our conceptualization of FTL, which is the only set of standards that is specific to the dynamics of immersive CBGL (Campus Compact, 2017b; Hartman, 2015a; Hartman et al., 2014). At the time of writing, The Forum on Education Abroad (2018a) was also in the process of releasing its first *Guidelines for Community Engagement, Service-Learning, and Volunteer Experiences Abroad.*

FTL Standards

FTL standards for ethical global campus–community partnerships were developed through a consultative process involving numerous long-standing GSL practitioners and community partners. There is substantial academic research, community experience, and diversity of input behind them, but they are written in the concise manner of standards, without citation. Though CBGL practice and research gave rise to these standards, the extraordinary growth in multiple forms of study abroad with marginalized communities around the world suggests a need for the broader assertion of standards for community-engaged international education (McNichols, Hartman, & Eccles, 2017; Hartman, Tansey, Ogden, & Kuhn, 2015).

The standards are separated into core principles, community-centered components, and student-centered components because it is often the case that different administrators, offices, leaders, or faculty members attend to these different foci. Yet the position expressed in this document is that student learning and community goals must reinforce and inform one another. Either is undermined by the absence of the other.

Readers and contributors have noted that the structure of the document often assumes that the university office or administrator holds more power in the relationship than the community partner. Although this is not always the case, the assumption throughout the document and in writing these standards has been that universities must take aggressive steps to create conditions of coplanning, comanagement, codirection, and codesign, because they often do unreflectively hold the larger share of power in global partnerships, particularly when partnering in marginalized communities.

These standards are intended as aspirational guidelines, not as limiting proscriptions. Although our strongest aspiration is that all programs would achieve the standards indicated here, we also recognize that program building and institutional change are most frequently characterized as journeys rather than revolutions. These guidelines, and examples from diverse programs profiled throughout this book, may show us a way forward. However, understanding the importance of cultural humility in this work and the process of shared meaning making, we have also developed corollary FTL queries, shown in Toolbox 5.3. The queries take the form of questions rather than standards, in an attempt to call attention to both the wisdom gathered through previous efforts and the importance of context and change in this work.

Core Principles

Dual purposes. Programs are organized with community and student goals and outcomes in mind, including the overall mission, vision, and purpose of the partnership. The ethics of integrating community development with student learning necessitates that as much attention is paid to community outcomes as to student learning. One purpose is therefore never primary. Rather, community-driven outcomes and student learning about ethical global engagement must be held in balance with one another.

Community voice and direction. Drawing on best practices in community development, service-learning, and public health, community-based efforts must be community driven. Community engagement, learning, program design, and budgeting should all include significant community direction, feedback, and opportunities for iterative improvements.

Twelve Queries for All Partnership Stakeholders Advancing Ethical Global Learning or FTL

1. Do stakeholders, including several and diverse community members, agree on long-term mutuality of goals and aspirations?

2. Do all stakeholders understand the nature of partnership commitments, including whether the partnership is ongoing or time bound and under what conditions or processes it might end?

3. Do community members have clear teaching and leadership roles, as well as clear roles in driving research direction, process, and publication with fair authorship rights?

4. Are vulnerable populations, such as children, clearly protected through appropriate safeguards and relevant training for all individuals involved in the partnership?

5. Do students' same-age peers from the community have financially underwritten opportunities to participate in programming (in an accredited way)?

6. In terms of community impact, are the reasons for the partnership understood and embraced by multiple and diverse stakeholders?

7. In terms of student learning, are the reasons for the partnership understood and embraced by multiple and diverse stakeholders?

8. Do recruitment and other outreach materials serve an educative function, shaping expectations for ethical engagement?

9. Do all stakeholders know whom to communicate with about what, through what channels, at all times?

10. For all interested community members and students, does carefully selected text and facilitated discussion support learning about responsible engagement, cross-cultural cooperation, and growth in global community before, during, and after community–campus engagements?

11. Is the economic impact of the partnership deliberately distributed among multiple stakeholders (e.g., community organization buildings where classroom space is secured, local restaurants that host students and community partners, and/or host families working with overnight programs)?

12. Do all stakeholders have access to information regarding financial commitments and disbursements that support the partnership, along with opportunities to openly and critically discuss those commitments with the other stakeholders?

Attention to the best practices referenced previously suggests practitioners should triangulate community voice, actively seek the voices of the marginalized, and otherwise be systematic about inclusion of broad community perspective and multiple stakeholders regarding purpose, goals, outcomes, process, and resource allocation to support agreed-on goals.

Commitment and sustainability. International education programming should be undertaken only within a robust understanding of how the programming relates to the continuous learning of the student and the community defined goals of the host community. For students, this translates as a relationship among the program, preparatory courses, and reentry programming. Such programming should support the development of the individual student and/or continuous connection to the community partnership or ethical questions addressed after returning to campus. Ideally, faculty, activities, and programs on campus support students' efforts to engage in ongoing global civic engagement and social change programming related to their immersion experiences. For community partners, this means clarity regarding the nature of the commitment with the university or international education provider, as well as a clear vision of likely developments in relationship, partnership, and community-driven goals for the next year, three years forward, and even as many as five years in the future.

Transparency. Students and community partners should be aware of how program funds are spent and why. Decision-making regarding program fund expenditures should be transparent. Lines of authority, roles, and responsibilities should be clear. Transparency should extend throughout CBGL relationships, from the university to and through any providers and to the community.

Environmental sustainability and footprint reduction. Program administrators should dialogue with community partners about the environmental impacts of the program and the balance of those impacts with program benefits. Together, partnership leaders must consider strategies for impact mediation, including supporting local environmental initiatives and/or opportunities for participants to travel to and from their program site in "carbon neutral ways" (e.g., by purchasing passes or "green tags").

Economic sustainability. Program costs and contributions should be aligned with local economies or social dynamics within the community. Donations or project support should reflect a sustainability perspective, thereby taking into account and/or developing the capacity of the community partner to manage funding effectively and ethically.

Deliberate diversity, intercultural contact, and reflection. The processes that enhance intercultural learning, appreciation, open-mindedness, inclusion, and acceptance involve deliberate intercultural contact and structured reflective processes by trusted mentors. This is true whether groups are multiethnic and situated domestically or composed of international participants, only students, or community members and students. Program administrators and community partners should work to enhance diversity of participants at all points of entry and should nurture structured reflective intercultural learning and acceptance within all programs.

Global community building. The program should point toward better future possibilities for students and community members. With community members, the program should encourage multidirectional exchange to support learning opportunities for locals, as well as continuous contact and commitment regarding local development and/or advocacy goals. With students, the program should facilitate a return process whereby learners have reflective opportunities and resources to explore growth in their understandings of themselves as global citizens capable of responsible and ethical behavior in a global context.

Proactive protection of the most vulnerable populations. Program stakeholders should be fully aware of the ways in which international volunteerism has at times created perverse incentives that undermine child development and patient safety. Orphanage volunteering and clinical medical volunteering settings for uncredentialed volunteers must be avoided. Together, stakeholders should discuss shared understanding of basic rights, vulnerable populations, and the local and international preparatory resources and training necessary to ensure ethical interaction between visitors and host community members.

Community-Centered Components

Purpose. Program administrators should engage in continuous dialogue with community partners regarding the partnership's potential to contribute to community-driven efforts that advance human flourishing in the context of environmental, economic, and social sustainability. Continuous dialogue should include at a minimum an annual evaluation and assessment of the partnership and its purposes based on mutually agreed-on and clearly designed program models with specific goals, objectives, methods, and metrics.

Community preparation. Community organizations and partners should receive clear preprogram clarity regarding expectations, partnership parameters through formal or informal memoranda of understanding, and sensitization that includes visitors' customs and patterns and the fullest possible awareness of the possible ramifications (both positive and negative) of hosting.

Timing, duration, and repetition. Program administrators should cooperate with community members to arrive at acceptable program timing, length, and repetition of student groups in communities. Different communities have demonstrated varying degrees of interest in the timing of programs, their duration, and their regularity of repetition. This, like all such conversations, must be highly contextualized within particular communities and partnerships.

Group size. Program administrators must discuss ideal group size with community members and arrange the program accordingly. Large groups of visiting students can have positive and negative effects on local communities, including undermining traditional cultural knowledge and distorting the local economy.

Local sourcing. The program should maximize the economic benefits to local residents by cooperating with community members to ensure program participant needs are addressed through indigenous sources. Community-engaged programs should categorically not parallel the economic structures of enclave tourism. Maximum local ownership and economic benefit is central to the ethos of community partnership. For example, consider the following:

- Transparently reimbursed host families offer stronger local economic development than hotels or hostels that are frequently owned by distant corporate organizations.
- Local eateries, host families, and/or local cooks should be contracted to support local economic development and offer opportunities to learn about locally available foods.
- Local guides and educators should be contracted to the fullest extent possible, including contracting with professionalized and credentialed, as well as nonprofessionalized and noncredentialed, educators who hold and understand local knowledge, history, tradition, and worldview.

Direct service, advocacy, education, project management, and organization building. To the extent desired by the community, the program involves students as service-learners, interns, and researchers in locally accountable organizations. Students learn from, contribute skills or knowledge to, and otherwise support local capacity through community improvement actions over a continuous period of time. Ideally, community members or organizations should have a direct role in preparing or training students to maximize their contributions to community work. Students should be trained in the appropriate role of the outsider in community development programs. They should also be trained on participatory methods, cultural appropriateness, and program design, with a focus on local sustainability and capacity development.

Reciprocity. Consistent with stated best practices in service-learning, public health, and development, efforts are made to move toward reciprocal relationships with community partners. These efforts should include opportunities for locals to participate in accredited courses; chances to engage in multidirectional exchange; and clear leadership positions, authority, and autonomy consistent with the ideals articulated in the previous "Community Voice and Direction" principle. Outcomes for communities should be as important as student outcomes; if this balance is not clear, program design adjustments should be made.

Student-Centered Components

Purpose. The program leaders instill an ethical vision of human flourishing by systematically encouraging student reflection and growth regarding responsible and ethical behavior in global context.

Student preparation. Robust learning in international education is clearly predicated on careful preparation for participating students. Student preparation should include pre- or in-field training that equips learners with the basic conceptual and experiential tools to optimize field learning. The program expects students to acquire a working knowledge of global political economy, the host country's political history, current events, group customs and household patterns, ethnographic skills, service ethics, and research methods, as well as culturally appropriate project design, participatory methods, and other community-based approaches and tools. This may require transdisciplinary courses and multidisciplinary cooperation among faculty members.

Connect context to course work and learning. The program leaders engage documented best practices in international education, service-learning, and experiential education broadly by systematically using reflection to connect experiential program components with course goals, global civic engagement goals, and intercultural learning goals.

Challenge and support. Program leaders embrace lessons learned regarding reflection in experiential education and intercultural learning by ensuring the living and learning environment is characterized by "challenge and support" for students.

- Student housing opportunities encourage sustained intercultural contact, opportunities for reflection, and connection to intercultural learning.
- Students are systematically encouraged to engage in contact with the local population that deliberately moves students out of "group cocoons" and into interpersonal relationships with a variety of local individuals.
- Service projects or community programs are conducted collaboratively, with students working alongside community members to maximize cultural understanding and local context knowledge.

Program length. Program design decisions recognize the strengths and limitations of different lengths of programming, and learning outcomes and educative processes are specifically calibrated to achieve outcomes consistent with program length.

Instruction and mentoring. The program provides the necessary external facilitation and supervision to keep students focused, active, and reflective in their learning. The field support system includes "mentor-advisers" drawn from the host community (e.g., host family members, service supervisors, language coaches, and research guides).

Communicative skills and language learning. On the basis of the length of the program and consultation with community partners, the program leaders choose the best possible strategy to improve current language and communication skills and spark interest in future language learning. The growth in short-term study abroad should in this light be seen as an opportunity to entice students toward language learning rather than as an excuse to avoid significant language development. More and deeper language learning is always optimal for improved communication and community partnership.

On-site learning and preparation for healthy return to home communities. Before, during, and after return, program leadership offers guidance, information, reflective opportunities, and exposure to networks intended to support students' growth as globally engaged, interested, and active individuals. This is part of both course planning and institutional support, as it should extend from the course into student programming and organizations, as well as career services and academic career opportunities.[1]

Conclusion

We close this chapter by recalling Korten's (1990) insight regarding one of the central flaws of NGOs (and, we would add, CBGL educators, and practitioners) in the Global North. That is, despite good intentions for helping communities in the Global South, development and CBGL practitioners and educators often do not have a well-developed understanding of their own approach to community development. This concern extends to local partnerships and includes consideration of all of the complexities that exist in community–campus partnerships at home and abroad.

Too often, practitioners fail to spend the necessary time and diligence gathering local knowledge on previous approaches to community development by nonprofit and for-profit organizations, neighborhood groups, and public institutions (Chambers, 1997). NGOs and CBGL programs need to have a clear understanding of not only their approach to community development but also the strengths and limitations of various approaches given the unique factors and conditions in specific contexts (Korten, 1990). We share this commitment to understanding development theory and coplanning with partners throughout the CBGL program planning processes, which is the subject of the next chapter.

Note

1. Special thanks to Richard Slimbach of Azusa Pacific University, whose "Program Design for the Common Good" was the first iteration of this set of written standards. In addition, we are appreciative of considerable written feedback from Slimbach himself, along with CBGL administrators, practitioners, and scholars, including Jeffrey Bouman, Lauren Caldarera, Brandon Blache-Cohen, Matthias Brown, Mireille Cronin-Mather, Junior Gasparini, Julia Lang, Nora Reynolds, and numerous individuals who provided feedback at the 2011 and 2012 International Association for Research on Service-Learning and Community Engagement Conferences, 2013 Forum on Education Abroad Conference, and 2013 Cornell/NYCC Global Service-Learning Institute.

6

IMMERSIVE COMMUNITY-BASED GLOBAL LEARNING PROGRAM DESIGN

What Are Your Team's Goals?

Planning an immersive program that takes place off campus, including developing sustainable partnerships with communities and arranging logistics, requires a tremendous amount of time and energy. As Hilary E. Kahn, associate director for the Center for the Study of Global Change at Indiana University wrote, it is "more arduous, time-consuming, and pedagogically complex than most curricular methods. Few would deny how demanding it can be for students, directors, instructors, researchers, as well as for local community members and service providers" (Kahn, 2011, p. 113). Though the rewards of CBGL can be significant, CBGL should not be taken up without a clear sense of program planning theory and practice and the commitments involved (Sandmann, Kiely, & Grenier, 2009).

This chapter moves from a broad overview of the institutional contexts in which immersive CBGL operates and proceeds to specific suggestions for actionable program planning. The broad context is vital, however, as individuals and networks advancing CBGL are so frequently engaging themselves and their collaborators in institutional change processes.

However planning is perceived at your institution, we encourage you to view planning and implementing your CBGL program as a collaborative and community-driven process to the fullest extent possible. We suggest you build a leadership *team* that will share vision, design, implementation, and evaluation responsibilities throughout the process. As we presented in chapter 5, community partners should play a significant role in planning a program and, eventually, evaluation and reconsideration processes after one cycle of the program is complete (Jacoby and Associates, 2003; Sandmann et al., 2009; Strand, Marullo, Cutforth, Stoecker, & Donohue, 2003). There is also a need for administrative involvement in this process. Administrators should understand the level of commitment and the kinds of support that will be needed by faculty and staff to effectively advance ethical global learning (Welch, 2016). Furthermore, administrators must keep their attention on the institutional commitments involved in engaged learning, commitments ranging from mitigation of any risk associated with the program to anticipation of long-term commitments to community partnerships formed during the planning process (Sandmann & Plater, 2013).

Recognizing why you, your partners, your colleagues, and your administrators see value in undertaking this program is an important first step. Yet your goals will not inform program development in isolation. The international education landscape is extraordinarily varied and characterized by distinct kinds of opportunities and limitations for faculty depending on their home institutions. We describe that environment briefly, with an explanation of how the institutional environment may inform program design choices. We then turn to an explanation of common models in CBGL.

The Institutional and Policy Environment: Who Are Your Partners?

Study abroad by U.S. higher education students has more than tripled in the past two decades (Institute of International Education, 2016). The conventional model of study abroad involves an agreement between two institutions of higher education in separate countries that stipulates that they will host one another's students. However, the increase in U.S. students abroad has occurred in other types of programming as more students opt for summer and other short-term experiences, which now comprise more than 50% of U.S. study abroad programming (Institute of International Education, 2016). As more students seek these kinds of programs, more faculty members are leading short-term programs that feature one course with a primary faculty leader or set of coleaders. These are termed *faculty-led programs*.

Even within faculty-led programs, there are multiple organizational possibilities. As with so many practices in our highly networked and largely privatized world, higher education institutions themselves frequently do not organize or implement study abroad programs independently. In the language of the sector, they contract with third-party providers (TPPs). TPPs, further discussed in Toolbox 6.1, are private sector or nonprofit organizations dedicated to managing international exchange programs of varying types, from ecology courses in Costa Rica to poverty seminars in Johannesburg,

TOOLBOX **6.1**
Working With a TPP

Working with a TPP often makes good sense for institutions interested in offering CBGL programming without the expense and responsibility of developing community partnerships and logistical planning. As Chisholm (2003) indicated, TPPs work with a model in which course instruction or program leadership is provided by the home institution.

Some colleges and universities use this option as a stepping-stone toward greater institutional commitment to CBGL, and others develop long-term relationships with the TPP and the community network it facilitates.

There are other benefits to working with TPPs. First, they have already done much of the labor-intensive work of identifying and building a relationship with a local community partner, thus ensuring that short-term projects will contribute toward the longer-term goals of the host community. Second, TPPs also typically handle housing, safety, health, food, and service projects. Local staff members are typically hired to coordinate projects. Depending on the type of partnership, TPPs can help with ongoing monitoring and assessment of shared projects and program quality.

When a provider takes care of logistics, faculty members can focus on teaching and addressing students' needs. Because the provider maintains the community partnerships, faculty members do not feel pressured into making a long-term commitment to the program; the provider ensures the long-term relationship with the community partner. In addition, and vitally, high-quality partner organizations bring expertise specific to the area of practice, such as global development or global health—expertise that is not always available through visiting faculty, staff, and students. The cost to students may be slightly higher, but the benefits to faculty and staff are often well worth the cost. Another option is for the host institution to provide pre- and post-CBGL program orientations and course work while the service work occurs with the TPP overseas (Chisholm, 2003; Kiely & Kiely, 2006). Even when working with TPPs, the FTL queries provide a useful evaluative tool for understanding commitments to community direction, collaboration, transparency, and other best practices.

South Africa, and history courses at the Great Wall of China (Hartman, Paris, & Blache-Cohen, 2013).

Several TPPs, such as Amizade, Child Family Health International, the Foundation for Sustainable Development, and the International Partnership for Service-Learning, formed or focused programming because of the recognition that an intermediary organization could help diverse higher education institutions maintain long-term and sustainable community partnerships around the world (Hartman & Kiely, 2014b). Other TPPs developed first as private sector study abroad providers and have lately sought community connections to cater to the growing market in service-learning and international volunteer programming (Hartman, Paris, & Blache-Cohen, 2014).

Understanding the role of TPPs is an important part of the picture. Other dynamics include the extent to which your institution has articulated international programming in its mission and provided resources to support study abroad programming. Although universities broadly claim support for internationalization of campus and community, the ways that they integrate best practices with the university mission and institutional incentives variy considerably, even though there is increasingly broad understanding of what constitutes best practices in internationalization (American Council on Education, 2017; NAFSA, 2017) and global learning (Association of American Colleges & Universities, 2017). At some institutions, individual faculty members still shoulder the entire burden of developing, leading, and evaluating a study abroad program. Other institutions have become increasingly strategic about sharing responsibilities for sustainable community partnerships over many years or appointing faculty members with primary responsibilities for specific partnerships. This kind of programming is emerging at a variety of institutions, from community colleges to Ivy League institutions.

At Harrisburg Area Community College in Pennsylvania, the Center for Global Engagement leverages limited funding and resources to maximize growing interest in international programming. Unlike the previously common practice of following faculty interests to support study abroad programming wherever individual faculty members proposed to take a new course, the center requires faculty members to demonstrate long-term vision for any proposed new site. At minimum, faculty members proposing new sites must identify at least two other faculty members interested in leading a course at the same site and commit to offering the course again two years after the pilot program. This decision requires team building among faculty, leverages scarce resources toward longer-term commitments, and increases stability of programming for the institution and for community partners.

Central College in Iowa has a long-standing institutional commitment to international study. More than 50% of the college's students study abroad, and the college also serves as a sending institution for numerous colleges throughout the United States. Central College has developed several institutional and community relationships through its program in Mérida, Mexico, to facilitate CBGL programming. An established presence in Mérida that included preexisting institutional relationships with higher education institutions and a continuous presence on the ground enabled staff to develop community organization partnerships as interest from students and faculty members increased. The college currently offers a diverse set of service-learning placements that include opportunities to work with senior and youth populations, teach English as a foreign language, and support public health programming. This set of opportunities, which flows from Central College's continuous presence and staffing resources in Mérida during the year, has clear implications for supporting short-term faculty-led programs during summer and winter breaks.

At Cornell University, the Global Health Program develops undergraduate students' skills to address global health issues through multidisciplinary research, service, and training (Moseley, Stoltzfus, & Kiely, 2017). The program's previous director, Rebecca Stoltzfus, a tenured professor (now president of Goshen College), spent a sabbatical year in Moshi, Tanzania, as part of an effort to develop a sustained relationship with Kilimanjaro Christian Medical College (KCMC). Through the resulting relationship, Cornell's global health students cooperate with KCMC students every summer, engaging in multidisciplinary research projects at the behest of local community organizations and medical institutions. The Global Health Program, through its leadership, has made this a clear ongoing commitment, and participating students must complete a field experience in Moshi or with another approved program. Crucially for program sustainability, there is a full-time staff member who works closely with students, faculty, and community partners to ensure that relationships are nurtured and maintained and essential planning and program components are coordinated well. This professional in the global health education and service-learning fields can respond to unpredictable events or programmatic concerns in a timely, professional, culturally sensitive, and nuanced manner. In addition, the faculty director of the program negotiated with central administration to retain the majority of tuition dollars for reinvestment in the program.

After the devastating 2010 earthquake in Haiti, five universities and Break Away came together to establish the Haiti Compact. At the center of the effort, they explicitly put a multiyear commitment to resource pooling and cooperation (Piacitelli, Barwick, Doerr, Porter, & Sumka, 2013).

The compact began with a 9-day exploratory trip attended by 16 student leaders and staff advisers from American University, the College of William and Mary, Loyola Marymount University, Indiana University, and the University of Maryland. During the visit, members of the delegation met with more than 20 community organizations as part of an effort to find and build productive partnerships with Haitian-led organizations. Since the founding of the compact, 4 of the 5 original schools have sent 9 successful alternative break trips to support partners in Haiti. The participating institutions indicate that the partnership model at the center of the compact has helped them build capacity for such programming, develop shared resources for themselves and for other campuses interested in participation, and create shared principles of social justice in the partnerships (Piacitelli et al., 2013).

These four programs make four different strategic efforts to address a challenging question in CBGL: How can resources be organized to increase the likelihood that programs are accessible for students, sustainable for academic institutions, and beneficial for community organizations? As we shared in chapter 5 and as established in the service-learning literature, commitment is a characteristic community organizations would like to see more frequently in partnerships (Larsen, 2015; Stoecker & Tryon, 2009; Welch, 2016). Each of the institutions mentioned made deliberate moves to enhance its commitments to particular organizations or locations.

Harrisburg Area Community College made a key innovation in managing faculty-led programming, ensuring that funds are committed only to programs with clear potential to be offered repeatedly. This small shift in policy transforms the Center for Global Engagement from an office serving individualized faculty travel and research to an office strategically seeding interdisciplinary, collaborative, and sustainable international partnerships and programming. The leadership of the Global Health Program director at Cornell University led to the establishment of an ongoing institutional commitment with a Tanzanian institution of higher education. The resulting community-engaged program is required for students and reinvests tuition back into the program. At Central College, presence in Mérida allowed the college to form partnerships with community organizations. The Haiti Compact offers a unique example of pooling the professional capacities and commitments of several institutions into one multiyear, focused alternative break commitment.

The discussion of the environment in which CBGL programs are offered has so far addressed the increasing interest in such programming, the role of TPPs, and the different kinds of institutional commitments that may strategically support CBGL. In addition to considerations of structure, third-party options, and institutional incentives, however, you must ultimately ask yourself one question: How will you design your program with adequate time, staffing, and resources to ensure quality in terms of academic integrity, student safety, meeting community commitments, ease of logistical processes (e.g., travel, board, and guest speaker fees), competent communication with partner organizations, program sustainability, and successful navigation of the challenging dynamics of power and privilege?

As the preceding discussion suggests, different institutions work to address this challenging question in different ways. We share Toolbox 6.2 to offer a few of the various factors involved in choosing an organizational model for CBGL partnership. We focus here on short-term programming options but will further discuss semester programs in the pages that follow.

Costs in Toolbox 6.2 are treated with an asterisk because, perhaps surprisingly, costs are understood in dramatically different ways at different institutions. Whether and how faculty salary and/or course release is budgeted as a "real cost" from within a study abroad office, within the cost of the program, or through cooperation with central administration funding varies. This variation in cost comprehension stems from the diversity of budgeting models at institutions of higher education. Many current directors of international education offices, or certainly individuals who hold titles such as vice president for global initiatives, began careers as faculty members at institutions that employed incremental budgeting. That budgeting system typically makes only incremental changes to program or departmental budgets once initiatives are established. In that environment, there is less need for precise understanding of costs than there is within several budgeting approaches that have emerged more recently (Hummell, 2012).

As institutions increasingly face declining state budgets and endowments, many have adopted responsibility-centered budgeting (RCB). RCB

> is guided by the statement, "Every tub has its own bottom" (Zierdt, 2009, p. 348). In this statement, the tub refers to academic units and the bottom refers to these units being responsible for their own revenue production. RCB shifts decision-making and financial accountability to units, such as departments or offices. (Hummell, 2012, p. 9)

As implied in Hummell's quote, institutions have historically not been as attentive to real costs in international programming as have been TPPs. This is partly because of the history of what critics would call unaccountable budgeting systems mentioned previously, but perhaps, more important, it is because the university has historically engaged in philanthropic,

TOOLBOX 6.2

Program Alternatives in Short-Term, Immersive CBGL

	Brief Description	Costs	Sustainability	Community Connection	Safety and Logistics
Faculty led, independent	The faculty member initiates the program and agrees to oversee all aspects (in cooperation with the study abroad office).	Preprogram site visits fall to the institution.* This is often more affordable for students, because faculty oversight is not always remunerated* beyond course overload.	It is dependent on the faculty member.	It is dependent on the quality of the individual faculty member's or leadership team's relationships and regularity of return.	They are dependent on the quality of the faculty member's site visit, relationships, and fact-checking in the community; responsibility falls with, the faculty leader(s).
Faculty led, third-party provider	The faculty member initiates and oversees academic components, plays a key role in student recruitment, and hands logistics to the third-party provider.	The third-party provider is continuously present on-site, so there is less need for pre-program visits. Real costs* accounting for community partnerships, logistics, and health, safety, and security oversight may drive student costs higher.	The continuous presence in the community improves the sustainability of relationships.	It is dependent on the quality of the third-party provider; assuming best practices, there is greater opportunity for community partnerships over time.	A broader network of support is available through the third-party provider's continuous presence in the community (assuming best practices).

University–community partnership	The university partners with community organizations.	There is more investment commitment than with faculty-led models at the outset, but it accrues some benefits with longevity of the partnership (e.g., fewer preprogram site visits).	Ongoing relationships and goal clarity must be central to the agreement.	It is dependent on the quality of the institutional commitment; assuming best practices, there is strong opportunity over time.	A broader network of support is available through the institution's continuous presence in the community (assuming best practices).
Institutional partnership	The university partners with a higher education institution in the host country.	The university can often reach agreement with the exchange institution regarding the number of student exchanges required to balance costs, but these traditionally common agreements do not typically include costs of community engagement.	Community partnership must be mutually understood. Goal complementarity is essential.	It is dependent on the quality of the institutional commitments. Partnership with the institution is not equal to partnership with the community.	A broader network of support is available through the institution's continuous presence in the community (assuming best practices).
Approved independent programs	The university encourages students to attend accredited programs organized through other institutions.	Students may choose a program based on ideal fit and costs. The university outsources these relationships.	It is entirely dependent on outside institutions.	It is entirely dependent on the quality of the program. Control extends only to choosing a list of approved programs.	They reside with the outside institution. The university embraces some risk with recognition of other programs.

public-serving activities, and it has done so at a cost (Merriman, 2010). Even today, the institution that is entirely dependent on tuition is unusual, creating a situation where "not even that very rare student who receives no financial aid from the college, will come close to paying what it is going to cost the college to educate" the student (Merriman, 2010).

In such a setting, institutions may still seed programs with start-up money, provide a budget incrementally, or dedicate an endowment to a particular initiative. If any of these things occur with your program, you are fortunate, but we urge you to continuously consider real costs, sustainability, and—even if only internally—your own understanding of RCB. This will ultimately improve your ability to guarantee your program's continued presence and possibly discover opportunities for equitable remuneration of off-campus partners. As discussed in Toolbox 6.3, given the diverse stakeholders recognized in CBGL, balancing economic sustainability is particularly challenging.

Because institutional models vary so greatly, being a clear, early, and articulate advocate for your initiative may support your program through the budget and policy process. Some institutions with mechanisms for offering courses at reduced rates, such as through continuing education or extension programs, have chosen to offer study abroad programs to students at these rates to further incentivize student participation in study abroad.

Other institutions, recognizing financial losses suffered when students are away from campus, require all students to pay home tuition for any international program participation, regardless of its real cost (Heitmann, 2007–2008). Still other institutions charge a study abroad fee on top of the home tuition cost. In a 2015 survey on program management in education abroad, with respondents representing 223 different U.S. higher education institutions, 56% of the study abroad offices that took part in the survey indicated the program fees they collected went to accounts not controlled by the education abroad office. Forty-four percent of offices, however, reported having control over the program fees gathered (The Forum on Education Abroad, 2015). As you consider sustainability for your program, accessibility for students, and equitable relationships with your community partners, it is important to understand the specific nuances of study abroad financing and budget accountability at your own institution. Institutional leadership that sees study abroad programming as central to the university mission can create a philanthropic enterprise that includes study abroad programming as part of the vision through which it invests in students. Alternatively, and at worst, faculty leaders, provosts, or presidents may see international education as superfluous, frivolous, or lacking in rigor.

TOOLBOX **6.3**
Balancing Costs and Equity

Considering costs and equity in CBGL is challenging. Different institutions arrange for the collection of fees and sharing of institutional monies in shockingly divergent ways. Particularly in respect to work with global engagement that does not benefit from the presences of any associated endowment funding, it is essential to become an informed advocate for your program's ability to keep any revenues and even secure additional monies to the extent that it advances institutional mission.

Depending on your institution and its student demographics, accessibility for students may be a significant concern. One strategy advanced to address this issue is driving program costs as low as possible. At times, institutional policies permit charging extraordinarily low per-credit fees and instead collecting a program fee. In these cases, faculty are free to volunteer to lead the course, thus trimming a small amount of overhead from the overall course cost. Alternative breaks, similarly, are often student led, with no remuneration beyond a discounted program fee. It is worth asking, however, how this affects program sustainability. Other programs follow a program fee model similar to that employed by many private institutions of higher education, where few students actually pay full tuition. This involves charging higher tuition that covers all costs comprehensively, including the generation of funding for some targeted student scholarships.

Student accessibility is also strongly affected by institutional policies regarding financial aid accessibility for CBGL programming, campus culture, and perceptions of international programming and whether international or immersion experiences are required. Requiring immersion experiences for degree completion often triggers the release of additional kinds of financial support, including veteran's benefits.

Institutions that serve students as primary customers have strong incentives to pursue the most affordable strategies possible when interacting with community partners. Yet any program dedicated to ethical partnership must consider not only what the market will bear but also what is fair and just for community partners. Driving student costs lower must be balanced with considering just community remuneration and even accessibility for community member course participation. (See the sections on FTL in chapter 5.)

It is important to balance concern for students and community members with the challenge of program sustainability. CBGL programs often begin with idealism, but they are most frequently sustained by matching that idealism with a sustainable approach to funding.

(Continues)

TOOLBOX 6.3 *(Continued)*

Most faculty members cannot dedicate substantial portions of their life to work that is unremunerated or remunerated at a rate well below their typical reimbursement. Although CBGL is movement building in a social justice tradition that "makes the road by walking," program leaders must keep an eye on financial sustainability for themselves and their collaborators if they wish to see programs transcend individual idealism.

In fairness to each of the three stakeholder groups mentioned previously, it is essential to understand your program's position within institutional economic incentives and policy and to try to leverage that understanding to your program's maximum benefit. Program benefit should be understood along each of these parameters: Does it enhance student accessibility? Does it improve program sustainability? Does it increase equitable outcomes for community partners?

In these cases, study abroad programs must anticipate raising all funds required for quality programming and perhaps even supporting a substantial portion of university core programming with study abroad fees. The extent of institutional support has clear implications for decisions about program structure, highlighted in Toolbox 6.2.

The growing inclusion of domestic study away in global learning offerings (Sobania, 2015) also presents significant questions in respect to shared institutional responsibility regarding curricular, safety, and budgetary questions as the field pivots to understand that global learning can occur anywhere. Though domestic civic engagement offices still frequently operate independently from study abroad offices, the conceptual rationale for taking a global approach is clear (Hartman & Kiely, 2014b; Longo & Saltmarsh, 2011; Sobania, 2015; Whitehead, 2015). The evaluation and assessment data on high-impact practices demonstrate that domestic engagement during the semester is associated with prosocial outcomes and deepened disciplinary learning in ways that parallel the power of study abroad (Kuh, 2008). As our understanding of CBGL continues to develop, we cooperate with numerous institutions to better understand how domestic community engagement, study abroad, and CBGL have similar or different effects on student learning in order to prioritize those programs that most clearly develop intercultural learning, cultural humility, global citizenship, and critical reflection capacities (Hartman, Lough, Toms, & Reynolds, 2015).

Whether it is accomplished through developing campus–community partnerships, institutional agreements, or independent faculty-led programming or by working with an established TPP, the planning and implementation process typically requires decision-making involving a number of common program areas. That process appears as an overview in Toolbox 6.4.

TOOLBOX **6.4**
Typical Planning and Implementation Cycle, Short-Term, Immersive CBGL Program

Proposal Preparation (two years before program implementation)

- Determine your and other stakeholders' primary goals with a CBGL program, both short term and long term.
- Familiarize yourself with institutional policies and capacities regarding study away and off-campus partnerships.
- In light of the institutional policies and best practices distilled throughout this book, develop an approach to community partnership, integration of learning goals, and travel logistics.
- Consider how you will know and demonstrate whether the program is a success.
- Submit a proposal through appropriate institutional channels, securing support from colleagues and administrators.

Promotion, Planning, and Vetting (year preceding program)

- Consider how you want the campus community and students to view your program, and determine how will you represent it.
- Engage recruitment with an understanding of the kinds of students you seek for your program.
- Undertake whatever promotion and vetting you are responsible for at your institution.
- Determine when students will receive the syllabus, gather course materials, and begin preparatory course work.
- Ensure your evaluation and assessment process relates strongly to program goals and stakeholder priorities.

Course Phase 1: Preimmersion (at least four weeks before travel)

- Ensure student orientation supports safety, prepares students for travel, and begins reflective learning.
- Engage students' reflective thinking on culture, human dignity, ethical community engagement and partnership, and the disciplinary content area.
- Foster an environment of trust and accountability.

(Continues)

TOOLBOX 6.4 (*Continued*)

Course Phase 2: Immersion (one to eight weeks)

- Adjust as necessary to respond to learning opportunities and community changes.
- Interrogate intersections among students' experiences, personal backgrounds and dispositions, course content, and learning goals through ongoing reflective practice.
- Determine interest in subsequent programming and/or improvements with community partners.

Course Phase 3: Postimmersion (within four weeks following travel)

- Encourage and support students' abilities to demonstrate learning experience and successfully reconnect in their home communities.
- Design final assignments to encourage students' ongoing critical global engagement.

Evaluation, Adjustment, and Continuous Communication

- Review program evaluation based on initial goals.
- Determine how program experience, community feedback, and student and institutional priorities suggest how future programs should be implemented.
- Make appropriate adjustments.
- Engage in continuous communication with community and institutional partners.

CBGL Program Factors

Regardless of what program model is chosen (see Toolbox 6.2), Kiely and Kiely (2006) provided CBGL educators with a number of factors to consider when selecting and developing a CBGL course or program, including location, time frame, level of immersion, link between service and academic content, faculty involvement and staffing, types of students, course and service, and resource and logistical considerations. Although these factors are discussed throughout this book, they are listed together in Toolbox 6.5.

TOOLBOX **6.5**
CBGL Program Factors

Factor	Description
Location	<ul><li>Political stability in region</li><li>Health and safety risks</li><li>Access to medical care</li><li>Availability of partner organizations, community groups</li><li>Availability of academic resources</li><li>Nature of problems and issues in the region</li><li>Language barriers</li></ul>
Time frame	<ul><li>Duration of trip</li><li>Time needed to develop meaningful relationships and complete service, academic work, reflection, and/or research</li><li>Summer, fall, spring</li></ul>
Type of course or program	<ul><li>Stand-alone, sandwich, capstone</li><li>Group or individual study</li><li>Disciplinary or research focus</li><li>Credit or noncredit</li></ul>
Type or purpose of partnership	<ul><li>Learning–project balance</li><li>Group or individual projects or combination</li><li>Direct or indirect service</li><li>Concurrent with study, sequenced or alternating</li></ul>
Level of immersion	<ul><li>Accommodation</li><li>Academics</li><li>Social opportunities</li><li>Collaborative projects</li><li>Other planned activities</li><li>Limits to immersion based on local context, participants' background, language skills</li><li>Number and diversity of community partners</li><li>Hotel, campus housing, host family</li></ul>
Critically reflective experiential learning	<ul><li>Readings</li><li>Oral and written reflection assignments</li><li>Group reflection on how experience informs understanding of subject matter and vice versa</li><li>Community-based research projects</li><li>Research papers</li><li>Dialogue</li><li>Opportunities for interaction with local leaders, experts, practitioners, community members</li></ul>

(Continues)

TOOLBOX 6.5 (*Continued*)

Community partnership	• Partnership with community leader, local service organization, third-party provider • Planned duration of partnership • Role of partner and community members in negotiating, implementing, and evaluating relationship • Partners from home institution
Staff and faculty	• Home campus, host community, or combination • Involvement of various departments or other faculty members • Institutional commitment • Time and level of commitment of lead faculty
Students	• Qualifications • Prerequisites • Recruitment • Application and admission procedures
Logistics	• Arrangements made by o Third-party provider o Community partner o Travel agent o Faculty director o Students o Combination of these
Resources	• Funding • Staffing • Faculty and/or institutional support • Program costs
Evaluation	• Student or participant learning • Community-driven outcomes

Note. Adapted from *International Service-Learning: What? Why? How?* by A. Kiely and R. Kiely, 2006. Paper presented at the NAFSA: Association of International Educators, 58th annual conference, Montreal, Canada.

Who Are Your Partners? Who Are Your Team Members?

Any approach to CBGL program design should proceed from both the imperatives of the institution and the role that the program will play in community development (Jones & Steinberg, 2011). Both at your institution and in the community, thinking deeply and broadly about whom to partner with to engage in service-learning will have important implications for the success of a service-learning program. We offer some considerations regarding the institutional leadership team before moving on to a community partner discussion, though of course these processes and decisions are intimately intertwined.

As the four examples shared previously make clear, institutions are adapting their global community engagement decisions to strategically leverage limited resources to increase the likelihood of long-term commitments and program sustainability. These examples present important questions for you to consider: Is your CBGL commitment individual, departmental, school-wide, or institutional? Who are the key stakeholders necessary for this commitment? How are stakeholders and potential allies regularly briefed and enrolled in continuous improvement efforts, from cooperating with risk management to working with the development office to enhance program sustainability? Toolbox 6.6 provides a list of potential collaborators on and off campus.

It is essential that throughout your program planning, implementation, evaluation, and iterative improvement processes, you systematically communicate with your key institutional, community, and other allies (Welch,

TOOLBOX **6.6**
A Partial List of Potential Stakeholders and Allies

Institution	Off-Campus Partners, Locally and Internationally	Supraorganization
• Alumni • Alumni association • Civic engagement • Department • Financial aid • Goals and performance rubrics • Institutional review board • Leadership • Parent association • Parents • Risk management • School • Student media • Study abroad • Trustees	• Businesses • Community organizers • Foundations • Government, faith, and community leaders • Host families • K–12 schools and educators • Peer colleagues • Peer students • People working directly with students in community, including any food or service provision partners, guides, drivers, and so on • Print, radio, and TV press • Rotary • Social sector staff members	• Accrediting bodies • Discipline or field • Large foundations • U.S. Department of State, including grant-making function and embassy • USAID

2016). Subsumed within the effort to strategically build institutional support and a strong team around CBGL programming, decisions must be made regarding specific commitments to course leadership capacity during each single course offering. Ensuring multiple leaders for each course offering, with clear responsibilities and shared authority, is clearly a best practice (Kiely & Nielsen, 2003). This ensures redundant capacity if one leader falls ill, if a health or safety issue at the site requires splitting the group, or if any other unforeseen circumstance arises.

Different programs achieve this redundancy of strong leadership capacity on-site in different ways. Some courses are team-taught by coinstructors from the home institution. Other programs hire host country faculty members or local site directors as coleaders throughout a course. This option is increasingly feasible as partnerships deepen. Amizade developed a three-pronged leadership model that built on community, faculty, and experiential educator strengths. This approach includes the clear commitments of a local site director, a faculty member with expertise in a particular discipline or course content area, and an experienced experiential educator from the service-learning or international education communities. The experiential educator holds the position of facilitator. This model is further discussed in chapter 7. In the model, the faculty member's area of expertise informs the content of a three-credit course called the *anchor course*, while the facilitator and faculty member cooperate to integrate additional CBGL learning in another three-credit course. In this arrangement, which we refer to as the Amizade Model (see Table 7.1), the facilitator is charged with working with the faculty member to integrate GSL theory and practice with the academic content of the anchor course and home discipline. This involves cultivating creative and critical thinking, focusing on learning with and through community interactions, considering the notion and application of community-driven service, as well as service more broadly, and exploring the notion of global citizenship.

The Amizade Model addresses capacity needs with clearly prepared individuals: a site director handles local logistics, community partnership processes, and local learning and lecturers; a faculty member brings expertise in a particular content area, along with familiarity regarding university learning and evaluation processes; and a facilitator supports the faculty member and site director in integrating their particular strengths into a cohesive, integrated, experiential learning experience. This model has worked well with demonstrably strong results for student learning (Hartman, 2014a) and community development (Hartman & Chaire, 2014), yet it is clearly resource intensive. The important questions for you as you develop your own course are as follows: How will you ensure that the necessary curricular and community development leadership capacities are available throughout the program? and How will you ensure redundancy in program leadership sufficient to address emergency situations or even faculty burnout (further discussed in chapter 7)? As vital as your institutionally recognized course leadership partner is your community-based leadership partner. Sometimes these are overlapping roles.

Whatever model you choose, it will be important to engage a systematic evaluation process. This can be challenging, because the format of immersive CBGL programming tends to spark hyperbolic self-report regarding personal change and transformation. The evidence is clear, however, that different programmatic approaches and program factors, as discussed throughout this volume, have different effects on learning outcomes. For a discussion of ongoing, mixed-methods, and evidence-based evaluation efforts underway through a network of institutions working with globalsl, see Toolbox 6.7.

On the basis of our experience facilitating programs in multiple community contexts with diverse institutions, TPPs, and community partners, we have found key steps that are useful in identifying and developing a mutually beneficial relationship with a community partner. Much of the process for choosing a partner depends on the type and purpose of the CBGL program. Faculty members often start with their course work and/or research interest in a specific discipline and begin to explore the relationship between their teaching and research interests and the global dimensions of community problems and issues. Sometimes the source of a partnership comes from ongoing relationships with community members and organizations built from conducting research abroad or from a connection with faculty colleagues at a college or university in another country. At times a specific request for service comes forward from an organization or community member, or your choice of partner might be dictated by existing partnership agreements with host country institutions in your department, college, or institution. Although alignment between the community-based program and faculty members' or students' personal, academic, and professional interests is ideal, this may not be the case, and CBGL educators should be prepared to adapt their goals and adjust them to align with community partner expectations.

As described earlier, working with a TPP can help to ensure this alignment. In the absence of such an arrangement, the institutional planning team will need to assume the responsibility for building a sustainable partnership very early in the planning process (Pigza & Troppe, 2003; Plater et al., 2009). This planning will usually involve a site visit to meet with potential partners (Kiely & Kiely, 2006). Such a visit will be fundamentally important for institutional risk management, logistical arrangements such as housing, and

TOOLBOX **6.7**
Program Evaluation

Evaluating CBGL outcomes and impact is challenging. Fortunately, the field has begun to mature, offering peer-reviewed examples of approaches to community-impact assessment (Larkin, 2015; Reynolds, 2014), global citizenship development (Hartman, 2014a), transformational learning (Kiely, 2004), and global learning broadly understood (Hartman, Lough, Toms, & Reynolds, 2015). Scholars are systematically drawing on lessons learned in this and related fields to suggest research frameworks and best practices for CBGL evaluation (Bringle, Hatcher, & Jones, 2011).

Although this recent work offers approaches to research on student and community outcomes of CBGL, individual program leaders may not wish to undertake the scope of such research. It is essential for every program director to determine

1. what program outcomes to track and
2. what kinds of evidence will count for the targeted stakeholder audiences.

Quantitative indices measuring intercultural learning may impress social science communities, demonstrably enhanced problem-solving capabilities may work for engineers, and filmed student and community member testimonials may appeal to generalist audiences. We encourage both qualitative and quantitative methods, as well as cultivation of the capacity to share stories, to evaluate program outcomes and impact. For program-level evaluation, it is important to have an evaluation plan that ties deliberately to program goals, to be systematic about gathering the kinds of data necessary for the question and for the audience, and to follow through carefully to implement the evaluation plan as necessary before, during, and after the travel experience. Visit https://compact.org/global-sl/ges// for a broad overview of the Global Engagement Survey, an evaluation tool that grew from the globalsl network.

instructional planning. The main aim will be to build a working relationship with off-campus partners. Among the important decisions to be made in such a visit will be the type of service project to engage and the roles and responsibilities for community members (Kiely & Kiely, 2006). If nothing else, such a visit can cement the role of community partners in the continuous planning process.

The importance of spending adequate time building a more meaningful relationship and clarifying roles, responsibilities, resources, costs, expectations, and logistics and working through any concerns or disagreements cannot be overstated. If such an approach seems overly daunting, you should reconsider partnering with a TPP to offer the program.

Program Models

The planning cycle detailed earlier suggests what is called a *short-term sandwich model of GSL programming*. Jones and Steinberg (2011) reviewed this and other approaches to international service-learning (ISL), identifying the program types enumerated next. Their chapter was published in Bringle, Hatcher, and Jones (2011), a helpful review of existing work in which the editors chose to employ *ISL* as the descriptive term. For the reasons mentioned previously, we are switching their analysis to reflect our philosophical commitment to CBGL, thus maintaining consistency within this book.

The common theme among CBGL program types is that, in any discipline, they offer unique and engaging learning opportunities. At times CBGL programs are opportunities to demonstrate a field's unique relevance to addressing a specific social issue, such as may be the case in public health, social work, education, and engineering. Alternatively, the tools of analysis and lenses of critique specific to anthropology, economics, literature, political science, and sociology may help students understand social issues with more nuance, identify structural issues, or process their comprehension of both (chapter 7 addresses academic planning).

Jones and Steinberg (2011) identified CBGL courses and programs employing a number of the approaches. The program types may be integrated in some cases. A summer engineering program focused on water harvesting, for example, could simultaneously be a sandwich program and a competency-based practicum.

- *All in the host country:* This experience occurs entirely in the host country; faculty may be from the home or host country institution. This is most common for programs longer than eight weeks. Although Jones and Steinberg (2011) focused on international experiences only, we add domestic CBGL semesters to this category. Azusa Pacific University (APU, 2017, further discussed in chapter 9), for instance, offers an entirely immersive Los Angeles Term, and the Higher Education Consortium for Urban Affairs (HECUA), in Minneapolis, offers several semester-length programs, such as "Intersections of Art, Identity, and Advocacy," "Ecology, Policy, and

Social Transformation," and "Policy, Community, and the Politics of Empowerment" (HECUA, 2017).

- *Sandwich 1:* This program has a pattern of several weeks of full-time study followed by travel for full-time service and concludes with another period of continued study, reflection, and evaluation. This may occur as a summer program or as part of a semester program with focused service during fall or spring break periods.
- *Sandwich 2:* This program is similar to Sandwich 1, but it includes domestic service in addition to service abroad.
- *Practicum:* Individual students study abroad as part of an intensive preprofessional learning experience. CBGL includes community-based work that goes beyond practicum requirements in terms of both required service and reflection. The practicum requires systematic supervision (on-site or online) and is common in teacher education.

In chapter 7 we explore a successful model of course leadership in depth and offer it as a model across disciplines, sites, and program lengths.

CBGL Program Protocols or Approval Processes

In addition to choosing a specific CBGL program model, each campus, institution, agency, or community partner may have its own process for approving new international study, exchange, or CBGL courses or programs. Institutional review and approval of CBGL programs is a vital component of risk management. (For more discussion of CBGL health, safety, and security, see chapter 8.) Although CBGL programs typically fall under the broader category of study abroad, there are important distinctions that require more in-depth assessment of the host country provider. In addition, there should be guiding criteria and an assessment of the level and type of preparation needed for students and faculty to be effective given their roles and responsibilities in undertaking a CBGL project.

The approval of new CBGL programs should be informed by a set of ethical guidelines and criteria based on good practices. We encourage faculty and administrators, in collaboration with community partners, to draw from FTL principles and queries (see chapter 5). Requiring additional information in the approval process ensures that new CBGL programs meet standards of best practice and protect the health and safety of students, faculty, and members of the host community.

Adapting the program approval process for CBGL programs may require the cooperation of several offices or departments on campus. Many institutions have an individual or office in charge of service-learning and another that manages study abroad and academic departments that over-see academic quality. It is important to negotiate clear roles for community engagement and study abroad professionals and academic departments that are involved in the approval process. Some universities establish a faculty advisory committee made up of individuals who have experience and exper-tise in CBGL. There are often opportunities to draw on existing expertise in service-learning and study abroad offices.

TPPs, host institutions, and community organizations frequently have existing protocols for program design and agreements, as well as outreach liaisons or coordinators who can be of great assistance in planning CBGL partnerships and preparing contracts, memoranda of understanding, and/ or agreed-on activities, costs, responsibilities, and resource sharing. These individuals can work with faculty, students, and administrators to develop policies and review new CBGL program proposals.

Effective collaboration on new program approvals will provide opportu-nities for each of the primary stakeholders involved in the CBGL planning process to be informed of new programs, offer input, provide feedback, and ensure quality. Holding periodic meetings between study abroad and service-learning professionals and curriculum and policy committees on campus can also facilitate effective communication and collaboration. In addition, com-munity partners should be involved in each step of the planning process. Having a planning process and structure in place will ensure that CBGL pro-grams maintain high-quality academic standards and that they are consistent with principles and standards of best practice in community-driven CBGL, risk assessment, health, and safety.

Recruitment and Preparation

As your program moves to approved status with an institution, you should be considering students you will recruit, how or why you will target them, and how you will encourage their entry into the program. Increasing numbers of institutions are requiring—or otherwise finding ways to strongly encour-age—student participation in international internships, immersion experi-ences, or study abroad. Program faculty and staff may have the opportunity through the application process to choose among several highly qualified applicants to determine what students will best represent the institution, help meet community goals, and benefit through their own personal and professional growth. CBGL program facilitators may also face the challenge of resistant participants, an area of growing concern and study as increasing numbers of institutions require experiential learning (Lassahn, 2015).

TOOLBOX **6.8**
Program Promotional Materials

> How do your materials represent strengths and dignity of off-campus stakeholders?
>
> How do program materials represent the work of service, development, and collaborative partnership with community-based, informal educators?
>
> Is there a structured application process to ensure participants who apply and who are selected understand the underlying guiding principles, goals, and expectations of the CBGL program and community partnership?

Program faculty and staff may be responsible for encouraging participation among individuals who associate travel with partying or with a population that sees study abroad as a luxury, travel outside the area code as noteworthy, or any extra expenditure as unnecessary or impossible. In any of the many cases regarding how students arrive, it is important to have a structured application and recruitment process in place to ensure participants are well prepared and support principles of good practice that underpin CBGL program goals expectations. See Toolbox 6.8 for questions that support careful recruitment guided by FTL principles. Whether other offices help support site visits, program planning, application, and recruitment, several early planning and recruitment decisions will determine not only the motivation and commitment of your students but also the way in which your program is perceived on campus and in the community.

There are several different good ways to represent CBGL programs, but of course anyone designing CBGL program materials should be aware of how such efforts affect existing stereotypes about external communities, development, service, and charity. This is the first opportunity to begin to shape student perceptions. You will want to strike a balance between the academic and experiential aspects of the program. Once students are recruited and assembled, the unfamiliar and rapid flow of a CBGL program really begins.

Systematic thinking about academic content, intercultural understanding, experiential learning, service and development, and common human dignity become more explicit and intentional as key dimensions of the course planning process, the subject of the next chapter.

7

PLANNING FOR IMMERSIVE GLOBAL LEARNING

I f your course or program involves travel, it begins with several types of disruption stemming from placing participants outside their comfort zones, daily habits, and routines. At the airport, some of your students will be nervous. One or two may be flying for the first time. All of your students will be in a heightened state: anxious, unsure, or excited. You will begin your experience of 24/7 immersion with them. If you are going to East Africa, your flights and connections will take more than 24 hours. Closer to home, you'll still be traveling all day. You'll get jet lag. They'll get jet lag. You'll land with a thud and—depending on the country—applause. You may deplane directly onto the runway—a first for many of your students—and walk across the tarmac into a holding space for immigration and customs. In the immigration line, your students will confer with one another, check in with you, and nervously approach the official. You'll all clear customs, and they'll stare in awe at the automatic weapons held by airport security as you greet an old friend or a site director with your name on a placard.

In a parking lot buzzing with activity, including women and children selling snacks and bottled water to taxi drivers and now your students, you'll all help load bags onto a minibus rooftop. You'll squeeze into the vehicle, spacious by local standards and inexcusably cramped according to American expectations. The driver will ease the large van onto the streets, some students peering out the windows with fervent curiosity, some falling asleep. The different stimuli that occur as students come into visceral contact with a different context cause different types and levels of physical, emotional, cognitive, and even spiritual responses. Knowing this is happening, as the program facilitator, when do you tell participants to journal in order to capture and reflect on the ways in which they are making sense and giving meaning to their experience? How do you ensure you are drawing on the experiential content of the program to strengthen students' learning and development? How can you be certain that your time in a place, engaged in cooperative learning and development, gives your students a stronger academic and meaning-rich experience than would be the case in a conventional classroom?

This chapter addresses academic design questions. We attended to intercultural, global civic, and service- and development-oriented learning earlier in this book, and the present chapter considers learning by design principles and multiple models for creating and facilitating the academic experience that are applicable across content areas. After sharing academic course and program design principles, we move on to provide tips for instructional delivery within the flow of a typical faculty-led sandwich course experience. Throughout, we offer specific recommendations for application.

Fortunately, understanding teaching and learning in this dynamic and challenging environment brings us to deeper awareness of best practices in course design. Coupling course design approaches such as backward design (Wiggins & McTighe, 1998) with the kinds of reflective practice approaches explained in chapter 3 unites two strands of best practice for fostering robust and purposeful CBGL experiences. According to Wiggins and McTighe (1998), course design should always begin with the end in mind. Starting with that premise, what are your aspirations for your students, in terms of

- academic content learning,
- academic skill development,
- abilities to integrate their intercultural learning insights with their development as professionals in the field, and
- interpersonal and other social skill development?

As this list implies, learning may take place in terms of foundational knowledge, application, integration, and even the "human dimension" (Dee Fink, 2013). The human dimension includes skills and capacities such as living by ethical principles, performing well on a team, becoming culturally sensitive, and contributing as a citizen (Dee Fink, 2013; University of New Mexico School of Medicine, 2005). In CBGL contexts, learning outcome possibilities are broad in terms of the kinds of knowledge, skills, attitudes, and behaviors one might be able to achieve given the length of time devoted to service and learning in a specific cross-cultural setting. When you are designing learning objectives that represent what you would hope to see your students know, feel, do, and consider as a participant in a course, aligning learning objectives with instructional strategies and assessment plans is essential to quality course and program design. In addition to alignment, learning objectives should be developmental and advance the level of cognitive, affective, emo-tional, and somatic complexity with appropriate support and scaffolding.

Bloom's taxonomy of learning provides a useful framework for design-ing course learning objectives that are both aligned and developmentally sequenced from simple memorization, recall, and comprehension to more advanced cognitive problem-solving to generating and applying knowledge through research (Ash & Clayton, 2009). Another useful (and mnemonic) device for developing learning outcomes is to design them to be SMART or "Specific, Measurable, Attainable, Results-focused, and Time-focused" (University of New Mexico School of Medicine, 2005). The key to devel-oping SMART learning objectives that are developmental and aligned is to think of the verb that best captures the meaning of the learning and experi-ence that you envision students will be engaged in. For example, start with "as a result of participation in this course, students will be able to *identify* and *practice* linguistic colloquialisms or cultural norms, *describe* important historical events, or *explain* factors that have influenced a particular local problem or issue."

Objectives like those listed previously would help students gain foun-dational knowledge and skills leading up to more advanced and challeng-ing learning such as "*conduct* interviews with residents to better understand perspectives on or approaches to a particular program or issue" or "*design* a website or health clinic in collaboration with community partners." Learning objectives such as *describe, explain,* and *practice* are in most instances precur-sors to learning objectives such as *application and design,* which would require some proficiency in the local language, cultural norms and customs, history, and previous approaches to a particular community program or issue. In addition, these more advanced outcomes of interest require some depth of relationship with local community members and organizations to facilitate effective collaboration. The globalsl.org website includes links to scores of action verbs associated with useful learning taxonomies and approaches that assist in the development of SMART learning objectives. As you consider the design of key learning outcomes for your students, remember that you must then articulate an instructional strategy and an assessment approach that is in alignment with the learning objectives to support students' achievement and articulation of each learning outcome (Ash & Clayton, 2009). Toolbox 7.1 demonstrates backward design of learning outcomes that are SMART, devel-opmental, and aligned with instructional methods and assessment in a CBGL course on community health in Nicaragua.

We recommend that faculty use the example course design template (see Toolbox 7.2) and complete this backward design exercise to develop learn-ing outcomes, instructional strategies, and an assessment plan for the CBGL

TOOLBOX 7.1

SMART Course Design: Community Health in Nicaragua

Learning Outcomes	Instructional Methods and Service Activities	Assessment
Upon completion of this course, what will students be able to do? • Describe and explain critical events in the history of Nicaragua and, in particular, the North Atlantic Coastal Region and their implications for the health and well-being of people living in this region • Identify and communicate social, economic, political, cultural, historical, and other factors that influence the social determinants of health • Create an electronic portfolio that demonstrates learning about self, others, and the source and solutions to community problems	*What instructional strategies or service activities will foster these outcomes?* • Readings • Face-to-face and online discussions • Journal entries • Lectures • Speakers • Independent and/or collaborative research • Instructor and peer feedback • Presentations • Sample ePortfolios	*What evidence measures do I plan to use to assess the achievement of this learning outcome?* • Rubric score on final reflection paper • Journal rubric score • Pre- and posttest of capacity to analyze challenges in respect to social determinants of health • Reflective essays rubric score • Portfolio rubric score • Poster rubric score • Publications • Presentation rubric score

TOOLBOX 7.2

What Are Your Targeted Course Outcomes and Instructional and Assessment Methods?

Learning Outcomes	Instructional Methods and Service Activities	Assessment
Upon completion of this course what will students be able to do? 1. – 2. – 3. – 4. – 5. –*	*What instructional strategies or service activities will foster these outcomes?*	*What evidence or (in)direct measures do I plan to use to assess the achievement of the learning outcomes?*

course or program they are developing. This not only requires systematic thinking about the relationship among instruction, assessment, and desired student learning and service outcomes but also compels faculty members to prioritize learning and service outcomes that are feasible given the program's time frame and community partner expectations. Alternatively, overly ambitious program leaders may try to "do it all" in every course, diluting numerous goals and focusing tightly on no specific outcome. The backward design process provides a useful visual and conceptual framework for discussion with community partners, clarifies purposes, and ensures alignment of expectations and feasibility (Ash & Clayton, 2009).

An important consideration in this process, of course, is the structure of your program as an academic experience. One of our core curricular insights through multiple experiences of trial and error is that learning about reflective practice (see chapter 3), service and community development (see chapter 5), cultural humility (see chapter 4), and critical global citizenship (see chapter 2) systematically occur only to the extent that curricular space is intentionally designed for the integration of each as key dimensions of the learning process. This insight first developed in the form of the Amizade Pedagogical Model (Hartman, 2008; Hartman, Friedrichs, & Boettcher, 2008; Hartman & Heinisch, 2003; Hartman & Kiely, 2004). The Amizade Model creates the time and curricular space for sustained, developmental, systematic, well-aligned, and integrated exploration of these core CBGL dimensions.

In its original formulation as a summer program, the Amizade Model (Table 7.1) was developed as a six-credit experience at institutions where three credits typically constitute a normal course. Three of the credits are from the faculty members' home discipline, and three create the space for the integration of CBGL theory and practice, enabling a fit between the considerable learning that takes place within this pedagogy and typical university credit-granting structures. The three credits from the home discipline,

TABLE 7.1
The Amizade Model: Anchor Course and CBGL

Three-credit anchor course in any disciplinary content area	Three-credit, transdisciplinary CBGL course
Home discipline content comparable to on-campus university course	Community-driven learning and/or service
	Critically reflective practice
	Development of cultural humility
	Seeking global citizenship

referred to as the *anchor course*, have sufficient academic content to stand alone in a manner similar to a comparable on-campus university course (Hartman, 2008, 2014a; Hartman et al., 2008).

Three CBGL credits then become the explicit space where the anchor course and experience are deepened through reflective activities, readings, discussion, and critical analysis regarding the notion and application of community-driven service, intercultural immersion and consideration of identity, the connection of experiential components to anchor course themes, and consideration of critical global engagement. Summer courses typically follow a model involving one month of online reflection, academic reading, writing, and preparation followed by one month of immersion, service, learning, and reflection in a specific community context. After return, students have an additional month to complete academic projects and reflective pieces, again online, as students often reside in different home communities (Hartman, 2008, 2014a; Hartman et al., 2008; see example syllabi at compact.org/global-sl/toolsandsyllabi/syllabi/).

Some institutions offer this CBGL course as a specific experiential course in the discipline, or they use a three-credit "special topics" designation. In other cases, institutions have developed a three-credit interdisciplinary service-learning course or "professional field experience" course. In this model, the CBGL course represents a kind of tool kit for connecting the experiential dimensions of the course with the anchor course in a specific discipline. This approach has the virtue of quantifying the varieties of credit-bearing work that go into CBGL, along with clarifying the curricular space for measuring student performance and assessing learning. When we have offered this model, course goals and objectives are so closely interrelated that we have often given the same grade for both courses. To be absolutely clear, in our programs academic credit is never granted for the act of doing service or participating in an experiential activity. Rather, credit is awarded on the basis of demonstration of systematically aligned critical analysis and demonstrable learning.

In addition to a specific academic project of the course with specific goals and learning outcomes, the anchor course can provide the broader intellectual structures and instructional occasions for the students to recall and reflect on the variety of experiences they undergo throughout the program. Placing the academic project within a CBGL program offers a special opportunity for instructors to present to their students the vitality of their disciplines for describing and interacting with the lived experience of the world.

For instance, Boettcher and Friedrichs developed a CBGL program in Belfast, Northern Ireland. The program paired a course in Irish literature with service work at youth centers in Belfast neighborhoods. CBGL creates a kind of reciprocal inquiry; in this course, the host community partnership invited a number of thematic focuses for the literature course, while the subjects and ideas of the literature created the terms for the students' engagement with community members when they arrived in Belfast. As one example, a persistent theme for Irish writers concerns the significant presence of history; this CBGL course structure brought that theme into stark reality that was not only an intellectual exercise but also concrete, palpable, and viscerally felt by participants. Students learned firsthand about the enduring presence of history as they spoke with cultural workers, some of whom were former members of Northern Ireland's warring factions now devoted to a process of peace and reconciliation.

The themes of the CBGL course complemented the goals of the Irish literature course in a number of ways. The students' learning about the cultures of Northern Ireland, for example, contributed to the course's investigation of the historical context of the literary works. Through service working with young people in Belfast neighborhoods, the students met with and developed deep connections with community members who offered perspectives about Northern Ireland's history and the historical context. Many of the community partner organizations also understood the intercultural import of their work. Following the implementation of peace agreements, some of the partner organizations have transitioned to serving other world communities in conflict. A course interrogating strains of narrow provincialism in Northern Irish identity opened for students into an inquiry into a subject of global significance.

A CBGL program will include both planned activities and unplanned events, and the latter can sometimes prove most significant. In a 2010 program in Northern Ireland, Boettcher's students were present for the delivery of the Saville Report on the events of Bloody Sunday in 1972 in which 14 protesters were killed by British paramilitary forces. It was a rare opportunity to participate in a history-making moment, and the students stood in solidarity with their community partners as the findings were read to a large crowd that had assembled in a city square to hear the report. The issuing of the findings spoke directly to the literary and historical course content the students had studied. Far beyond that, it offered much opportunity for reflection as the students worked through what the event meant to their community partners on the various sides of the reconciliation process, as well as their own role as witnesses. This is just one example of the kinds of chance opportunities for teachable moments we have encountered during CBGL programs.

Since the development of the Amizade Model, numerous institutions and programs have embraced the structure, adding a few variations along the way. To accommodate differing program lengths and credit structures, we offer in Figure 7.1 examples of transdisciplinary CBGL programs and in Figure 7.2 an interdisciplinary, semester-length CBGL program.

Figure 7.1. Transdisciplinary CBGL program.

One- to three-credit CBGL course
Community-driven learning and/or service
Critically reflective practice
Development of cultural humility
Seeking global citizenship

Figure 7.2. Interdisciplinary CBGL semester.

Discipline course		Community-driven learning and/or service
Discipline course	**Three-credit CBGL course**	Critically reflective practice
Discipline course		Development of cultural humility
Discipline course		Seeking global citizenship

The transdisciplinary CBGL program model can be used to intensify the experiences of programs organized around the service, travel, and intercultural experiences. In this model, students participate in significant community engagement and service. They also participate in regular and structured reflection on the program experiences. This reflective work encompasses the experiential components of the program. Learning in the program also connects the program experiences in the host community with the students' lived experiences in their home communities. Students should leave the program better able to perceive and knowingly operate within the various cultural, economic, and political structures connecting these communities.

This CBGL curriculum has been used to transform a wholly volunteer alternative spring break into a more significant learning experience. Specific learning activities are adapted to fit with immersion experiences of varying length. (Visit compact.org/global-sl/toolsandsyllabi/syllabi/ for several syllabi examples.)

This interdisciplinary semester model links several courses with a significant service experience conducted throughout the term. A semester model has the virtue of extended immersion and extended classroom study, creating greater opportunities for sustained work and intercultural exchange. It also allows for the creation of an interdisciplinary project in which the various disciplines can inform one another. In a Tanzania semester program, for example, students engage in community-driven project management and fund-raising in collaboration with local women's rights and sustainable development organizations, while studying the philosophy of global justice (three philosophy credits), international development (three political science credits), East African history (three history credits), and Swahili (three modern language credits). These four distinct disciplinary content courses are integrated and applied through the community projects, and reflective integration and application is advanced and supervised through the CBGL course (three credits). Though this semester model with Amizade has been engaged in many locations around the world, other organizations (HECUA, 2017) and institutions (Azusa Pacific University, 2017) offer domestic versions. As discussed in chapter 9, some institutions are even beginning to offer ongoing experiential curricular pathways that make CBGL part of institutional offerings during a "typical" college experience.

For the purposes of further discussion, this chapter proceeds with a description of the Amizade Model. Though this model was originally designed for a sequence that features a month of preparation, a month of immersion, and a month of academic and reflective work following return, the typical program flow is applicable to models of any type. No matter what course format you are teaching, we strongly advise that you build your course to be sequenced developmentally with the immersion experience that is sandwiched in a structured learning experience that prepares students for their travel and immersion and then guides them in reflecting on and learning from their CBGL experiences afterward. Employing the Amizade Model, a summer short-term program typically follows this structure:

- Four weeks preprogram, online, blended, in-person learning
- Four weeks in country
- Four weeks postprogram with a capstone project

This kind of model can be extended to a classroom course with a travel component over a break, or it can be compressed so that the pre- and postprogram components are conducted as an intensive retreat immediately before and after travel. Likewise, both components can be conducted as independent or directed studies or online or blended studies. Even semester programs, majors, and minors benefit from sequencing curricula that entail a form of preimmersion orientation and preparation and postimmersion study. Universities are increasingly recognizing the importance of sequencing CBGL curricula and pre- and postimmersion courses as part of the undergraduate curriculum during semesters before and after abroad semesters (Hartman, 2017b). Extended, deliberate learning before and after experiential learning deepens the learning significantly (Vande Berg et al., 2012). The following sections describe the variety of activities you will want to engage in during these distinct pre-, during-, and postengagement phases of any experience.

Supporting Student Capacity Development Throughout the Program Experience

Once you have accepted and assembled a group of students for your program, your first concrete course step beyond syllabus preparation and clarifying academic responsibilities will be your role in providing an introduction to the program and the work the students will be doing. Even the most adventurous students will have major concerns and questions about the program, and they will bring different levels of expectations about the way you plan and communicate your plans. Wherever possible, work to anticipate students' concerns and questions as a way to shape their expectations and perceptions of you and the program. The more that you are able to anticipate and address foreseeable concerns, the better the program will accomplish its goals and objectives overall. This includes developing students' capacities for dealing with unforeseeable events, including building their capacities for dealing with the stressors of dissonance and uncertainty, likelihood of change, and comfort with both unscheduled time and unpredictable environments. We provided an orientation tip list in Toolbox 7.3. The more you build the tone as a competent leader from the beginning of the course, the smoother it will go.

Preengagement

It is useful to think of the first weeks of the program as you would a conventional class. We generally recommend using the preprogram work to cover as much of the academic classroom content as possible, depending on your discipline and course. A rule of thumb is especially helpful for short-term programs: You should only plan on-site academic work such as reading, instruction, and other activities that will directly inform or be informed by the course experiences. It is often effective to introduce material well before travel and then to return to it on-site. In other words, the more work students can accomplish before they leave, particularly in terms of reading or acquisition of basic knowledge about the CBGL program's goals and expectations, the academic dimension of the course, and the local context where the service will take place, the more productive their analysis, synthesis, and critical reflection on-site.

TOOLBOX **7.3**

Develop a Comprehensive Orientation

Orientation Tip #1: Plan sufficient time to address all of the elements adequately. Most immersive CBGL programs hold multiple orientation sessions prior to departure. It is also possible to communicate information to participants and facilitate dialogue and learning online before departure. Ideally, students participate in a credit-bearing predeparture course that provides academic and practical preparation for participation in the program.

Orientation Tip #2: Present important program information in writing. Students will not remember everything that is said during orientation sessions, and many of them depend on their parents for help with preparation for the experience. Comprehensive and organized written materials provide a resource to which students and their parents can refer. Written materials can also limit institutional liability.

Orientation Tip #3: Include team-building activities in the orientation program. Participants will need to rely on each other and work together as soon as they arrive in the host country. Providing opportunities for students to get to know each other and build trust is a vital component of the predeparture orientation. Team-building activities may include the following:

- Participating in a local community engagement project as a group
- Completing a ropes course or similar activities
- Planning and implementing fund-raisers for the program
- Social gatherings related to the host culture (e.g., preparing and eating foods common to the region, celebrating a holiday)
- Developing a group agreement (see Toolbox 7.4)
- Doing a scavenger hunt related to the host country and program (i.e., participants work in groups to find specific information, resources, and supplies)
- Engaging in face-to-face or web-based dialogues, research, and reflection activities

Orientation Tip #4: Plan reflection activities to surface the participants' values, assumptions, and expectations. (Examples are offered throughout this book.)

Orientation Tip #5: Invite guest speakers who are or have significant experience in the host community to talk with participants about aspects of the culture and history, community issues, or academic focus of the program.

TOOLBOX **7.3** (*Continued*)

Orientation Tip #6: Show slides and videos to provide some exposure to the sights and sounds participants will encounter when they arrive in the local community. If possible, Skype with community partners.

Orientation Tip #7: Engage students in role-playing activities. Although it is impossible to prepare students for all of the situations they may encounter, role-playing can help them anticipate some of the challenges they will face and provide them with an opportunity to brainstorm possible responses and solutions. Cross-cultural dilemmas and challenges related to service projects provide fodder for role-playing situations.

Orientation Tip #8: Administer a preservice questionnaire related to students' backgrounds and experiences and course learning goals to establish a baseline for students' preparation, experience, and learning. The questionnaire helps students reflect on their expectations and assumptions, and faculty can gain a better understanding of students' level of knowledge, skill, experience, or proficiency relative to course learning and any service goals and expectations. A follow-up questionnaire helps students and instructors evaluate the program and the learning they experienced through the program. Comparative pre/post mixed method survey opportunities are available through globalsl. See Toolbox 6.8.

Orientation Tip #9: Predeparture readings and assignments must help students prepare for the global learning experience. Participants need to have background on the history and culture of the host country, as well as academic knowledge and skills to participate effectively in experiential learning and/or service projects. The orientation program must address these topics, but students should also do some independent reading, research, and reflection before the program begins. Students can participate in online dialogues about readings and issues.

Orientation Tip #10: Provide an opening for students to talk about their expectations and fears regarding program participation. A discussion of expectations can help program leaders better prepare students for the realities they will face. An open and honest dialogue about fears enables program leaders to assist students during the program and may also serve as a team-building activity.

Note. Orientation tip list adapted from Kiely and Kiely (2006).

Build in other materials to ensure that the CBGL portions of the course are productively covered prior to travel. This work should include introductions to the culture, language, history, and economic background of the region and area to which you will be traveling. This can be accomplished through readings, direct instruction, and activities, but it is also helpful to model the kinds of activities students will engage with on-site. We have invited invite guest speakers familiar with the community site, showed multimedia presentations to demonstrate clearly what life is like in the host community, and utilized role-play to anticipate challenges.

Develop students' reflective practice capacities immediately as you begin the course. This will include activities such as instructing students on setting up a journal and setting some ground rules for group interaction. Establish an environment that is safe and in which students feel comfortable putting words to what they are thinking and feeling. Toolboxes 7.4 and 7.5 share a process for including students in establishing a democratic course environment with high expectations. This environment will be extremely important when you are on-site and students are dealing with challenges they are not quite able to comprehend. Likewise, it will be important for students to analyze and articulate their preexisting assumptions and document where they are now in regard to the CBGL program goals; their expectations; the place where they are going; their assumptions about the language and culture; the factors that influence the problem that the CBGL is focused on; specific theories, models, and approaches; and so on. In essence, the preparation is an opportunity for students to learn about each other, the program, the problem, and the place; to engage in self-reflection; to learn how to surface their assumptions; and to state their thinking both so that they can return to it later and so that they can chart their progress.

Good preparation for critical reflection on their own and others' assumptions will also encourage students to practice the skills and habits of mind they will need when they are on-site. Establishing a journal-writing schedule, for example, can form a habit of regular writing that they will be familiar with when they arrive. We also have developed introductory "ethnography exercises" that prepare students for the intercultural components of the course and assist them in developing more advanced skills in tapping into all of their senses to better document—with the help of observation guides and field notes and key aspects or characteristics of the setting and interactions—their experience and the experiences of others in a specific cross-cultural context. These assignments ensure students visit places that carry them outside their comfort zones or engage in interactions to practice talking with people, a useful tactic to prepare some of our quieter students. An example assignment is included in Toolbox 7.6.

TOOLBOX **7.4**
Create a Group Agreement

Engage democratic, reflective classroom practice early. During orientation or during your first class meeting, we suggest setting aside at least 30 minutes for a facilitated discussion regarding the characteristics of the ideal living, learning, traveling, and serving community. As students share characteristics they would like to see in one another and in the group as a whole, write those traits on the board. Stimulate their thinking by asking them to think about times they have flourished within groups and times they have felt constrained by groups. As you collectively develop a list of positive traits, discuss the tensions within them. Use this list to write a group agreement with which everyone agrees. Provide ample opportunity for disagreement. Make clear that this agreement will form the standard of community behavior. Return to the agreement as needed throughout the program to help students stay conscious of their own ideals.

CBGL groups developed the commitments in the following list as part of the agreements they generated together. Each of the statements was part of a larger agreement and is included here simply as an example. Toolbox 7.5 offers suggestions for how to facilitate group agreement. The following are sample statements from a previous agreement:

- Write questions in your journals throughout the day—and then find out the answers!
- Ask questions of people outside the course! Gain knowledge from community members on a daily basis.
- Share inspiration and frustration with the group.
- Act consciously and compassionately.
- Sleep well, eat well, and take care of your physical and emotional needs to be healthy and 100% involved in this experience.
- Stick to functional complaints (e.g., "It's hot" is not productive). Take complaints to someone who can do something about it.
- "Okay, good!" is our motto. When we miss our train and are left standing at the station, we'll say, "Okay, good!" Flexibility is key!

This and similar activities also create incentives for students to closely observe their home communities, noticing and documenting aspects that they might consider anew in light of their travel experiences. Having students write about, draw, or take pictures of their communities to introduce themselves to each other is a good way to facilitate this work.

TOOLBOX 7.5

Facilitating a Group Agreement

Process	Example Prompt	Facilitator Comments
Ask participants to brainstorm individually about times they flourished or felt constrained through group membership.	"Think about a time you were in a group and it did not go well. What were some of the issues?"	It's often easier for people to think about a negative group experience than a positive one.
Develop statements for the group agreement.	"Now let's each come up with some statements that would address those issues."	Try to stay fairly quiet at this point. The actual wording matters; the group will take more ownership if statements are in their words.
Have each participant share their statements, clarifying meaning.	"Tyrone said, 'Respect each other,' and Laura said, 'Don't oppress anyone.' Are those the same? How are they different? How would those look as actions?"	There will often be a lot of overlap in their ideas. Point that out to begin building consensus.
Decide what the leadership wants to contribute to the list.	"Having led CBGL trips in the past, I have learned one statement that we've found helpful is 'be on time'; is that something we could all agree on?"	This can be a great place to insert critical ideas that the group may not think of independently, yet it is also vital that the students understand they are empowered to question and discuss all proposed ideas.

Develop a final list of 8 to 10 statements.	"So, here's what we have: Honor confidentiality Show respect Stay aware of your privilege Be on time . . . ."	It is vital to build consensus at this point. The group can strike statements, revise the wording, combine ideas, and so forth to get there, but everyone should buy in.
Take a vow.	"Let's all write down the group agreement. Now, raise your hand if you agree to abide by this document."	Each member needs to feel that he or she has made a public commitment to the group agreement. Another option is signing it.
Revisit the group agreement regularly.	"Today, we had a tough day. Let's take a look at our group agreement and see how we are doing at upholding it. Is there anything we need to add or change?"	Use the group agreement as a tool for checking in on team dynamics. Ask the students to assess how they are doing individually and together at upholding it. Revise and amend as needed.

TOOLBOX **7.6**

Seven Strangers

This experiential learning assignment can be conducted in the pretravel phase of a CBGL course or used while in a host community. The goal is to have participants practice engaging in conversation with people, as this will be a key technique for learning while on their CBGL course. You may choose to incorporate this assignment into a larger ethnography and provide the participants with resources in ethnographic interviewing technique (Spradley, 1979).

The Assignment
Over the course of seven days, you are to engage with seven strangers in meaningful conversation. The goal with these conversations is to go beyond basic scripts such as "How are you? Fine. It's cold out. Yeah." or "What would you like to order? I'll have the burger." Ask open-ended questions that generate meaningful responses and conversations from those around you. Practice active listening skills. Don't interrupt, encourage people to elaborate, and generally be the quieter one in the conversation.

You may engage in these conversations with just about anyone—a person you see every day but never talk to (e.g., at the bus stop or the gas station) is one choice. If you typically do not see a lot of people during a day, you'll need to find an environment in which to complete this activity, such as an event, a restaurant, or another public location. If you are on your CBGL experience, you may have challenges completing this assignment because of language barriers, but try it anyway. You may end up learning a lot about how to communicate even when you don't share language fluency with a person.

After completing the assignment, reflect on your experience:

- Describe at least one encounter you found particularly meaningful or interesting.
- Was this assignment challenging for you? Why or why not? In thinking about your challenges, what will you do to better engage with individuals during your CBGL experience?
- Did you struggle with accents or language barriers? If so, how did you manage them? What did you learn about communicating in that context? How might you apply that during your CBGL experience?
- What worked as conversation starters? Why? What kinds of discussions did you have that were unexpected? How did these develop?
- What did you learn from your conversations? How did this learning help you better understand the person's culture, your own ideas (stereotypes, biases, and knowledge), and areas where you would like to learn more?

Community Engagement

Whatever the program or course format and structure, CBGL experiences frequently feel relentless in their onslaught of unfamiliar experience. As students arrive at the location, they will experience new sounds, smells, sights, and cultural expressions of personal space, warmth, and public space—all while engaging in a new service experience with unfamiliar people. Academic work takes place within this overarching, rapid, and radically new experience. Academic work will necessarily share time with other important group activities, including unplanned reflection sessions and meetings to discuss and plan logistics. Instructors see students throughout the day, at each meal, during scheduled service, at community events, whenever they have a question or concern, and of course during structured class time. In this environment, it becomes a challenge to set aside clear time for academic course content and associated learning experiences.

There will be no shortage of things to do and invitations to participate in a variety of community events. Especially as a program begins, students will feel strongly about taking advantage of every opportunity. Structured and unstructured downtime will become increasingly important for the health and balance of each individual and the group as a whole. Structured downtime, although contradictory at first glance, can create space for healthy pause and reflection, something that our students are increasingly socialized away from. Being attentive to the need for downtime will be essential as fatigue sets in, and it can be a significant learning experience for students. It is also essential to continue to set clear expectations regarding deliberate and guided reflection and journaling, as captured in Toolbox 7.7.

Learning early, through the group agreement process or otherwise, what students perceive as their individual needs for downtime, alone time, exercise, or spiritual maintenance can help you respond in a way that is sensitive to your

TOOLBOX **7.7**
Journal the Sensory Experience Upon Arrival

Immediately after arrival, require students to go to a public space in the community, such as a plaza, to sit quietly alone and to record the sensory experience in their journals for one hour. Encourage them to focus on basic sensory description, recording their sense of sight, sound, smell, feel, and taste in this new environment. This deliberate effort to set aside space for processing counterbalances what can easily feel like the frenetic pace of any program and develops students' basic descriptive skills as part of their reflective experiences.

specific students' needs. Students' responses to the stresses and, in some cases, the perceived freedom of the travel will also benefit from different leadership approaches. Having a leadership team (discussed in chapter 6) with complementary interpersonal skills will make for a balanced approach to students.

Faculty and staff facilitators will play a special role in most CBGL programs. In some of the cultures where we have conducted courses, faculty and staff hold a much higher status than is the case in the United States. These dynamics often shape the first meetings with community partners, and they can often happen in the midst of jet lag if not immediately after travel. In any case, faculty members often are expected to act as representatives of the group—and by extension the institutional or organizational partnership—so faculty should be prepared to represent and speak for the group in many greetings and ceremonial occasions.

Particularly early in the travel experience, all of your students will be looking to you, more or less consciously, for cues on how to respond to experiences. As indicated in Toolbox 7.8, your approach to facilitation, positive disposition, flexibility, and intentional role modeling will set the tone for their responses; in this way, faculty members are far more than teachers on CBGL trips.

Along with being a role model, perhaps the most important concept for the travel and cultural immersion portion of the course is the idea of teachable moments. Such moments range from the experience of security at the airport to the students' lived experience of fatigue. Encourage your students to be attentive to their responses to experiences, and take such experiences as the subject of group reflection. It is important to be conscious of the ways in which students need both challenge and support for effective learning and reflection, as indicated in Toolbox 7.9. A chance moment waiting for a bus or relaxing after a day of service can be a good moment to raise a simple question for everyone to answer: What was your favorite moment today? What have you been most surprised by?

This engages the first stage of the DEAL reflective process (see chapter 3). If time permits, move into the second stage by asking students why these moments were their favorites or how those experiences related to their perceptions of the host country before the program.

As the end of the program comes into view, a new challenge will present itself: returning home with the insights gained by living and working for a short time in the host community. The usual student concerns about completing a program will likely be eclipsed by students' ideas about how to rejoin their life in their home communities, often with new and very earnest civic and ethical commitments. Similarly, your thoughts will likely turn toward your professional life at your home institution, perhaps toward taking steps to sustain and intensify the partnership with your host community.

TOOLBOX **7.8**
Setting the Tone

Students are most receptive to your leadership at the beginning of the course. They are in an unfamiliar environment with a group they have only recently met. Decisions you make early will determine expectations throughout the course.

- Set a routine and stick to it. Being busier in the beginning is often best because everyone gets used to the pace. Later, you can be the benevolent leader by recognizing when the group has reached an energy limit.
- Choose timing for classes that is sensitive to the environment and the group's energy level (not when everyone is exhausted or when the classroom is awfully hot). Make sure you have enough time for all classes.
- Engage multiple and diverse modes of reflection from the outset (see chapter 3).
- Build a culture of compassionate critique to prevent specific students from dominating and having assumptions being accepted as the norm.
- Prevent the formation of cliques by mixing people in room assignments and seat assignments at first. Have students work in partners, but be subtle about assigning them.
- Check in with community and site directors to make sure things are going well.
- Remind students of their ambassadorship throughout the experience.
- Cultivate the recognition that you are compassionate, prudent, and eager to address actionable issues. This means not only that you care about students, their safety, and their concerns but also that you develop expectations with students that they should not bring you concerns over persistent comfort issues you cannot address (e.g., it's hot, it's dusty, the Internet is slow). They should simultaneously understand your limits and your definitive willingness to address important health and safety issues. Health and safety are discussed in detail in chapter 8.
- Encourage consciousness of physical and spiritual health. Provide opportunities for exercise and spiritual quietude or attendance at local religious ceremonies.
- Encourage students to monitor themselves and one another and to share concerns about dehydration, inability to eat, or insomnia.
- Continue to engage students as peers and colleagues in respect to behavioral norms and consequences. Refer to the group agreement. Encourage students to be responsible for themselves as a team.

(Continues)

TOOLBOX 7.8 (*Continued*)

- The imperative to engage students as colleagues includes frank discussions about nonnegotiable issues such as commitment to safety standards and abstinence from illegal drugs. It also includes unconventionally open discussion about the emotional and physical risks of alcohol abuse and sexual involvement with other students or with community members during a program.
- Be cognizant and intentional as a role model in your interactions with students, community members, and local staff. How you respond to stress, unpredictable events, emergencies, sickness, food, cultural norms, customs, and language is essential to maintaining a quality program guided by principles of good practice.

Consult Toolbox 7.10 for insights and reminders on how to systematically wind down the program.

Conclusion

As CBGL educators, the overall impact of the program experience on our students is often the most gratifying component of our professional lives. We have assessed it in quantitative and qualitative ways, and we are struck by compelling empirical evidence and our own personal observations or powerful anecdotes of students who have steered a new life course as a response to their experiences in our programs. Although we do not encourage uncritical conversion to a specific ideological or political affiliation, we are gratified by critically reflective commitments and the thoughtful engagement of our students with their life in their home communities after participation in CBGL.

Aside from considering our own civic involvements and our commitment to our host community partners, we recognize that the CBGL experience does nothing if not activate students to see themselves and their world in a different light and sometimes in transformative ways. It activates them to return to their home communities eager to put to work what they have learned in their imaginings of a better world. However, the process of learning transfer postprogram is often a neglected dimension of program design often influenced by the nature of how curriculum and syllabi are structured with a beginning and end point. Therefore, being mindful of how to assist participants in translating their CBGL learning experience into meaningful action and ongoing reflection upon return is crucial. In the final chapter, we consider teaching and learning practices that facilitate the process of reconnecting at home, and we close with reflections on charting a path forward. Before moving to those concluding comments, we focus in the next chapter on safety.

TOOLBOX **7.9**

Challenge and Support

Challenge and support are two essential commitments in CBGL program leadership. Although students must be challenged to engage in continuous reflective thinking, they must also be supported where they are in their own journeys in respect to both comfort level and personal processing. The following tips support the creation of a healthy environment that facilitates simultaneous challenge and support.

- Be aware that immersion affects different people in different ways. Some students "go native" and deeply embrace the culture, whereas others disparage locals offhandedly. Target reflective questioning to encourage individual students to move beyond their initial responses and embrace deeper nuances.
- Praise the group regularly for their flexibility and inclusion of each other in the beginning of a program so those practices become norms. Employ the group agreement (Toolbox 7.4) and fist-to-five (Toolbox 3.1) activities to consciously develop group identity and self-awareness.
- Remember that travel and change increase stress levels for most people. Center responsible compassion in all of your interactions.
- Activate students by providing specific tools and practice in actively listening, sharing, serving, and taking in the inundation of the new world around them.
- Respond to breakdowns, both emotional and academic. Give people a day off when it's obviously needed. Break with the schedule if it means an enriching activity or needed downtime.
- Ensure students know and hear regularly that the best way to maintain good health is to maintain a strong immune system by eating regularly, drinking plenty of water, and getting adequate sleep.
- Rearrange assignments and activities to address pressing issues. A discussion about responsible philanthropy, for example, should be moved to respond to students' concerns and questions regarding their new experiences of stark poverty or persistent begging.

(Continues)

TOOLBOX 7.9 *(Continued)*

- Present students with questions that illustrate synthesis of course content and experience, or, alternatively, present paradoxes stemming from a discrepancy between theory and practice. Although students should ultimately develop many similar insights themselves, your early example will help them develop their practice.
- Remember students will have to go home and incorporate this experience into their lives. Continuously remind them of that eventuality, and surface discussion on how they will engage in service from their home communities.
- Again, be an example and role model with intention. Your tone sets the tone for the course. Model flexibility, engagement with the community, continuous curiosity, concern for others, and the ability to deal with issues calmly.

TOOLBOX 7.10
Winding Down

Your final weeks or days of immersion present several important opportunities to spark students' reflective thinking about returning home with abilities to communicate about the experiences. These opportunities may productively catalyze students' continued pursuit of theoretically robust and actionable global civic efforts. In addition, this is a key time for cementing community relationships and looking to the future together.

- Acknowledge individual contributions from students and from community partners.
- Provide a final thank-you event, and encourage both groups to share with each other what they learned.
- Programs sometimes conclude in greater proximity to more conventional tourist locations. This brings to light many contradictions and challenges for students to think about how they want to see and engage with the world. Use this as a teaching moment and spark for critical reflection.
- Be sure you are aware of contact info for any new community contacts, and discuss whether and how you will stay in touch.
- Engage in discussion about how the experience has affected students and how that will affect their life at home.

- Use reflective activities, articles, and discussion designed to stimulate critical thinking on human dignity, other-affiliation, and civic responsibility (see chapter 9).
- Prepare students to employ multiple modes of communication to share their experience after returning home (see chapter 9).
- Remind students of the seriousness of their online course responsibilities after return, if applicable.

8

STAYING SAFE,
HEALTHY, AND HAPPY

The world is rife with risk. In our life at home, we take conscious and unconscious steps to mitigate risk every day. We speak at the right times, walk in the right areas, and wear the right clothing. Our subconscious, deep, and nuanced understanding of the everyday culture of our home communities informs us of the risk–reward calculus involved in speaking out, exploring new streets and alleys, or pushing beyond "normal" with our clothing choices. The impact of everyday decisions on study abroad safety must not be underestimated. Yet travel brings unique and specific challenges as well.

A cursory review of the U.S. Department of State's travel advisories is enough to give many leaders pause. Risks highlighted (several of which exist inside the United States as well) include malaria, kidnapping, travelers' diarrhea, forced marriage, yellow fever, dengue, bilharzia, polio, natural disaster, terrorism, pickpockets, altitude sickness, police impersonators, road safety, sexual harassment, protests, strikes, and roadblocks. This is not, of course, an exhaustive list. Fortunately, there are many practical, preventative steps that increase program safety.

This chapter shares those steps and offers additional important resources. Furthermore, leaders must understand that they are not alone in their efforts to ensure student safety. From programming planning to travel and through return, there are numerous institutional resources available to support your program's safety. We begin with an example, using it to highlight typical processes for responding to crisis. We then move on to share global resources at your disposal as a leader. From global resources we return to preventative steps available to you and your students. Finally, we examine considerations, opportunities, and challenges specific to GSL, as well as opportunities for integrating safety considerations with intercultural learning processes. We close with health and safety questions that must be addressed at an institutional level.

The Importance of Preparation, Process, and Networks

Off the east coast of Africa, on the island of Zanzibar, in the small village of Bweju, students danced around a bonfire on the beach late into a Saturday night. Their program was nearly over. The faculty members had been traveling with them for almost one month. The students had proven themselves responsible and conscientious. Hartman and another faculty member each felt comfortable, therefore, going to bed while the students continued to talk, dance, and sing with trusted Tanzanian friends in an enclosed space. As the students moved around the fire, dropping their feet to the beat of the drum, following their Tanzanian friends' instructions, an anomalous event occurred—a student broke a small bone in the top of her foot, simply while dancing.

It was late Saturday night, moving into early Sunday morning. They were far from Zanzibar's only major city, Stone Town. And because the Zanzibar experience was an excursion at the end of the trip rather than the focus of the experience, they lacked deep community networks or firsthand knowledge of the local medical facilities. They had a U.S. student with an injured foot, a dark weekend night, and a great deal of distance to the nearest hospital. Fortunately, resources were (and always are for responsible study abroad programs) at their fingertips.

Those resources consisted of strong program leadership and preparation coupled with knowledge of international networks at their disposal. Strong leadership in a moment of possible crisis stemmed from several deliberate moves earlier in the program. Before application and departure, the students were thoroughly briefed on the geographically remote quality of the program. The program leaders had deliberately developed strong rapport and trust with the students. And the program leaders had a positive working relationship and trust in one another. These factors combined to ensure all program participants remained calm and supportive of one another despite the possible severity of the swelling foot, the time of night, and the isolated location.

Although remaining calm, cool and collected is certainly important, it may not be enough when medical facilities, technologies, and/or emergency care are needed immediately. Fortunately, major study abroad international insurance providers, such as HTH Worldwide and FrontierMEDEX, couple insurance coverage with emergency evacuation and assistance. These companies staff phones with qualified individuals around the clock, 365 days a year. All major university study abroad programs choose an insurance provider. From Zanzibar, one faculty leader took charge of the injured student's situation, while the coleader maintained ongoing group programming and attentiveness to the other students. When Hartman called the insurance provider, he immediately learned that the highest rated hospital with an X-ray machine near the area was the Aga Khan Hospital in Dar es Salaam. (International evacuation providers actually assist with evacuation in acute emergencies, from civil unrest to medical emergencies.)

Several improvisations were necessary to get the student to the hospital. In an area generally low on ice, faculty members and students teamed up to make some ice and find other cold products to reduce the swelling. The faculty member and student used several taxis that weren't part of the original plan as arrangements were made to get from Zanzibar back to the mainland and then to the hospital. Once the student's foot was diagnosed, the care instructions included buying crutches (not available at the hospital) and resting the foot as much as possible. Hartman navigated the city with the student, finding crutches through the local pharmacy network and making sure the student was comfortable once she returned to the hostel with her crutches and reconnected with the rest of the group. All the while, the other faculty member and participants continued with the program as scheduled.

While this process was underway, faculty members were also certain to follow the emergency procedures specified by the university–nonprofit partnership they represented. Precise procedures vary by institution but typically trace the critical questions and contacts included in Toolbox 8.1.

In the particular scenario described to open this chapter, most of the solutions came through the faculty members on the ground cooperating with the students and learning about the best hospital available through the international insurer. Yet communicating with home offices was also essential. Maintaining calm during an acute incident includes extraordinary attention to information management. It is essential that responsible parties at the home university and nonprofit partner (if applicable) know about and understand any crises before they get inquisitive phone calls from parents or loved ones. Carefully following the procedures in Toolbox 8.1 ensures that

- students' health and safety comes first, including immediate mobilization of any necessary emergency resources;
- information is systematically gathered to support medical professionals' response and enhance home office and family understanding of the situation; and
- home office personnel are apprised of the situation as soon as possible, with full detail; therefore, they additionally become able to offer support and communicate responsibly with loved ones.

TOOLBOX **8.1**
Acute Incident Response Process

1. Ensure the safety and security of all program participants, determine whether the emergency is real or perceived, and communicate to participants that resources are available and will be contacted as soon as the situation is stabilized. If emergency medical attention is needed,
   a. in the United States, call 911;
   b. outside the United States, call the institution's insurer, Provider Travel Insurance.
2. Gather information:
   a. What is the specific situation?
   b. Is anyone still in danger? Is everyone on the program safe?
   c. On what day and at what time did this occur?
   d. Who is involved?
   e. What is the impact of this on students?
   f. What action has already been taken?
   g. What other information is critical?
   h. Who has already been contacted? What additional information do you have that is useful in making a decision? (Make sure to record the names and phone numbers of pertinent people, so that they can be passed on to the institution's staff.)
3. Contact the institution once you have ensured the safety and security of all program participants, contacted any necessary emergency health service providers, and gathered pertinent information.

Students often wish to call their parents during such situations. Although we in no way suggest that students should be encouraged to underreport the severity of any situation, it is important to remind students of their role in the situation before they call home, if possible. In the Tanzania case, the faculty member again checked to be sure the student was comfortable with the steps taken, reminded her that all her parents would know about the situation would be what she would tell them, and encouraged her to communicate comfort clearly if that is what she felt. If, alternatively, she did not feel comfortable with the steps taken or felt something else should be addressed, he asked her to please share that with him directly as well. This kind of direct communication in challenging moments depends on the strength of established relationships and clear communication pathways that should be established early in any CBGL program.

Our years of experience with CBGL programs have exposed us to the example described previously and several possibly more acute emergencies. We write "possibly" because it is essential to maintain a calm disposition during emergency situations and recognize that there is an important difference between perceived risk and real risk. In all cases, it is vital to understand and be comfortable with available support networks and crisis management procedures before the arrival of an acute event.

Global Support Networks

Several global and domestic institutions exist that expressly wish to support your effort to lead a safe CBGL program. The earlier you develop familiarity with these institutions, their capacities, and the manner in which they communicate, the better you will be served by their resource offerings. In several cases, you should specifically make contact with representatives of the institutions.

The U.S. Department of State offers web-based resources in several ways. The Consular Information Program provides country-specific information, travel alerts, and travel warnings. Program leaders should review Department of State information on the countries they plan to visit as far in advance as possible. The Department of State's information is three tiered. The country-specific information provides a broad overview of threats to safety and security, medical facilities, road and traffic safety, and more. A travel alert is issued if the department is concerned about the effects of an event it anticipates as temporary. A travel warning indicates the department's judgment questions any elective travel to the country in question.

Readers will grow accustomed to the tone of the Department of State's information and therefore become better, more educated readers of the content. At the time of publication, international educators are readjusting to new State Department Travel Advisory classifications, with most institutions continuing programming in countries classified as Level 1 or Level 2, conducting special review for programs in countries classified as Level 3, and avoiding programs in countries classified as Level 4.

Leaders should also be sure to register their program dates and participants with the Department of State's Smart Traveler Enrollment Program (STEP). STEP is a free service provided by the U.S. government to American citizens. By registering with the program, participants increase the government's ability to assist them in the event of an emergency and become eligible to receive regular updates about the region through which they travel from the closest embassies and consular offices.

A recent and important addition to the Department of State's online offerings, and this one is targeted specifically at students, is Students Abroad. Using language, photos, and scenarios designed to appeal specifically to younger audiences, the website is an excellent preparatory review of risks and responsible behaviors for students.

Perhaps the most interesting for the leaders and participants, establishing contact with the U.S. embassy and requesting a presentation about the country while visiting provides excellent opportunities. Participants hear the Department of State's perspective and gain exposure to one more kind of international career while your program gains an introduction to an important regional network. Embassies have occasional opportunities to allocate funding to development projects and frequently wish to share information on connections between U.S.-based institutions and local community organizations. If your partners are interested in such recognition and possible funding, connecting with the embassy may open some doors.

The Centers for Disease Control (CDC) is the authoritative resource for health-related travel information. The CDC provides information about appropriate vaccinations, health risks, and related medicines. Program participants will ask you for your advice on vaccinations. Our practice is to refer participants to the CDC site (www.cdc.gov) and encourage conversation with their own doctors. For particularly complicated or isolated locations, leaders sometimes share their own health choices with participants, but the choice (with the exception of some required vaccinations that vary by country) is ultimately a personal one. Participants should review the website carefully before visiting their own medical professional, who may or may not have strong knowledge of the particular country or international travel.

The final global network resource that deserves emphasis is the insurance and evacuation provider of choice. As indicated in the narrative that opened this chapter, those companies staff phones continuously with the express intent of addressing policyholders' crises. The companies regularly review, rate, and confirm the location of health clinics and hospitals around the world. Before departure, program leaders must be certain to review the chosen provider and clarify how to contact it from abroad and how its services work.

An Ounce of Prevention Is Worth a Pound of Cure: Enrolling Program Participants

Implicit throughout the preceding section is that it is imperative that you and your program participants systematically grow your understanding of health, safety, and security in the country you plan to visit. Several other relevant tips were discussed in chapter 7, including offering careful and systematic orientations, being clear and honest about alcohol and drug policies, and creating a foundational group understanding through a group agreement process. Throughout our reflective practice, there is an ongoing effort to grow group cohesion and accountability for one another.

Leaders should, through the group development process, consciously enroll participants in what must be a shared effort to guarantee a safe and healthy group. Discussing accountability to one another, designating buddies in areas with high population density, and emphasizing the importance of speaking up to avoid unnecessary risk are three ways to enhance students' accountability to one another and the group. Examples of important moments to speak up during a program include the following:

- One participant's observations that another student has stopped eating regularly should be shared with the other participant and with program leadership. Although speaking up may be uncomfortable and even risk misunderstanding or confrontation, health takes precedence. Opening a conversation about eating allows the concerned participant and program leadership to devise ways to ensure that participants are comfortable enough with the diet offered to eat regularly.
- If program leaders believe participants are prepared to journey to the market and through the community individually, but an individual participant is not yet comfortable with that, she or he must be encouraged to speak up. Participants can still be permitted to experience the community in pairs, allowing them many important community interactions with the support of another group member.
- If, as is true of many programs, students are permitted to consume alcohol, they will likely do so. And on programs where students are not permitted to consume alcohol, they sometimes continue to do so as well. In both cases, many students rightfully continue to take their responsibilities as representatives of their home communities seriously, and many students also acknowledge the reality that status as an inebriated foreigner puts them at a distinct disadvantage and substantial risk. When responsible students notice other students consuming too much alcohol or becoming drunk, their responsibility to speak up and encourage moderate drinking is stronger than that responsibility at home. Students must be encouraged to speak up and be accountable for one another.

A CBGL Strength: Local Resources

Continuously returning to the same community, with the same trusted community partners, has extraordinary benefits. Depending on the program design and partnership situation, local leaders may have explicit safety and security roles as well. Even if there are no such specific role designations, local leaders often have the most recent information about local doctors and health-care resources. They should, therefore, be continuously consulted about program safety.

Similarly, homestay opportunities in CBGL present both unique strengths and weaknesses. It is essential, of course, to carefully prepare students for their upcoming accommodation experiences during orientation. Although living with local families may be an important part of the learning experience, it is essential to take every step to ensure students are in safe environments. However, study abroad homestay review policies often do not apply in CBGL contexts. We share a homestay checklist in Toolbox 8.2.

Often to an even greater extent than is the case in the United States, visible forms of identity have implications for interactions in the community during CBGL programs. This should be shared and discussed at orientation in a manner that is deeply rooted in the host community context. Many resources are available that specifically address female travel safety, such as the U.S. Department of State's Information for Women Travelers page. These kinds of resources, as well as institution-specific documents, policies, and support systems, should be introduced to students at orientation (see chapter 7). Perhaps even more important, ongoing reflective practice (see chapter 3) and related safe exploration of self as a cultural being (see chapter 4) should create the environment where students grow in understanding of the relationship between their identities and the societal contexts in which they will operate. This is not to excuse harassment in a host community or to suggest exploration itself yields greater safety but rather to note that these processes can be intertwined to develop students' identities, awareness of societal contexts, and proactively safe behaviors in the host community. See Toolboxes 3.5 and 4.1 for frameworks for advancing intercultural learning related to social diversity and oppression, and integrate these activities with discussions of proactive personal and group safety measures.

LGBTQ travelers may wish to consult several different resources potentially relevant to their travel. The International Lesbian, Gay, Bisexual, Trans, and Intersex Association publishes global maps of sexual orientation laws and an annual state-sponsored homophobia report (ILGA, 2018). NAFSA: The Association of International Educators has a special interest group that

TOOLBOX **8.2**
Homestay Checklist

Date of Visit: _____

Name of Family: _____

Ages of Residents: _____

Accommodations
- Private room? Y/N
- Room furnishings: type of bed, dresser, phone, TV, bathroom? (Explain)
- Adequate study space? Y/N
- Smoke detectors? Fire escape? Fire extinguishers? Y/N
- Locks on doors? Locks on windows? Y/N
- Who ordinarily lives in the house? Who has access to the house? (Explain)
- Describe the cooking utensils and appliances available for use. (Explain)
- Fan or air-conditioning? Y/N
- Electricity or lighting? Y/N
- Computer access? Internet access? Y/N
- Expectations as far as provision of supplies for cleaning, towels, linens, laundry, bathroom? (Explain)
- Pets? What type? (Explain)
- Keys? Y/N
- Laundry facilities? Y/N
- Mailing address?
- Any history of crime on the premises? What type, and who did the crimes involve?
- Any safety or security issues with the accommodation that should be discussed?

Transportation and Area
- How far from the nearest public transportation stop is the residence?
- What type of public transportation is available?
- How far is the residence from the hospital, the grocery store, restaurants, and so on?

Lifestyle
- Is the family willing to host a student of a different religion?
- Has the family's religion been conveyed to the student?
- Does the family speak any English? How much?

(*Continues*)

TOOLBOX 8.2 (*Continued*)

- Are there any family-particular expectations that the student would need to follow?
- Has anyone in the house been convicted of a felony, imprisoned, or convicted of a crime involving bodily injury or a sexual offense?
- Has the family provided references? Have the references been contacted and questioned about the family?
- Has the family hosted foreign students previously? Are there any references from those students?
- Is there housework that is expected of the student?
- Is smoking permitted? Are there smokers in the house?

continuously compiles and updates resources relevant for international and study abroad students who identify as LGBTQ (Rainbow Sig, 2018). Columbia University's Office of Global Programs offers leading examples of resources relating to diversity while abroad. Its LGBTQ Guide to Studying Abroad page offers information on relevant cultural differences, legal rights, program-specific advice, and links to outside resources for safe LGBTQ study abroad and travel (Columbia University, 2018). All of these resources are searchable and linked from the globalsl website.

We have thus far focused on leadership practice in cooperation with institutional, community, and student resources. Another important set of questions addresses essential health, safety, and security questions to ask on a programmatic and institutional leadership level. The Forum on Education Abroad (2011) is the leading standards-development, training, and professional association in this area. See Toolbox 8.3 for questions that the forum encourages institutions to have ready and clear responses.

The forum and related professional and institutional networks provide resources to develop institutional response capacities and systems, while CBGL offers specific kinds of strengths and challenges with health, safety, and security that we have worked to address previously.

After facilitating safe travel experiences and responding to emergencies as they arise, you may breathe a sigh of relief. But the work of CBGL does not end when travel concludes. Indeed, CBGL may include ongoing activities near campus. What is essential to recognize whether experiential activities take place nearby or farther away is that transformative learning requires carefully facilitated support as students reconnect with family members and peers. Supporting that ongoing, postcourse journey is the subject of our next and final chapter.

TOOLBOX **8.3**
The Forum on Education Abroad Health, Safety, Security, and Risk Management—Queries

1. What are the health, safety, and security risks that your students face? How are these risks considered in program development, implementation, and management?
2. Do you regularly conduct risk assessments for program sites and activities?
3. Do you maintain written emergency plans and protocols, and do they utilize both U.S. and local authorities and resources?
4. How does your organization routinely access a range of resources, including but not limited to the U.S. Department of State and other applicable U.S. and in-country governmental agencies, to monitor and advise on health, safety, and security issues? How do you ensure that all participants receive timely updates on health, safety, and security issues?
5. How are staff trained to anticipate and respond to student health, safety, and security risks?
6. How are your students trained to responsibly manage their own health, safety, and security while abroad?
7. What measures are in place to routinely monitor and advise students on health, safety, and security risks?
8. Do you maintain appropriate kinds of insurance for your programs at recommended levels?
9. Do you operate in compliance with local laws and regulations?
10. What are your procedures for reporting critical incidents? Are these procedures aligned with best practices and applicable laws?

Note. From *Standards of Good Practice: Health, Safety, Security, and Risk Management—Queries*, by The Forum on Education Abroad, 2018b, Carlisle, PA: Author. Retrieved from https://forumea.org/resources/standards-of-good-practice/standard-8/

9

THE JOURNEY CONTINUES

Stepping Forward

Wee begin our closing chapter with two stories of CBGL that catalyzed personal and professional learning and actions aimed at positive social change.

In Pittsburgh, a student enrolls in a course through which his volunteerism directs him to ongoing service at a drop-in center for individuals who are homeless. Though he is from a working-class family in the immediate area, he has never before been in extended dialogue with community members who have had to adjust to life on the streets. More than a decade later, he becomes the executive director of Amizade, a nonprofit that inspires empathy, catalyzes social action, and links diverse communities through FTL. He insists that enrolling in a course that focused on rights and citizenship, which required related service at the drop-in center, contextualized many things for him in a way that was deeply influential and further clarified his path toward public-serving, system-changing work. That person, Brandon Blache-Cohen, continues to serve Amizade, the city of Pittsburgh, and the region beyond as a tireless citizen advocate for global citizenship and social justice.

Four U.S. students participating in a semester-long social justice CBGL program in northeast Thailand are moved by their experiences learning from rural farmers displaced by hydroelectric dams, fishermen facing environmental threats, and urban dwellers affected by a growing sex industry. Throughout the program, they participate in regular critical reflection that causes them to challenge their assumptions and helps them see the connections between the U.S. government, multinational corporations, and the lives of people in Thailand. They also realize that once they return home, their positions of privilege and power will distract them from continuing to address the injustices they witnessed. With the support of CBGL program faculty and staff, the students establish a nonprofit organization, called ENGAGE, focused on international solidarity. Seventeen years later,

ENGAGE has evolved to "emphasize connecting returned students to existing members' community-organizing efforts in the U.S. as a basis for building bridges with international movements and inspiring new and veteran activists in our network" (www.engagegrassroots.org/who-we-are.html). Through ENGAGE, returning students are able to reintegrate back to the United States after their CBGL program with support from others committed to global solidarity and justice. One of the students, Jessica Friedrichs, advances CBGL programming in Pittsburgh and beyond through her work at Carlow University and with Amizade.

The learning that results from the high-intensity dissonance that can occur in CBGL, along with ongoing critical self-reflection and dialogue with like-minded others, frequently compels students to make significant changes in their life to foster social justice (Kiely, 2005). This chapter begins with a summary of this book, reviewing the experiential, theoretical, facilitative, and programmatic components that advance ethical global engagement at home and abroad. It then builds on that foundation to offer resources that support students' continuing growth and reflection following CBGL. Significant personal change that leads to a commitment to social justice, however, is frequently difficult and rarely, if ever, as tidy as is implied in the opening example. Often, journeys such as the previous two involve challenging existing social, cultural, and institutionalized norms and in many cases result in continuous resistance from family members, friends, and even broader cultural expectations. As this chapter develops, it considers the ways in which transformative personal growth may lead individuals to locations of creative maladjustment, where the mismatch between what is and what might be compels them to become change agents.

Understanding that transformative, life-changing events and journeys, like critical reflection, are ongoing, intergenerational, and lifelong, we then shift the focus from students to faculty and institutional reimagination as this chapter nears its conclusion. Finally, following this exploration of institutional reforms and emerging possibilities, we close with a call to action: imagining CBGL as a central organizing pedagogy and partnership process in higher education.

The Path We Have Walked

We arrived at this point by looking seriously at how universities might contribute to the development of global citizens, individuals who cooperate across difference to celebrate and advance shared dignity with conscientiousness and care, who aim to address challenging social and environmental issues at home and abroad. As we detailed throughout the introduction and chapter 1, the call to create global citizens has often been connected with study abroad and ISL. Although some excellent programs have emerged, much of the programming advanced has been undertheorized and even harmful to communities and counter to the important, aspirational ideals of global citizenship.

Throughout this book, our analysis has moved from theory to practice, citing the literatures informing specific concepts and specific instances of practice with students, colleagues, and off-campus partners in the United States and around the world. Considering the social and environmental challenges before us and drawing on scholars, activists, and international associations of higher education, we demonstrated the importance of a theoretically robust understanding of global learning today, one that is inclusive of domestic engagement and local environmental and social challenges. We introduced our motivating and animating ideal—advancing a critical global citizenship—and indicated its roots in theoretical traditions of critical reflection and cosmopolitanism. As we shared in chapters 1 and 2,

> Global citizenship is a commitment to fundamental human dignity, couched in a critically reflective understanding of historic and contemporary systems of oppression, along with acknowledgment of positionality within those systems; it connects with values, reflection, and action. A critical global citizenship calls us all to humble, careful, and continuous effort to build a world that better acknowledges every individual's basic human dignity (Hartman & Kiely, 2014a). (this volume, pp. 56–57)

Chapter 1 provided further detail regarding the global citizenship efforts we have been part of, specifically offering a definition of *CBGL* and detailing its seven essential components. The first five of those components are (a) community-driven learning and/or service, (b) intercultural learning and the development of cultural humility, (c) seeking global citizenship, (d) continuous and diverse forms of critically reflective practice, and (e) ongoing attention to power, privilege, and positionality throughout programming and course work. These components should be carefully integrated and facilitated to ensure (f) deliberate and demonstrable learning within (g) safe, transparent, and well-managed programs. We defined *CBGL* as

> a community-driven learning and/or service experience that employs structured, critically reflective practice to better understand global citizenship, positionality, power, structure, and social responsibility in global context. It is a learning methodology *and* a community-

driven development philosophy that cultivates a critically reflective disposition among all participants. (this volume, p. 21)

Our work has largely been as university educators, and our CBGL programs have most often been accredited, yet the principles and concepts we shared are relevant for ethical engagement through cocurricular programs such as alternative breaks, as well as global citizenship education and advocacy efforts outside of higher education. Chapters 2, 3, and 4 explored theoretically robust and empirically tested methods to advance intercultural learning, cultural humility, and global citizenship. As is true for all of the chapters in this book, these three chapters are best understood in ongoing conversation with one another.

Global citizenship, explored through several theoretical traditions in chapter 2, can be understood as little more than an imaginative conceptual exercise if engaged without targeted personalizing, connecting, and critical questioning through critically reflective practice, the topic of chapter 3. That chapter offered theoretical frameworks and practical resources for advancing specific cognitive, affective, disciplinary, prosocial, and potentially other learning goals through systematic reflective practice. We then clarified the conceptual roots of critically reflective practice and its central role in CBGL through its commitment to recognizing hegemonic narratives, structures, and assumptions and changing the harmful parts of the systems and institutions we are part of through ongoing investigation and cocreation of a more just and equitable world.

In chapter 4, we integrated the theoretical insights of the literature on intercultural learning with literatures on cultural humility and critical reflection to share tools and resources for advancing all three throughout the complicated work of local and international CBGL. This integration leads to our understanding of cultural humility as

> a commitment to critical self-reflection and lifelong reevaluation of assumptions, increasing one's capacities for appropriate behaviors and actions in varying cultural contexts. This capacity for appropriate, culturally relevant action is coupled with awareness of one's positionality within systems of power and aligned in service of collaboratively reconsidering and reconstructing assumptions and systems to enact a deeper and broader embrace of shared dignity, redressing historic inequities. (pp. 96–97)

We turned in chapter 5 to consider how an embrace of cultural humility combines with a commitment to critical global citizenship and the ethos of CBGL to inform off-campus partnerships. It is only through continuous attention to collaborating, connecting, and committing that inherently evolving and dynamic partnerships may coalesce to make meaningful progress on shared goals for learning, development, and/or social change. We shared FTL principles to offer a demanding and ethically grounded approach to partnership that engages the challenging economic structures of CBGL partnerships, particularly immersive partnerships.

In chapter 6, we considered the institutional and economic contexts in which CBGL often takes place and provided examples and strategies for sustaining such programming. Sustaining robust partnerships often requires new kinds of institutional commitments, policies, practices, and understanding. We offered several tactics for on- and off-campus organizing to support movement toward institutional embrace of CBGL. Following consideration of economic sustainability, stakeholders, and allies throughout CBGL planning cycles, in chapter 7 we offered tools for planning specific immersive global learning programs. Although many of these tools are transferrable to nonimmersive programs in local contexts, several of the tips and techniques are specific to the 24/7 living, learning, and inquiry environment of immersive CBGL. We shared models of immersive CBGL connected to a specific discipline, engaged through a transdisciplinary course, or utilized as a component of a partnership throughout a semester. In chapter 8, we provided tips and resources for ensuring that groups remain safe, healthy, and happy during immersive CBGL experiences. We now turn to the final moments of a CBGL course or program, during which facilitators should provide multiple opportunities to prepare for integrating learning with ongoing personal development and change.

Continuing Growth and Reflection

In chapter 2 on global citizenship, Mary was overwhelmed by the resource inequities in global health, as that previously abstract classroom-based topic was embodied in the lives of people she worked with in Nicaragua. Similarly, the student in Chapter 4 who witnessed the work of the women's rights organization in Tanzania felt newly grounded and convicted in respect to her relationship to specific women and the broader women's rights movement. Lang's (2013) story following her return from community-engaged work in Ecuador, which began chapter 3, demonstrated how challenging it can be to communicate with friends and family following these deeply meaningful and disruptive experiences. Still other students have returned from immersive and/or local CBGL experiences in West Virginia, South Dakota, Pittsburgh, and New York City with a sense of having been *changed*, an overly general term possibly signaling profound new insights and paradigmatic shifts personally, politically, socially, culturally, intellectually, morally, and spiritually (Hartman & Kiely, 2014a; Kiely, 2015).

Whether we are faculty, students, or staff, after high-dissonance visceral learning experiences, everything around us suggests that it's time to return to *normal living*, a term that signifies life as it is and, implicitly, life as it should be. The mismatch between these strong environmental pressures to return to normal and our own deeply felt changes can lead to varying degrees of what the study abroad literature has referred to as *reverse culture shock* (Martin, 1998).

This process is experienced and felt viscerally. It is often gut-wrenching and heart-wrenching. Kiely (2002, 2004, 2005) documented this thoroughly with his articulation of the chameleon complex, which describes how returning travelers look the same to their friends and family members but very frequently feel so fundamentally changed that they are surprised that others cannot see their new identity. As Kiely's (2004) longitudinal research indicated, the "chameleon complex suggests that a transformation in one's worldview is a necessary, but not a sufficient condition for changing lifestyles, challenging mainstream norms and engaging in collective action to transform existing social and political institutions" that he or she has come to understand as unjust and oppressive (p. 16). Like a chameleon, returning travelers spend much of their time changing colors as a defense mechanism, without displaying their true colors and authentic self, frustrated by those around them who do not maintain a similar worldview. Although returning travelers are typically not conscious of this contrast in such explicit terms, struggle with the process of returning is common.

Struggle is common, but thoughtful course-based processes and resources to support that cognitive, emotional, and ontological struggle are rare. Others have noticed the extraordinary potential in learning from these uncomfortable moments. In an article on innovative international experiential education programs, Peterson (2002) asserted that international educators too frequently treat reverse culture shock "as a sort of temporary pathology that we must help students work through, rather than one of the most pregnant learning moments students" ever experience (p. 202).

More recently, CBGL scholar-practitioners have articulated the important realization that in aspirational, justice-oriented, global-citizenship-seeking education, it is not for educators to readjust students to the world as it is. Kiely (2017) noted, "You can't inoculate against the dissonance that grows from the insight that we must transform dominant cultural norms" that are oppressive and unjust. Separately, Richard Slimbach observed, "Hope amidst dire circumstances is sustained by first-rate madness. Which is why Martin Luther King Jr. called for the 'creative maladjustment of a nonconforming minority.' Few colleges and universities educate for creative maladjustment" (personal communication, August 8, 2017).

Indeed, what is frequently missed in dialogue about reentry and reverse culture shock that can result from participation in CBGL programs focused on social change is that travelers (whether old or young) struggle because they have learned that the world as they understood it was incomplete at best, inaccurate and fundamentally exploitative at worst. In many CBGL programs, these new insights come in the context of severe injustices.

Travelers return and desperately wish that their friends and loved ones would understand that they met wonderful and kind people in, for example, Detroit, rural South Dakota, or Tanzania. They wish others could know that many of those people work as hard and dream as beautifully as "we" do and that because of circumstances beyond their control, they nonetheless frequently have far fewer options than those individuals who have made it into CBGL programs. And they often wish people knew that the situation can change through policy advocacy, targeted giving, or other means.

When friends, family, and even educators suggest that students (and faculty) should get "back to normal," they're asking lifelong learners to deny new insights and ways of seeing and being in the world. Several assignments and activities, however, can systematically target and support this important learning, growth, and interpersonal advocacy. These assignments encourage individuals to develop their own stories and share them with individuals important to them. In this sense they engage with the growing understanding that it is story rather than facts, data, or reason(s) that lead us to empathy, understanding, and shared action (Ganz, 2009; Hsu, 2008). Toolboxes 9.1 and 9.2 feature specific examples.

While the assignments in Toolbox 9.1 focus on communication capacities and narrative development in interpersonal relationships and may prompt students to explain both personal and academic insights, the need for developing communication skills can also support opportunities for summative evaluation of the course learning experience. This is a question faculty members frequently want to ask students at the end of courses: "What have you learned?" And this is precisely the right question to ask after a CBGL experience. Part of the assignment, however, should be to arrange a venue where the presentation will be shared with six or more people. This can be done by using online tools, developing a video, and posting it on Facebook or Twitter. Or it can be achieved by organizing a group of six or more friends (e.g., on the dorm floor), family members, faith institution members, or other members of the home community. Students thus have to engage in the civic act of organizing an audience as they develop an opportunity to share their learning with members of their community who are important to them. Toolbox 9.2 provides an example of such an assignment. An additional compelling assignment at this

TOOLBOX **9.1**

Assignments to Communicate Ongoing Learning

The Elevator Speech

Ask students to prepare a 30-second response to the question "How was it?" ("It" being the students' trip or engaged learning experience.) Prepare them for this important moment, and practice the speeches. This activity serves multiple purposes. It develops individuals' communication capabilities, strengthens a skill necessary in the nonprofit and private sectors, and supports individuals in their efforts to reconnect with friends and family. Crafting and sharing an elevator speech forces students to consider what was most important about their learning and what they most want to share with others. Ideally, the speech inspires listeners' curiosity and leads to more conversation.

The Letter to a (Skeptical) Loved One

"Why are you going over there or doing that?" Almost everyone has at least one skeptic in his or her life: the person who does not understand why travel is appealing or (even more frequently) why someone would do volunteer service "with those people." Ask participants to craft a letter to the skeptic in their life, a good exercise to foster and improve communication skills. (This letter does not need to be sent, and sending the letter should certainly not be a requirement.) They should be encouraged to consider the values they share in common with that person, the good and positive values that person holds, and how their community-based learning relates to those values. Then they should practice communicating in the context of those values. Almost everyone ultimately has a values basis that suggests common human dignity. The importance is often finding the right way to communicate how CBGL is in itself supporting and advancing an important process of peace by pieces.

time is returning to reflections on the activity in Toolbox 2.1 ("Global Civic Action?"). How might we consider next steps together?

The assignments featured in Toolboxes 9.1 and 9.2 help participants integrate their insights from the experience with their lives at home. Yet programming can continue beyond the arc of a few post-immersion assignments and, ideally, take the form of a reentry course, capstone project, or well-sequenced curriculum in the form of a community-engaged major, minor, or certificate. Following the completion of course assignments, students may continue to

TOOLBOX **9.2**
The Public Presentation: "What Have You Learned?"

Capstone Presentation

Prepare a presentation for a group in which you are involved. This could be a club or an organization, a church, a class that you have access to, or a media outlet you follow. If you'd prefer, make a YouTube video and get at least six of your friends and family members to watch it and comment. Synthesize your own experiences and what you've learned in a format that is memorable and accessible and helps others see what opportunities may exist for them. The presentation should be at least 10 minutes long. You will do the presentation in the final class meeting, but you should prepare in light of the audience to whom you will eventually present it at home.

Presentation Grading Rubric

___/10   The presentation is at least 10 minutes long.

___/10   The visual presentation is crisp, professional, engaging, and without error.

___/10   The presentation clearly identifies community engagement, location, concise history, and languages.

___/30   The presentation clearly addresses the student's individual experience, what he or she learned, why it should be important to others, and what the student and his or her audience can do about the social issues involved.

___/20   The presentation clearly provides the audience with next steps for addressing pressing social issues and/or learning about other cultures.

___/10   The presentation demonstrates the ability to engage in critical reflection (i.e., using the DEAL model or another critical reflection framework).

___/10   The student capably and professionally responds to questions.

have interest in addressing the issues they witnessed or supporting the community they visited. These kinds of impulses may be leveraged into on-campus activities and events, such as Water Walks, participation in the Two Dollar Challenge, or other specific events, as described in Toolbox 9.3.

Campus Activities and Events That Support Geographically Distant CBGL Partnerships

Students returning from CBGL programs are frequently compelled to support the communities where they were involved in addressing specific challenges. At times, students want to imagine a big event, a new organization, or a fund-raiser. The examples that follow demonstrate diverse instances of this kind of effort and also provide more recent students with models to consider.

Amizade Water Walks provide annual opportunities for students from several campuses to raise awareness about global water issues, draw attention to specific sites, and raise funds for Tanzanian water systems. Individual students and student groups cooperate to organize the event, secure donations, and develop publicity. In Morgantown, West Virginia, and Pittsburgh, Pennsylvania, these events have resulted in hundreds of people carrying five-gallon water buckets over a predetermined course to raise awareness in the community and dedicate registration costs to future water systems at Amizade's partner site in rural Tanzania. Students from Carlow University, Duquesne University, and West Virginia University have played significant roles in raising the events' profiles on their campuses.

Water for Waslala is a nonprofit organization founded by graduates of Villanova University. A small group of young people, at the end of their senior year, organized a service trip to Waslala, Nicaragua. While they were there, community members approached them about raising funds for a local water system. They completed that effort and soon reflected on their opportunity to do more. In the years that followed their return home, they founded an organization that now supports year-round indigenous water system development and maintenance in Waslala and serves as the conduit for occasional visits by Villanova CBGL programs, primarily in engineering as well as nursing and other departments. Every year, the organization organizes a Water Walk fund-raiser on Villanova's campus. Their efforts have supported clean water access for more than 2,000 people.

Several campuses have also enrolled in the Two Dollar Challenge, an initiative that aims to raise funds and awareness about global poverty through educational programming, grassroots network mobilization, and an annual challenge of living on less than US$2 per day for a week. The challenge specifically recognizes that most campus-based participants "as outsiders, are: Imperfectly Informed, Culturally and Geographically Distant, and engaged for relatively Short-Duration" (Two Dollar Challenge,

2016). This kind of challenge can nonetheless provoke campus dialogue on global poverty and draw students who may not have been interested in such topics into conversation with students who have been drawn to questions of justice and/or CBGL programs. Oxfam Hunger Banquets, in which participants are randomly assigned a meal according to the distribution of resources in the world (some people do not eat), have a similar effect (Oxfam, 2016).

A range of reentry assignments and campus activities may support students' capacities for continuing connection with an individual experience as part of a longer learning journey. As interest in applied, community-engaged, globally contextualized learning continues to grow, several campuses are developing experiences that continue throughout the college learning process. Together, these shifts and changes show routes of institutional reimagination, as transformational learning moves students and faculty to advocate for new structures of higher education.

Curricular Pathways and Institutional Reimagination

This book grounds itself in the moments around specific community-based learning experiences at home and abroad. In the broader higher education landscape, the AAC&U and other national organizations have worked to specify the institutional and curricular pathways that support sustained, repeated, and developmentally sequenced experiences of high-impact practices throughout a four-year college experience (AAC&U, 2017; Kuh, 2008). This work, in many ways, is frequently the work of faculty and students who have had transformative experiences and are now working to transform the institutions where they work and learn (Kiely, 2017). Efforts to reimagine higher education have led to several systematic initiatives to advance public purposes and global learning.

Campus Compact (2017b) has advanced civic institutionalization, while NAFSA and the American Council on Education (ACE, 2017) have placed a focus on internationalizing campuses, from student and faculty recruitment through course work, programming, tenure incentives, and postgraduate support. These efforts place attention on the importance of sustained focus on, among other things, the critical inquiry and consequential action of seeking global citizenship. Several campuses have made strides in developing programs or campus-wide initiatives that deliberately scaffold the increasing complexity of CBGL (Nair & Henning, 2017).

Continuous Global Learning Through Major Pathways

At Azusa Pacific University (APU), a faith-based institution near Los Angeles (LA), California, students in the global studies major must complete a global learning term. The global learning term is a "self-directed, full-immersion learning experience that integrates community-based residence, study, service, and research within different 'majority world' contexts (mostly nations in Latin America, Africa, and Asia)" (APU, 2017). Before being permitted to enter this semester experience, however, students must first achieve upper-class standing in the global studies major and successfully complete the LA Term. The LA Term is geographically close to the APU campus, but the semester is deliberately immersive away from campus. Students experience language immersion through homestays with families that speak Spanish, Tagalog, and Black English vernacular. The students are required to use public transit rather than their own cars, and they cooperate with community-based organizations through service and experiential learning. To move to a global learning semester opportunity, students must not only complete an LA Term but also complete it well, as evaluated by community organization staff members, host families, and the faculty director (R. Slimbach, personal communication, August 12, 2015).

At Providence College in Rhode Island, students may choose to major in global studies, an interdisciplinary program that emphasizes "collaborative learning, participatory research, community engagement, activism, and cross-cultural competency" in the process of cultivating "global citizens who think critically and are equipped to respond to the challenges of a diverse, complex, and globalized world" (Providence College, 2017). Students in the global studies program have multiple opportunities for cross-cultural community engagement, locally and internationally, and continuously return to reflective work on their individual roles within global systems over a four-year period. While APU and Providence College offer models for staggered learning throughout four-year experiences for declared majors, other institutions have chosen to design staggered learning experiences available to a broader population of students over a shorter period of time.

Staggered Learning Following Extended Summer Experiences

Since 2003, Haverford College has developed several courses through its Center for Peace and Global Citizenship (CPGC) that offer students opportunities to integrate summer internship experiences with academically grounded learning and critical reflection. These courses follow a yearlong process of advising, application, selection, intensive cocurricular preparation, and summer experience. As the entire course falls after the immersion experience, assignments frequently investigate experiences as a kind of text that opens questions for deeper inquiry. Among choices for reentry courses during the 2017 fall term was the following:

> *Reentry Course Option 1: Development, Human Rights, and Transnational Injustices.* What are the worldwide obstacles to peace and justice? How can we surmount them? This course examines theories of some of the leading obstacles to peace and justice worldwide and of what global citizens can do about them. In doing so, it invites returning CPGC interns to interpret their experience in light of some of the most important concepts and theories driving debates over international activism and global citizenship. The three problems we will consider are colonialism and its legacies, whether we live in a global racial order, and whether the global economic order harms the poor and does them a kind of violence. The two solutions we will consider are the practice of human rights and the project of economic and social development. The course has three main goals: (a) to give students some of the knowledge they will need to address these problems and be effective global citizens; (b) to understand some of the major forces that shape the present world order; and (c) to hone the skills in analysis, theory-building, and arguing that are highly valued in legal and political advocacy, in public life and the professions, and in graduate school.

The development and human rights course includes significant theoretical investigation and as such could stand independently as a course in political science or human rights. To better integrate experiential learning with that strong theoretical foundation and academic inquiry, returning interns receive several prompts that specifically integrate both. In addition to these response papers, course discussion and presentation opportunities return continuously to consider summer experiences in light of broad political, economic, social, cultural, and historical structures.

Another reentry course for the 2017 fall term was the following:

> *Reentry Course Option 2: Bodies of Injustice: Health, Illness, and Healing in Contexts of Inequality.* This course is designed for students returning from internship experiences who wish to deepen their understanding of social justice, health, and health care. The course integrates experiential learning with humanities and social medicine readings on witnessing and representing inequalities, cultural conceptions of health, structural determinants of health, and addressing health inequalities in the United States and other countries. Structural determinants include education, food resources, markets, medical and social services, governments, environments, transportation, cultures, languages, and more.

The syllabus indicates clearly, "All course graded activities, including reading responses, an internship presentation, an internship critical reflection essay, and a next steps project, center on integrating internship experiences with relevant critical readings in the humanities and social sciences" (Hartman, 2017b).

Readings and dialogue within the course highlight health as a human right, as understood in the 1946 Constitution of the World Health Organization; the 1948 Universal Declaration of Human Rights; and the 1966 International Covenant on Economic, Social, and Cultural Rights. Course questions and dialogue extend to the United States' historic and continuing reluctance to engage health as a right, the relevant civil policy structures in place to support health as a right at the internship sites (in the United States and abroad), and the next steps in organizing and advocacy for supporters of health as a human right (Hartman, 2017b).

Engaging students in courses such as these provides theoretically grounded, academically rewarded, ongoing opportunities that increase the likelihood that students will understand their community-engaged experiences in light of broader legal, cultural, economic, and social forces. The courses also encourage increasingly sophisticated academic inquiry, and many of the students continue with additional research, leading to senior theses (all Haverford students must complete a substantive senior thesis for graduation). Center for Peace and Global Citizenship internship programming is offered to nearly 20% of Haverford's campus population and across a growing diversity of reentry course disciplines, and the Providence and APU programs provide great depth for small cohorts of learners over a 4-year period. Yet it is also possible to imagine simultaneous breadth and depth with respect to institutional commitment to CBGL.

Campus-Wide Dedication to CBGL During a Four-Year Experience

Many CBGL proponents complain that experiential learning remains a fringe activity, and most of the initiatives referred to so far in this chapter involve reforming existing systems to move toward engaged learning (ACE, 2017; Campus Compact, 2017b); however, there are examples of institutions founded with global learning and public purposes as central ideals. One such example is California State University, Monterey Bay, where through institutional requirements in lower and upper division courses across all majors, students work to develop the knowledge, skills and attitudes to participate sensitively in multicultural communities, and to work effectively to address deep-seated social inequities. The goal is to help CSUMB students become multicultural community builders: students who are able to work sensitively and effectively in a diverse society to create more just and equitable workplaces, communities and social institutions. (CSUMB, 2017)

CSUMB's model is inspiring in many ways. It engages students across all majors; it includes faculty development opportunities in all disciplines; it features long-standing partnerships; it is grounded in the ethos of reciprocal social justice work; and students are prepared carefully for engaged learning through an early career, lower division course before being challenged to undertake engaged learning in their chosen major in an upper division course. The number of higher education institutions that are changing their institutional policies, support structures, curricula, and approaches to support engaged scholarship are growing (Butin & Sieder, 2012). The potential for more work of this kind with a focus on seeking global citizenship offers promise for a better, more equitable, and sustainable world. But this work is not merely about accredited spaces.

It's Not Academic: Making the Road by Walking

Much of this book has been about the ways in which targeted programming can support targeted learning and community-driven development. Learning is not merely cognitive—affective, emotional, moral, political, spiritual, cultural, situational, and humanistic learning are too often left out of curricular planning. Through intentional course and program design, we can increase the likelihood that participants will understand themselves as cultural beings, possess the capacity to criticize hegemonic assumptions that are harmful, and cultivate the lifestyle and civil society networks necessary to build more just and sustainable communities.

Yet as much as we may share best practices that are sometimes data driven and other times the result of hard-earned wisdom through a global network of collaborators, we also know that we are small players in overlapping communities that simply want more shared understanding and more sustainable ways of being. We are always walking into the unknown.

The theories and practices described here engage the process of practitioner-scholar reflection as part of broader, profound inquiry into questions of justice in the world. For many academics, this step into general questions of justice involves a challenging move away from a highly structured and disciplined space, a space that has been systematically disentangled from the world as it is. Community-engaged learning requires movement into a problematically overlapping, difficult-to-isolate tangle with broad civic, social, and environmental questions.

As engaged faculty, students, community members, and civil society activists know, there is something beautiful and special in this broad inquiry into how we may work together to build integrative education, to engage in deep reflective conversations that bring disparate communities together to build "relational trust" (Palmer, 2010, p. 46), and to be part of a learning process that seeks solutions for a better world. The capacity to work across disciplines and address real issues as they exist is a skill that higher education is currently reemphasizing, contrary to disciplined approaches (Taylor, 2009; Worcester Polytechnic Institute, 2017). Yet this could go too far. One of the wonderful things about academic integration and the accumulation of knowledge is that knowledge can thoughtfully and systematically discipline and respond to specific portions of broad, general questions, as exhibited in the global health and human rights course examples in this chapter or the engineering examples earlier in this book. Disciplining can save the vital work of addressing challenging issues from vague and undertheorized appeals to what feels right. Like so much of this work, locating the correct balance between a generalist inquiry and a disciplined approach is often situational, operating in the tension between important principles that frequently compete with one another. Universities are indeed only beginning to grapple with the ways in which CBGL opens new possibilities for methodology, epistemology, and purpose (DelNero & McGregor, 2017; Hartman, 2016).

As we work within our own institutions and across them, sometimes building new programs or even choosing to leave higher education, those of us committed to seeking a critical approach to global citizenship will continuously find ourselves challenging and compromising with systems we are part of while building more just possibilities. A broad network of community organizations, campus programs, nonprofit organizations, community members, and growing global citizens suggests to us that CBGL may be mutually beneficial when grounded in community-driven practices, seeking global citizenship, intercultural learning and cultural humility, and continuous critical reflection (globalsl, 2017a; see also chapter 1).

Not to Survive, But to Thrive

As we see the value in CBGL, and also see with clear eyes the distance that many of our institutional and cultural assumptions are from embracing it, we must also consider the possibility of not *reforming* but *preforming*. That is, through complex systems of accreditation, endowment, reputation, and other factors, higher education is a decidedly conservative sector. Some nonprofit organizations, foundations, and social sector innovations embrace and support CBGL because it advances important learning and cocreation of knowledge, and they are willing to do this work without the imprimatur of accreditation. Many of these organizations are building possibility from the ground up rather than reforming from institutions founded with classroom-based, nonexperiential pedagogical and structural commitments at their core.

Amizade, which employs CBGL as an intervention for youth labeled as at-risk in Northern Ireland and Pittsburgh, is unconcerned with accreditation because it is focused on the ways in which the pedagogical processes reduce involvement in violence and enhance positive identity development (Perry Abello, 2016). Omprakash is similarly an initiative that reimagines what is necessary for shared learning and cooperative community improvement. As an online platform, it connects community organizations around the world with potential interns. It does so without "middlemen," which it continuously critiques. Omprakash is therefore able to connect community organizations and individuals without what it believes are the perverse incentives of placement fees (Oppenheim, 2017).

Though the teenagers it works with in Northern Ireland and Pittsburgh are not perceived to be college bound, Amizade connects them with profound engaged learning and community-building experiences. Though organizations and individuals on opposite sides of the world have previously had few opportunities to learn from and collaborate with one another, Omprakash is experimenting with a model to facilitate that. These two organizations, which insist on learning without accreditation and community building without institutionalization, call the CBGL movement to ask itself not what it is against (orphanage tourism, service without learning, tenure systems that struggle to recognize robust CBGL) but rather what it is for. What will it pursue, advance, and advocate for? The globalsl network offers some answer to this question by supporting global learning that reveals our common humanity; implicates each of us as socially responsible actors in interconnected systems; celebrates diverse traditions of knowledge, faith, and wisdom; and calls us to humble, collaborative action to cocreate more just and sustainable communities.

This view of mission and possibility invites new thinking. What if we were to embrace higher learning not as a place of reform but as a place of possibility? What if higher education were to maximize its transformative potential as a dynamic, complex, responsive, living system? In this possibility, working in higher education is not about achieving tenure or institutional preservation but about the work of seeking equity and justice—seeking critical global citizenship and collaborative community partnerships.

This justice-seeking orientation has already led to partnerships that bring community members, students, and faculty into collaborative working relationships that have yielded increased access to water (Fleischman, 2017); broader support for human rights norms (Lough & Matthew, 2014); increased recognition of historically marginalized communities (Reynolds, 2014); ongoing economic investment in local, small-scale public infrastructure (Hartman, Paris, & Blache-Cohen, 2014); and general support from off-campus partners (Hartman, 2015c; Larsen, 2015; Toms, 2013).

These impacts have been achieved while simultaneously supporting students' transformative learning (Kiely, 2004, 2005, 2011; Monard-Weissman, 2003) and increasing intercultural learning, cultural humility, global civic engagement, and capacities for critical reflection (Hartman, 2014a; Hartman, Edwards, & Vandermaas-Peeler, 2017; Hartman, Lough, Toms, & Reynolds, 2015; Kiely, 2015; Oberhauser & Daniels, 2017; Ogden, Chieffo, & Hartman, 2017).

CBGL, we know from experience, anecdotal evidence, and qualitative and quantitative evaluations by multiple, independent researchers, is a pedagogy and partnership approach that supports student and community growth into better versions of themselves. We look forward to continuing to seek global citizenship and social justice, individually, institutionally, and systemically, with colleagues and collaborators in our home communities and around the world.

ABOUT THE AUTHORS

Eric Hartman, PhD, is curious about the ways in which social transformation is simultaneously personal and structural, and he is working on both as executive director of The Center for Peace and Global Citizenship at Haverford College. He previously served as executive director of Amizade, a community-driven global nonprofit organization, and taught on human rights and transdisciplinary research methods in diverse academic programs at several universities. Hartman has advanced cross-cultural development practice and critical global education in communities around the world. He cofounded globalsl.org and the global engagement survey, initiatives that support best practices in global learning and cooperative development within community-campus partnerships.

Richard Kiely, PhD, is a senior fellow in the Office of Engagement Initiatives at Cornell University. In 2005 he was recognized nationally as a John Glenn Scholar in Service-Learning for his longitudinal research that led to the development of a transformative service-learning model. Kiely is a cofounder of globalsl.org, a multi-institutional hub supporting ethical global learning and community-campus partnerships. As a community-engaged scholar and practitioner, he is interested in learning about and contributing to the different ways people work together to have a positive impact on the world.

Christopher Boettcher, PhD, is an associate professor of English at Castleton University. He previously worked with Amizade to design and teach community-based global learning courses in Brazil, Australia, Northern Ireland, and Montana. With research interests spanning Irish literature and pedagogy, he specializes in general education instruction and integrative learning.

Jessica Friedrichs, MSW, MPA, is an assistant professor of social work and coordinator of the Just and Merciful World Curriculum at Carlow University. She previously worked with Amizade, where she cofacilitated courses in Bolivia, Jamaica, the Navajo Nation, Northern Ireland, and Tanzania. She also worked as a refugee advocate and leadership trainer. She is interested in social justice issues, including within higher education, and has published research on the service-learning experiences of first-generation college students. She currently connects students to global justice by exploring diversity, women's rights, and immigration in their U.S. communities.

REFERENCES

350.org. (2016). Homepage. Retrieved from https://350.org/

ABET. (2012). Criteria for accrediting engineering programs. Retrieved from http://www.abet.org/uploadedFiles/Accreditation/Accreditation_Step_by_Step/Accreditation_Documents/Current/2013_-_2014/eac-criteria-2013-2014.pdf

Aga Khan Development Network. (2007). About us. Retrieved from http://www.akdn.org/about.asp

Allport, G. W. (1954). *The nature of prejudice*. Reading, MA: Addison-Wesley.

Alonso García, N., & Longo, N. (2013). Going global: Re-framing service-learning in an interconnected world. *Journal of Higher Education Outreach and Engagement, 17*(2), 111–136.

Alonso García, N., & Longo, N. (2015). Community voices: Integrating local and international partnerships through storytelling. *Partnerships: A Journal of Service-Learning and Civic Engagement, 6*(2), 1–18.

Alter, C. (2014). New global study calls violence against women "epidemic." *Time Magazine*. Retrieved from http://time.com/3598444/lancet-violence-against-women-global/

American Council on Education. (2017). Mapping internationalization on U.S. campuses. Retrieved from http://www.acenet.edu/news-room/Pages/Mapping-Internationalization-on-U-S-Campuses.aspx

American Jewish World Service. (2016). 2013 annual report. Retrieved from https://ajws.org/who-we-are/publications/2013-annual-report-hope-action-change/

Amizade. (2017). Philosophy and history. Retrieved from https://amizade.org/about/mission-vision-and-values/

Andreotti, V. (2006). Soft versus critical global citizenship education. *Policy and Practice: A Development Education Review, 3*, 40–51.

Andreotti, V. (Ed.). (2014). *The political economy of global citizenship education*. New York, NY: Routledge.

Andreotti, V., & de Souza, L. M. T. M. (2008). *Learning to read the world through other eyes*. Derby, UK: Global Education Derby. Retrieved from https://www.academia.edu/575387/Learning_to_Read_the_World_Through_Other_Eyes_2008_

Appiah, K. A. (2006, January). The case for contamination. *The New York Times Magazine*, p. 30+.

Arends, J. (2014). "Just collecting data for the White guys": Community impacts of service-learning in Africa. Retrieved from http://globalsl.org/just-collecting-data-white-guys-community-impacts-service-learning-africa/

Ash, S. L., & Clayton, P. H. (2009). Generating, deepening, and documenting learning: The power of critical reflection in applied learning. *Journal of Applied Learning in Higher Education, 1*(1), 25–48.

Association of American Colleges & Universities. (1998). Statement on liberal learning. Retrieved from https://www.aacu.org/about/statements/liberal-learning

Association of American Colleges & Universities. (2014). *VALUE: Valid assessment of learning in undergraduate education.* Washington, DC: Author.

Association of American Colleges & Universities. (2017). Global learning. Retrieved from https://www.aacu.org/resources/global-learning

Ausland, A. (2010a). Poverty tourism: A debate in need of typological nuance. *Staying for tea.* Retrieved from http://stayingfortea.org/2010/08/17/poverty-tourism-a-debate-in-need-of-typological-nuance/

Ausland, A. (2010b). Poverty tourism taxonomy 2.0. *Staying for tea.* Retrieved from http://stayingfortea.org/2010/08/27/poverty-tourism-taxonomy-2-0/

Austen, C. (1986). *Cross-cultural reentry: An annotated bibliography.* Abilene, TX: ACU Press.

Azusa Pacific University. (2017). Global learning term. Retrieved from https://www.apu.edu/global-learning-term/

Balusubramaniam, R., Hartman, E., McMillan, J., & Paris, C. (In press). Ethical global partnerships: Leadership from the global south. In D. E. Lund (Ed.), *Handbook of service-learning for social justice.* Hoboken, NJ: Wiley.

Battistoni, R., Longo, N., & Jayanandhan, S. R. (2009). Acting locally in a flat world: Global citizenship and the democratic promise of service-learning. *Journal of Higher Education Outreach and Engagement, 13*(2), 89–108.

Baxter Magolda, M. B. (2003). Identity and learning: Student Affairs' role in transforming higher education. *Journal of College Student Development, 44*(2), 231–247.

Benford, R. (2015). The accidental activist scholar: A memoir on reactive boundary and identity work for social change within the academy. In B. Reiter & U. Oslender (Eds.), *Bridging scholarship and activism: Reflections from the frontlines of collaborative research* (pp. 31–48). East Lansing, MI: Michigan State University Press.

Bennett, M. (1993). Towards ethnorelativism: A developmental model of intercultural sensitivity. In R. M. Paige (Ed.), *Education for the intercultural experience* (pp. 21–72). Yarmouth, ME: Intercultural Press.

Bennett, M. (2012). Paradigmatic assumptions and a developmental approach to intercultural learning. In M. Vande Berg, R. M. Paige, & K. Hemming Lou (Eds.), *Student learning abroad: What our students are learning, what they're not, and what we can do about it* (pp. 90–114). Sterling, VA: Stylus.

Bergdall, T. (2003). *Reflections on the catalytic role of an outsider.* Evanston, IL: ABCD Institute, Northwestern University. Retrieved from http://community-wealth.org/sites/clone.community-wealth.org/files/downloads/paper-bergdall.pdf

Braskamp, L. A., Braskamp, D. C., & Merrill, K. (2009, Fall). Assessing progress in global learning and development of students with education abroad experiences. *Frontiers: The Interdisciplinary Journal of Study Abroad, XVIII*, 101–118.

Bringle, R. G., & Clayton, P. H. (2013). Conceptual frameworks for partnerships in service-learning: implications for research. In P. H. Clayton, R. G. Bringle, & J. A. Hatcher (Eds.), *International service learning: Conceptual frameworks and research, Volume 2B: Communities, institutions, and partnerships.* Sterling, VA: Stylus.

Bringle, R. G., & Hatcher, J. A. (1996). Implementing service learning in higher education. *Journal of Higher Education, 67*, 221–239.

Bringle, R. G., & Hatcher, J. A. (1999). Reflection in service learning: Making meaning of experience. *Educational Horizons, 77*, 179–185.

Bringle, R. G., & Hatcher, J. A. (2011). International service learning. In R. G. Bringle, J. A. Hatcher, & S. G. Jones (Eds.), *International service learning: Conceptual frameworks and research* (pp. 3–28). Sterling, VA: Stylus.

Bringle, R. G., Hatcher, J. A., & Jones, S. G. (Eds.). (2011). *International service learning: Conceptual frameworks and research.* Sterling, VA: Stylus.

Brislin, R. (1993). *Understanding culture's influence on behavior.* Fort Worth, TX: Harcourt Brace College.

Brookfield, S. (1995). Adult learning: An overview. In A. Tuinjman (Ed.), *International encyclopedia of education* (pp. 375–380). Oxford, UK: Pergamon Press.

Brookfield, S. (2000). Transformative learning as ideology critique. In J. Mezirow & Associates (Eds.), *Learning as transformation: Critical perspectives on a theory in progress* (pp. 125–148). San Francisco, CA: Jossey-Bass.

Brookfield, S. (2009). The concept of critical reflection: Promises and contradictions. *European Journal of Social Work, 12*(3), 293–304.

Brownell, J. E., & Swaner, L. E. (2009). High impact practices: Applying the learning outcomes literature to the development of successful campus programs. *Peer Review, 11*(2). Retrieved from https://www.aacu.org/publications-research/periodicals/high-impact-practices-applying-learning-outcomes-literature

Bruce, J. (2016). (Beyond) the death of global service-learning and the White saviour undone. Retrieved from https://compact.org/resource-posts/beyond-the-death-of-global-service-learning-and-the-white-saviour-undone/

Burbules, N., & Berk, R. (1999). Critical thinking and critical pedagogy: Relations, differences, and limits. In T. Popkewitz & L. Fendler (Eds.), *Critical theories in education* (pp. 45–65). New York, NY: Routledge.

Burleson, K. (2015). *A guidebook for the development of cultural mindedness.* Retrieved from http://www.interculturalservice.org/online-guidebook/

Butin, D. (2008). Saving the university on his own time: Stanley Fish, service-learning, and knowledge legitimation in the academy. *Michigan Journal of Community Service Learning, 15*(1), 62–69.

Butin, D. W., & Sieder, S. (2012). *The engaged campus: Majors, minors, and certificates as the new community engagement.* New York, NY: Palgrave MacMillan.

Cafferella, R., & Merriam, S. (2000). Linking the individual learner to the context of adult learning. In A. L. Wilson & E. Hayes (Eds.), *Handbook of adult and continuing education* (pp. 55–70). San Francisco, CA: Jossey-Bass.

California State University, Monterey Bay. (2017). Catalog: Service-learning. Retrieved from https://csumb.edu/catalog/service-learning

Camacho, M. (2004). Power and privilege: Community service learning in Tijuana. *Michigan Journal of Community Service Learning, 10*(3), 31–42.

Cameron, J. (2014). Grounding experiential learning in "thick" conceptions of global citizenship. In R. Tiessen & R. Huish (Eds.), *Globetrotting or global citizenship? Perils and potential of experiential learning* (pp. 21–42). Toronto, Canada: University of Toronto Press.

Campus Compact. (2012). *A praxis brief: Campus Compact's response to a crucible moment: College learning and democracy's future.* Boston, MA: Campus Compact.

Campus Compact. (2017a). globalsl. Retrieved from https://compact.org/global-sl/

Campus Compact. (2017b). Campus Compact's indicators of engagement: Themes and indicators. Retrieved from https://kdp0l43vw6z2dlw631ififc5-wpengine .netdna-ssl.com/wp-content/uploads/indicators/Indicators_Themes.pdf

Carter, A. (2001). *The political theory of global citizenship.* New York, NY: Routledge.

Cervero, R. M., & Wilson, A. L. (2006). *Working the planning table: Negotiating democratically for adult, continuing and workplace education.* San Francisco, CA: Jossey-Bass.

Chambers, R. (1997). *Whose reality counts? Putting the first last.* London, UK: Intermediate Technology Publications.

Chambers, R. (2012). Why don't all development organizations do immersions? *From poverty to power.* Retrieved from http://oxfamblogs.org/fp2p/robert-chambers-why-dont-all-development-organizations-do-immersions/

Chavez, V. (2012). Cultural humility. Retrieved from https://www.youtube.com/ watch?v=SaSHLbS1V4w

Chickering, A. W. (1969). *Education and identity.* San Francisco, CA: Jossey-Bass.

Chisholm, L. A. (2003). Partnerships for international service-learning. In B. Jacoby & Associates (Eds.), *Building partnerships for service-learning* (pp. 259–288). San Francisco, CA: Jossey-Bass.

Christian Peacemaker Teams. (2015). History. Retrieved from http://www.cpt.org/ about/history

Clayton, P., Bringle, R., Senor, B., Huq, J., & Morrison, M. (2010). Differentiating and assessing relationships in service learning and civic engagement: Exploitative, transactional, or transformational. *Michigan Journal of Community Service Learning, 16*(2), 5–22.

Collier, J. (Ed.). (2014). *Community engagement and intercultural praxis: Dancing with difference in diverse contexts (Critical Intercultural Communication Studies).* New York, NY: Peter Lang.

Collier, P. J., & Williams, D. R. (2005). Reflection in action: The learning–doing relationship. In C. M. Cress, P. J. Collier, & V. L. Retenauer (Eds.), *Learning through serving* (pp. 83–97). Sterling, VA: Stylus.

Columbia University. (2018). Identity and diversity abroad. Retrieved from http://ogp .columbia.edu/studyabroad/steps/identity-and-diversity?FuseAction=Abroad .ViewLink&Parent_ID=BFD46F4A-BCDE-E7F3-538519FF4740AB28& Link_ID=89CC54ED-26B9-58D3-F508ECBBAFBD7969

Comhlámh. (2012). Code of good practice for volunteer sending agencies. Retrieved from http://www.volunteeringoptions.org/WhatWeDo/CodeofGoodPractice/ tabid/75/Default.aspx

Comhlámh. (2014). Comhlámh's volunteer charter. Retrieved from http://www .comhlamh.org/volunteer-charter-2/

Community Campus Partnerships for Health. (2013). Community-based participatory research. Retrieved from http://depts.washington.edu/ccph/commbas.html

Council on Social Work Education. (2015). Educational policy and accreditation standards. Retrieved from https://www.cswe.org/getattachment/Accreditation/ Accreditation-Process/2015-EPAS/2015EPAS_Web_FINAL.pdf.aspx

Crabtree, R. (2008). Theoretical foundations for international service-learning. *Michigan Journal of Community Service, 15*(1), 18–36.

Cruz, N., & Giles, D. (2000). Where's the community in service-learning research? *Michigan Journal of Community Service Learning, 7*(1), 28–34.

d'Arlach, L., Sánchez, B., & Feuer, R. (2009). Voices from the community: A case for reciprocity in service-learning. *Michigan Journal of Community Service Learning, 16*(1), 5–16.

Deans, T. (1999). Service-learning in two keys: Paulo Freire's critical pedagogy in relation to John Dewey's pragmatism. *Michigan Journal of Community Service Learning, 6*, 5–29.

Deardorff, D. (2006). Identification and assessment of intercultural competence as a student outcome of internationalization. *Journal of Studies in International Education, 10*(3), 241–266.

Deardorff, D., & Edwards, K. (2013). Framing and assessing intercultural competence in service-learning. In P. Clayton, R. Bringle, & J. Hatcher (Eds.), *Research on service-learning conceptual frameworks and assessment* (pp. 157–186). Sterling, VA: Stylus.

Dee Fink, L. (2013). *Creating significant learning experiences: An integrated approach to designing college courses.* San Francisco, CA: Jossey-Bass.

DelNero, P., & McGregor, A. (2017). From patients to partners. *Science, 358*(6361), 414.

Deshler, D., & Grudens-Schuck, N. (2000). The politics of knowledge construction. In A. Wilson & E. Hayes (Eds.), *Handbook of adult and continuing education* (pp. 592–611). San Francisco, CA: Jossey-Bass.

Dewey, J. (1916). *Democracy and education.* New York, NY: Macmillan.

Dinges, N., & Baldwin, K. (1996). Intercultural competence. In D. Landis & R. Bhagat (Eds.), *Handbook of intercultural training* (pp. 106–123). Thousand Oaks, CA: Sage.

Doerr, E. (2011). Cognitive dissonance in international service-learning: Possibilities and challenges for service-learning pedagogy. In B. J. Porfilio & H. Hickman (Eds.), *Critical service-learning as revolutionary pedagogy: A project of student agency in action* (pp. 71–94). Charlotte, NC: Information Age Publishing.

Donnelly, J. (2003). *Universal human rights in theory and practice.* Ithaca, NY: Cornell University Press.

Dower, N., & Williams, J. (2002). *Global citizenship: A critical reader.* Edinburgh, Scotland: Edinburgh University Press.

Dugan, J. P., Turman, N. T., & Torrez, M. A. (2015). Beyond individual leader development: Cultivating collective capacities. *New Directions for Student Leadership, 2015*(148), 5–15. Retrieved from https://doi.org/10.1002/yd.20149

Edwards, M. A., & Post, S. G. (Eds.) (2008). *The love that does justice: Spiritual activism in dialogue with social science.* Stony Brook, NY: Unlimited Love Press.

Eliasoph, N. (2013). *Making volunteers: Civic life after welfare's end (Princeton Studies in Cultural Sociology).* Princeton, NJ: Princeton University Press.

Engle, L., & Engle, J. (2012). The American University of Provence experiment in holistic intervention. In M. Vande Berg, R. M. Paige, & K. Hemming Lou (Eds.), *Student learning abroad: What our students are learning, what they're not, and what we can do about it* (pp. 284–307). Sterling, VA: Stylus.

Enos, S., & Morton, K. (2003). Developing a theory and practice of campus community partnerships. In B. Jacoby & Associates (Eds.), *Building partnerships for service-learning* (pp. 20–24). San Francisco, CA: Jossey-Bass.

Escobar, A. (1994). *Encountering development: The making and unmaking of the Third World.* Princeton, NJ: Princeton University Press.

Esteva, G., & Prakash, M. S. (1997). From global thinking to local thinking. In M. Rahnema & V. Bawtree (Eds.), *The post-development reader* (pp. 277–289). New York, NY: Zed Books.

Evert, J. (2014). How does global service-learning become a dis-service in healthcare settings? Commentary from Child Family Health International. Retrieved from http://globalsl.org/cfhi/

Eyler, J., & Giles, D. (1999). *Where's the learning in service-learning?* San Francisco, CA: Jossey-Bass.

Eyler, J., Giles, D., & Schmiede, A. (1996). *A practitioner's guide to reflection in service learning.* Nashville, TN: Vanderbilt University.

Falk, R. A. (2000). *Human rights horizons: The pursuit of justice in a globalizing world.* New York, NY: Routledge.

Farmer, P. (2003). *Pathologies of power: Health, human rights, and the new war on the poor.* Berkeley and Los Angeles, CA: University of California Press.

Farmer, P., Gutiérrez, G., Griffin, M., & Weiss Block, J. (2013). *In the company of the poor: Conversations with Dr. Paul Farmer and Fr. Gustavo Gutiérrez.* Maryknoll, NY: Orbis Books.

Festinger, L. (1957). *A theory of cognitive dissonance.* Stanford, CA: Stanford University Press.

Fitch, P., Steinke, P., & Hudson, T. (2013). Research and theoretical perspectives on cognitive outcomes of service learning. In P. H. Clayton, R. G. Bringle, & J. A. Hatcher (Eds.), *Research on service learning: Conceptual frameworks and assessment, Vol. 2A: Students and faculty* (pp. 57–83). Sterling, VA: Stylus.

Fleischman, T. (2017). AguaClara opens its 14th Honduras plant, debuts micro system. *Cornell Chronicle.* Retrieved from http://news.cornell.edu/stories/2017/03/aguaclara-opens-its-14th-honduras-plant-debuts-micro-system

The Forum on Education Abroad. (2011). *Standards of good practice for education abroad* (4th ed.). Carlisle, PA: Author.

The Forum on Education Abroad. (2015). State of the field survey report. Retrieved from https://forumea.org/wp-content/uploads/2014/08/ForumEA-2015-State-of-the-Field-Survey-Report.pdf

The Forum on Education Abroad. (2018a). *Guidelines for community engagement, service-learning, and volunteer experiences abroad.* Carlisle, PA: Author.

The Forum on Education Abroad. (2018b). *Standards of good practice: Health, safety, security, and risk management—Queries.* Carlisle, PA: Author. Retrieved from https://forumea.org/resources/standards-of-good-practice/standard-8/

Freire, P. (2000). *Pedagogy of the oppressed.* New York, NY: Continuum.

Friedman, M. (1982). *Capitalism and freedom.* Chicago, IL: University of Chicago Press.

Friesen, D. (2000). *Artists, citizens, philosophers: Seeking the peace of the city: An Anabaptist theology of culture.* Scottdale, PA: Herald Press.

Gallardo, M. E. (Ed.). (2014). *Developing cultural humility: Embracing race, privilege and power.* Los Angeles, CA: Sage.

Galtung, J. (1969). Violence, peace, and peace research. *Journal of Peace Research, 6*(3), 167–191.

Ganz, M. (2009). What is public narrative: Self, us and now (public narrative worksheet). Working paper. Retrieved from http://nrs.harvard.edu/urn-3:HUL.InstRepos:30760283

Gazley, B., Littlepage, L., & Bennett, T. A. (2012). What about the host agency? Nonprofit perspectives on community-based student learning and volunteering. *Nonprofit and Voluntary Sector Quarterly, 41,* 1029–1050.

Gelmon, S. B., Holland, B. A., Driscoll, A., Spring, A., & Kerrigan, S. (2001). *Assessing the impact of service-learning and civic engagement: Principles and techniques.* Providence, RI: Campus Compact.

Glendon, M. A. (2001). *Catholicism and human rights: The Marianist award lecture.* Dayton, OH: University of Dayton.

Gorski, P. (2008). Good intentions are not enough: A decolonizing intercultural education. *Intercultural Education, 19*(6), 515–525.

Green, G. P., & Haines, A. (2002). *Asset building and community development.* Thousand Oaks, CA: Sage.

Green, P. M., & Johnson, M. (Eds.). (2014). *Crossing boundaries: Tension and transformation in international service-learning.* Sterling, VA: Stylus.

Greenwood, D. J., & Levin, M. (1998). *Introduction to action research: Social research for social change.* Thousand Oaks, CA: Sage.

Gullahorn, J., & Gullahorn, J. (1963). An extension of the U-curve hypothesis. *Journal of Social Issues, 14,* 33–47.

Gutierrez, G. (1988). *A theology of liberation: History, politics and salvation.* Maryknoll, NY: Orbis Books.

Hammersley, L. (2014). Volunteer tourism: Building effective relationships of understanding. *Journal of Sustainable Tourism, 22*(6) 855–873.

Hansen, F. B., & Clayton, P. H. (2014). From *for* to *of:* Online service-learning as both disruption and doorway to democratic partnerships. In S. Crabill & D. Butin (Eds.), *Community engagement 2.0: Dialogues on the future of the civic in the disrupted university* (pp. 12–25). New York, NY: Palgrave Macmillan.

Hartley, M. (2011). Idealism and compromise and the civic engagement movement. In J. Saltmarsh & M. Hartley (Eds.), *To serve a larger purpose: Engagement for democracy and the transformation of higher education* (pp. 27–48). Philadelphia, PA: Temple University Press.

Hartman, E. (2008). *Educating for global citizenship through service-learning: A curricular account and theoretical evaluation* (Doctoral dissertation). University of Pittsburgh. Retrieved from http://d-scholarship.pitt.edu/9657/

Hartman, E. (2011). Becoming more human: Building a better world. *Community Works Journal.* Retrieved from http://www.communityworksinstitute.org/cwjonline/essays/a_essaystext/hartman-human.html

Hartman, E. (2014a). Educating for global citizenship: A theoretical account and quantitative analysis. *American Democracy Project eJournal of Public Affairs Special Issue on Global Engagement, 3*(1). Retrieved from http://ejournal.missouristate .edu/2014/04/educating-global-citizenship/

Hartman, E. (2014b). *Learning into cultural humility and social change.* Keynote presentation at the Fourth Intercultural Horizons Conference, New York, NY. Retrieved from http://globalsl.org/learning-into-cultural-humility-and-social-change/

Hartman, E. (2015a). Fair Trade Learning: A framework for ethical global partnerships. In M. A. Larsen (Ed.), *International service learning: Engaging host communities* (pp. 215–234). New York, NY: Routledge.

Hartman, E. (2015b, May–June). Global citizenship offers better solutions. *International Educator,* pp. 74–79. Retrieved from http://www.nafsa.org/_/File/_/ ie_mayjun15_forum.pdf

Hartman, E. (2015c). The utility of your students: Community partners' critique. In V. Jagla, J. Strait, & A. Furco (Eds.), *Service-learning pedagogy: How does it measure up?* (pp. 231–256). Charlotte, NC: Information Age Publishing.

Hartman, E. (2016). Bridging scholarship and activism: Reflections from the frontlines of collaborative research [Review]. *Journal of Higher Education Outreach and Engagement, 20*(3), 186–195.

Hartman, E. (2017a). Community-engaged scholarship, knowledge, and dominant discourse: A cautionary tale from the global development sector. *Journal of Leadership Studies, 11*(1), 1–7.

Hartman, E. (2017b). Sustained rights inquiry: Before, during, and after summer internships. In C. Colon, A. Gristwood, & M. Woolf (Eds.), *Civil rights and inequalities* (pp. 189–198). Boston, MA: CAPA Global Education Network.

Hartman, E., & Chaire, C. (2014). Market incentives and international volunteers: The development and evaluation of Fair Trade Learning. *Journal of Public Scholarship in Higher Education, 4*, 31–56.

Hartman, E., Edwards, A., & Vandermaas-Peeler, M. (2017). *Global engagement survey: Assessing intercultural competence, civic engagement, and critical reflection.* Presentation at the Association of American Colleges and Universities Conference: Global Engagement and Social Responsibility: Higher Education's Role in Addressing Global Crises, New Orleans, LA.

Hartman, E., Friedrichs, J., & Boettcher, C. (2008, November). *Taking students from me to we: A global citizenship course model for students participating in service-learning.* Paper presented at the Vermont Campus Compact 2nd Annual Global Citizenship Conference, Burlington, VT.

Hartman, E., & Heinisch, R. (2003, November). *Fostering civic attitudes and an appreciation for diversity through international service-learning: A qualitative and quantitative analysis.* Paper presented at the International Conference on Civic Education Research, New Orleans, LA.

Hartman, E., & Kiely, R. (2004, November). *Understanding the theory and practice of international service-learning: A comparative case study of three program models.* Paper presented at the International Association for Research on Service-Learning and Community Engagement, East Lansing, MI.

Hartman, E., & Kiely, R. (2014a). A critical global citizenship. In M. Johnson & P. M. Green (Eds.), *Crossing boundaries: Tension and transformation in international service-learning* (pp. 215–242). Sterling, VA: Stylus.

Hartman, E., & Kiely, R. (2014b). Pushing boundaries: Introduction to the global service-learning special section. *Michigan Journal of Community Service Learning, 21*(1), 55–63.

Hartman, E., & Kiely, R. (2017). Global service learning: Definition, theoretical lineages, and application efforts. In C. Dolgon, T. D. Mitchell, & T. K. Eatman (Eds.), *The Cambridge handbook of service learning and community engagement (Cambridge Handbooks in Psychology)* (pp. 321–334). Cambridge, UK: Cambridge University Press.

Hartman, E., Lough, B., Toms, C., & Reynolds, N. (2015). The beauty of global citizenship: The problem of measurement. In B. Oomen, E. Park, M. Sklad, & J. Friedman (Eds.), *Going glocal: The theory, practice, evaluation, and experience of education for global citizenship* (pp. 125–142). Amsterdam, the Netherlands: Drukkerij Publishing.

Hartman, E., Paris, C. M., & Blache-Cohen, B. (2013). Tourism and transparency: Navigating ethical risks in voluntourism with Fair Trade Learning. *Africa Insight*, *42*(2), 157–168.

Hartman, E., Paris, C. M., & Blache-Cohen, B. (2014). Fair Trade Learning: Ethical standards for international volunteer tourism. *Tourism and Hospitality Research*, *14*(1–2), 108–116.

Hartman, E., Sanchez, G., Shakya, S., & Whitney, B. (2016). New public scholars. In M. Post, E. Ward, N. Longo, & J. Saltmarsh (Eds.), *Publicly engaged scholars: Voices of the next generation of engagement* (pp. 156–168). Sterling, VA: Stylus.

Hartman, E., Tansey, J., Ogden, A., & Kuhn, L. (2015). *International education and ethical community partnerships: Considering Fair Trade Learning.* Paper presented at The Forum on Education Abroad, New Orleans, LA.

Hatcher, J. A., & Bringle, R. G. (1997). Reflection: Bridging the gap between service and learning. *Journal of College Teaching*, *45*, 153–158.

Haubert, J., & Williams, G. (2015). The Rocha, Nicaragua project: Using research to build relationships in international service-learning. *Humanity and Society*, *39*(2), 170–188.

Heitmann, G. (2007–2008). The opportunity cost of study abroad programs: An economics-based analysis. *Frontiers: The Interdisciplinary Journal of Study Abroad*, *XV*, 57–66.

Herbert, D. (2002). *Religion and social transformation.* New York, NY: Ashgate.

Hermann, S. L. (2011). Holding on to transformation: Reflections on global service-learning. In B. J. Porfilio & H. Hickman (Eds.), *Critical service-learning as revolutionary pedagogy: A project of student agency in action* (pp. 273–296). Charlotte, NC: Information Age Publishing.

Higgins-Desbiolles, F., & Russell-Mundine, G. (2008). Absences in the volunteer tourism phenomenon: The right to travel, solidarity tours, and transformation beyond the one-way. In K. D. Lyons & S. Wearing (Eds.), *Journeys of discovery in volunteer tourism: International case study perspectives* (pp. 182–194). Oxfordshire, UK: CABI.

Higher Education Consortium for Urban Affairs. (2017). Study USA. Retrieved from https://hecua.org/study-usa/

Hilliard, M. J. (2011). *Stories and cultural humility: Exploring power and privilege through physical therapists' life histories* (DePaul University, UMI Order AAI3458780). Retrieved from http://via.library.depaul.edu/cgi/viewcontent.cgi?article=1033 &context=soe_etd

Hoff, J. (2008). Growth and transformation outcomes in international education. In V. Savicki (Ed.), *Developing intercultural competence and transformation: Theory, research, and application in international education* (pp. 53–73). Sterling, VA: Stylus.

Holligurl. (2008). Giving back: The volunteers descend on Ghana. *Aidworkers Network*. Retrieved from http://www.aidworkers.net/?q=node/1603

Hovland, K. (2014). *Global learning: Defining, designing, demonstrating.* Washington, DC: Association of American Colleges & Universities.

Howard, J. P. F. (1998). Academic service learning: A counternormative pedagogy. In R. A. Rhoads & J. P. F. Howard (Eds.), *Academic service learning: A pedagogy of action and reflection* (pp. 21–29). San Francisco, CA: Jossey-Bass.

Hsu, J. (2008). The science of storytelling: Why we love a good yarn. *Scientific American.* Retrieved from https://www.scientificamerican.com/article/the-secrets-of-storytelling/

Hummell, J. D. (2012). Financing higher education: Approaches to funding at four-year public institutions (Ohio University Center for Higher Education Working Paper Series CHEWP.1.2012). Retrieved from https://www.ohio.edu/education/centers-and-partnerships/centers/center-for-higher-education/loader.cfm?csModule=security/getfile&PageID=2149085

ILGA. (2018). International lesbian, gay, bisexual, trans, and intersex association. Retrieved from https://ilga.org/

Ignatieff, M. (2003). *Human rights as politics and idolatry*. Princeton, NJ: Princeton University Press.

Illich, I. (1968, April). *To hell with good intentions*. Paper presented at the Conference on InterAmerican Student Projects (CIASP), Cuernavaca, Mexico.

Institute of International Education. (2015). Profile of U.S. study abroad students, 2003/04–2013/14. *Open Doors Report on International Educational Exchange.* Retrieved from http://www.iie.org/opendoors

Institute of International Education. (2016). Open doors data. Retrieved from http://www.iie.org/research-and-publications/open-doors/data

The International Ecotourism Society. (2011). International voluntourism guidelines for commercial tour operators. Retrieved from http://www.icrtourism.org/wp-content/uploads/2012/09/TIES-Voluntourism-Guidelines.pdf

International Volunteer Program Association. (2016). IVPA principles and practices. Retrieved from http://volunteerinternational.org/wp-content/uploads/2015/11/IVPA-PRINCIPLES-AND-PRACTICES.pdf

Irie, E., Daniel, C., Cheplick, T., & Phillips, A. (2010). *The worth of what they do: The impact of short-term immersive Jewish service-learning on host communities.* Berkeley, CA: BTW Consultants.

Jackson, S. A., & Smothers, L. (1998). The Southern Volunteer Corps at West Virginia Wesleyan. In J. L. DeVitis, R. W. Johns, & D. L. Simpson (Eds.), *The spirit of community in liberal education* (pp. 102–120). New York, NY: Peter Lang.

Jacoby, B. (2015). *Service-learning essentials: Questions, answers, and lessons learned.* San Francisco, CA: Jossey-Bass.

Jacoby, B., & Associates. (2003). *Building partnerships for service-learning.* San Francisco, CA: Jossey-Bass.

Jacquez, F., Ward, E., & Goguen, M. (2016). Collaborative engagement research and implications for institutional change. In M. Post, E. Ward, N. Longo, & J. Saltmarsh (Eds.), *Publicly engaged scholars: Voices of the next generation of engagement* (pp. 76–95). Sterling, VA: Stylus.

Jameson, J. K., Clayton, P. H., & Bringle, R. G. (2008). Investigating student learning within and across linked service learning courses. In M. A. Bowdon, S. H. Billig, & B. A. Holland (Eds.), *Advances in service-learning research: Scholarship for sustaining service-learning and civic engagement* (pp. 3–27). Charlotte, NC: Information Age Publishing.

Jenkins, K., & Skelly, J. (2004, Winter). Education abroad is not enough. *International Educator Subject Index.* Retrieved from http://www.nafsa.org/ieindexctrl .aspx?t=s&v=Global+Citizenship

Jones, S. (2003). Principles and profiles of exemplary partnerships with community agencies. In B. Jacoby & Associates (Eds.), *Building partnerships for service learning* (pp.151–173). San Francisco, CA: Jossey-Bass.

Jones, S. R., Robbins, C. K., & LePeau, L. A. (2011). Negotiating border crossing: Influences of social identity on service-learning outcomes. *Michigan Journal of Community Service Learning, 17*(2), 27–42.

Jones, S. G., & Steinberg, K. (2011). An analysis of international service-learning programs. In R. G. Bringle, J. A. Hatcher, & S. G. Jones (Eds.), *International service learning: Conceptual frameworks and research* (pp. 89–112). Sterling, VA: Stylus.

Kahn, H. (2011). Overcoming the challenges of international service learning: A visual approach to sharing authority, community development, and global learning. In R. G. Bringle, J. A. Hatcher, & S. G. Jones (Eds.), *International service learning: Conceptual frameworks and research* (pp. 113–124). Sterling, VA: Stylus.

Kant, I. (2012). *Groundwork of the metaphysics of morals.* Cambridge, UK: Cambridge University Press. (Original work published 1785)

Kateb, G. (2014). *Human dignity.* Cambridge, MA: Harvard University Press.

Kegan, R. (1982). *The evolving self: Problem and process in human development.* Cambridge, MA: Harvard University Press.

Kegan, R. (1994). *In over our heads: The mental demands of modern life.* Cambridge, MA: Harvard University Press.

Kegan, R. (2000). What "form" transforms? A constructive developmental approach to transformative learning. In J. Mezirow & Associates (Eds.), *Learning as transformation: Critical perspectives on a theory in progress* (pp. 35–69). San Francisco, CA: Jossey-Bass.

Kiely, R. (2002). Toward an expanded conceptualization of transformational learning: A case study of international service-learning in Nicaragua (Doctoral dissertation). Cornell University. Dissertation Abstracts International, *63*(09A), 3083.

Kiely, R. (2004). A chameleon with a complex: Searching for transformation in international service-learning. *Michigan Journal of Community Service Learning, 10*(2), 5–20.

Kiely, R. (2005). A transformative learning model for service-learning: A longitudinal case study. *Michigan Journal of Community Service Learning, 12*(1), 5–22.

Kiely, R. (2011). Study abroad, intercultural learning and international service-learning. In R. Bringle, J. Hatcher, & S. Jones (Eds.), *Research perspectives in international service-learning* (Vol. 1, pp. 243–273). Sterling, VA: Stylus.

Kiely, R. (2015). Considering critical reflection. Retrieved from http://globalsl.org/ criticalreflection/

Kiely, R. (2017). *Transforming global engagement and social responsibility: The theory to practice nexus.* Keynote presented at the Association of American Colleges & Universities Global Learning Conference, New Orleans, LA.

Kiely, R., Hartman, E., & Nielsen, D. (2005). Understanding the theory and practice of international service-learning: A comparative case study of three program models. Presentation at the Proceedings of the 5th Annual International Service-learning Research Conference. Michigan State University, East Lansing, MI.

Kiely, A., & Kiely, R. (2006). *International service-learning: What? Why? How?* Paper presented at the NAFSA: Association of International Educators, 58th Annual Conference, Montreal, Canada.

Kiely, R., & Nielsen, R. (2003). International service-learning: The importance of partnerships. *Community College Journal, 73*(3), 39–41.

Kim, Y. Y. (1991). Intercultural communication competence: A systems-theoretic view. In S. Ting-Toomey & F. Korzenny (Eds.), *Cross-cultural interpersonal communication* (pp. 259–275). Newbury Park, CA: Sage.

Kim, Y. Y. (2001). *Becoming intercultural: An integrative theory of communication and cross-cultural adaptation.* Thousand Oaks, CA: Sage.

Kleingeld, P., & Brown, E. (2013). Cosmopolitanism. In E. N. Zalta (Ed.), *The Stanford encyclopedia of philosophy.* Retrieved from http://plato.stanford.edu/archives/fall2013/entries/cosmopolitanism/

Kolb, D. A. (1984). *Experiential learning: Experience as the source of learning and development.* Englewood Cliffs, NJ: Prentice Hall.

Korten, D. (1990). *Getting to the 21st century: Voluntary action and the global agenda.* Bloomfield, CT: Kumarian Press.

Koth, K., & Hamilton, S. (1993). *How do you define service?* Paper presented at the Washington Campus Compact Conference, Tacoma, WA.

Kretzmann, J. P., & McKnight, J. (1993). *Building communities from the inside out: A path toward finding and mobilizing a community's assets.* Evanston, IL: Asset-Based Community Development Institute, Institute for Policy Research, Northwestern University.

Kristoff, N., & WuDunn, S. (2009). *Half the sky: Turning oppression into opportunity for women worldwide.* New York, NY: Vintage Books.

Kuh, G. D. (2008). *High-impact educational practices: What they are, who has access to them, and why they matter.* Washington, DC: Association of American Colleges & Universities.

Lambert, R. D. (1994). Parsing the concept of global competence. In R. D. Lambert (Ed.), *Educational exchange and global competence* (pp. 11–24). New York, NY: Council on International Educational Exchange.

Landorf, H., & Doscher, S. (2015). Defining global learning at Florida International University. *Diversity and Democracy, 18*(3). Retrieved from https://www.aacu.org/diversitydemocracy/2015/summer/landorf

Lang, J. (2013, March). Culture. Shock. Service. Study abroad. Global citizenship? New master's thesis with provocative data. Retrieved from http://globalsl.org/

culture-shock-service-study-abroad-global-citizenship-new-masters-thesis-with-provocative-data/

Larkin, A. (2015). I am because we are: Rethinking service learning and the possibility of learning from Ubuntu. In M. A. Larsen (Ed.), *International service learning: Engaging host communities* (pp. 252–262). New York, NY: Routledge.

Larsen, M. A. (Ed.). (2015). *International service learning: Engaging host communities*. New York, NY: Routledge.

Lasker, J. N. (2016). *Hoping to help: The promises and pitfalls of global health volunteering*. Ithaca, NY: Cornell University Press.

Lassahn, D. (2015). *A necessary evil? Barriers to transformative learning outcomes for resistant participants in required experiential learning activities* (Doctoral dissertation). ProQuest database. Retrieved from http://media.proquest.com/media/pq/classic/doc/3730215601/fmt/ai/rep/NPDF?_s=If758snU3RLNxFn3QCbBEC mzHVk%3D

Laubscher, M. R. (1994). *Encounters with difference: Student perceptions of the role of out-of-class experiences in education abroad*. Westport, CT: Greenwood.

Lawrence, J. (2000). The Indian Health Service and the sterilization of Native American women. *American Indian Quarterly, 24*(3), 400–419.

Lebedko, M. (2014). Interaction of ethnic stereotypes and shared identity in intercultural communication. *Procedia: Social and Behavioral Sciences, 154*, 179–183.

Lewin, R. (Ed.). (2009). *The handbook of practice and research in study abroad: Higher education and the quest for global citizenship*. New York, NY: Routledge.

Li, T. M. (2007). *The will to improve: Governmentality, development, and the practice of politics*. Durham, NC: Duke University Press.

The Life You Can Save. (2010). The life you can save in 3 minutes by Peter Singer. Retrieved from https://www.youtube.com/watch?v=onsIdBanynY

Lillehaugen, B. D. (2016). Why write in a language that (almost) no one can read? Twitter and the development of written literature. *Language Documentation and Conservation, 10*, 356–392.

Liu, E. (2013). Why ordinary people need to understand power [Video file]. Retrieved from https://www.ted.com/talks/eric_liu_why_ordinary_people_need_to_understand_power

Locklin, R. B. (2010). Weakness, belonging, and the Intercodia experience: The logic and limits of dissonance as a transformative learning tool. *Teaching Theology and Religion, 13*(1), 3–14.

Longo, N. V., & Gibson, C. (2016). Collaborative engagement: The future of teaching and learning in higher education. In M. Post, E. Ward, N. Longo, & J. Saltmarsh (Eds.), *Publicly engaged scholars: Voices of the next generation of engagement* (pp. 61–75). Sterling, VA: Stylus.

Longo, N., & Saltmarsh, J. (2011). New lines of inquiry in reframing international service learning into global service learning. In R. G. Bringle, J. A. Hatcher, & S. G. Jones (Eds.), *International service learning: Conceptual frameworks and research* (pp. 69–88). Sterling, VA: Stylus.

Lough, B. J., & Matthew, L. W. (2014). *International volunteering and governance.* Bonn, Germany: United Nations Volunteers and the International Forum for Volunteering in Development. Retrieved from http://forum-ids.org/2014/10/unv-forum-paper#discussion_paper

Lysgaard, S. (1955). Adjustment in a foreign society: Norwegian Fulbright grantees visiting the United States. *International Social Science Bulletin, 7,* 45–51.

Madsen-Camacho, M. (2004). Power and privilege: Community service learning in Tijuana. *Michigan Journal of Community Service Learning, 10*(3), 31–42.

Mangis, P. (2011). How the chameleon overcame its complex: ENGAGE and the formation of a prefigurative social movement. *Master's Capstone Project, 14.*

Martin, C. (2016, January 11). The reductive seduction of other people's problems. *BRIGHT Magazine.* Retrieved from https://brightthemag.com/the-reductive-seduction-of-other-people-s-problems-3c07b307732d

Martin, J. N. (1986). Communication in the intercultural reentry: Student sojourners' perspectives of change in reentry relationships. *International Journal of Intercultural Relations, 10,* 1–22.

Martin, J. N. (1993). The intercultural reentry of student sojourners: Recent contributions to theory, research and training. In R. M. Paige (Ed.), *Education for the intercultural experience* (pp. 301–328). Yarmouth, ME: Intercultural Press.

Massachusetts Institute of Technology. (2016). Poverty Action Lab. Retrieved from https://www.povertyactionlab.org/

McAllister, L., Whiteford, G., Hill, B., Thomas, N., & Fitzgerald, M. (2006). Reflection in intercultural learning: Examining the international experience through a critical incident approach. *Reflective Practice, 7*(3), 367–381.

McGuire, L., Ardemagni, E., Wittberg, P., Strong, D., Lay, K., & Clayton, P. H. (2007). *Faculty learning, student learning, and the relationship between them: A collaborative scholarship of teaching and learning project.* Indianapolis, IN: Assessment Institute.

McIntosh, P. (1989). White privilege: Unpacking the invisible knapsack. *Peace and Freedom Magazine,* pp. 10–12. Philadelphia, PA: Women's International League for Peace and Freedom.

McMillan, J., & Stanton, T. (2014). "Learning service" in international contexts: Partnership-based service learning and research in Cape Town, South Africa. *Michigan Journal of Community Service Learning, 21*(1), 64–78.

McNichols, A., Hartman, E., & Eccles, P. (2017). *Ethical global partnerships: Sparking campus-wide commitment.* Paper presented at the Association of International Education Administrators Conference, Washington, DC.

Measure of America. (2009). Maps: Life expectancy by county. Retrieved from http://www.measureofamerica.org/maps/

Merriman, D. (2010). The college as a philanthropy. Yes, a philanthropy. *The Chronicle of Higher Education.* Retrieved from http://www.chronicle.com/article/The-College-as-a-Philanthropy/125176

Messmore, N., & Davis, J. (2016). *"White savior complex": Using critical race theory in alternative breaks.* Paper presented at the NASPA Conference, Indianapolis, IN.

Mezirow, J. (1991). *Transformative dimensions of adult learning.* San Francisco, CA: Jossey-Bass.

Mezirow, J. (1995). Transformation theory of adult learning. In M. Welton (Ed.), *In defense of the lifeworld: Critical perspectives on adult learning* (pp. 39–70). Albany, NY: SUNY Press.

Mezirow, J., & Associates. (2000). *Learning as transformation.* San Francisco, CA: Jossey-Bass.

Mitchell, T. (2008). Traditional vs. critical service-learning: Engaging the literature to differentiate two models. *Michigan Journal of Community Service Learning, 14*(2), 50–65.

Monard-Weissman, K. (2003). Fostering a sense of justice through international service-learning. *Academic Exchange Quarterly, 7*(2), 164–169.

Montague, D. (2012). *Tania Mitchell: Celebrating the heart of service learning at Stanford.* Stanford, CA: Center for Comparative Studies in Race and Ethnicity, Stanford University. Retrieved from https://ccsre.stanford.edu/sites/default/files/images/2012sa-ccsre-service-learning.pdf

Morais, D. B., & Ogden, A. C. (2011). Initial development and validation of the global citizenship scale. *Journal of Studies in International Education, 15*(5), 445–466.

Morrison, E. (2015). How the I shapes the eye: The imperative of reflexivity in global service-learning qualitative research. *Michigan Journal of Community Service Learning, 22*(1), 52–66.

Morton, K. (1995). The irony of service: Charity, project, and social change in service-learning. *Michigan Journal of Community Service Learning, 2*(1), 19–32.

Moseley, J., Stoltzfus, R., & Kiely, R. (2017). Understanding service-learning basics and best practices. In A. N. Arya & J. Evert (Eds.), *Global health experiential education: From theory to practice* (pp. 85–94). London, UK: Routledge.

Murphy, J. (2015). Resipwosite as a guiding framework for rethinking mutual exchange in global service learning partnerships: Findings from a case study of the Haiti Compact. In M. A. Larsen (Ed.), *International service learning: Engaging host communities* (pp. 175–188). New York, NY: Routledge.

Musil, C. M. (2006). Assessing global learning: Matching good intentions with good practice. Retrieved from http://www.aacu.org/SharedFutures/documents/Global_Learning.pdf

NAFSA. (2017). Internationalizing higher education. Retrieved from http://www.nafsa.org/_/File/_/cizn2011_execsummary.pdf

Nair, I., & Henning, M. (2017). *Models of global learning.* Washington, DC: Association of American Colleges & Universities. Retrieved from https://www.aacu.org/publications/models-global-learning

National Task Force on Civic Learning and Democratic Engagement. (2012). *A crucible moment: College learning and democracy's future.* Washington, DC: Association of American Colleges & Universities.

Nelson, E. (2010). *A community perspective on volunteer tourism and development in South Africa* (Unpublished master's thesis). Miami University, Oxford, OH.

Niehaus, E., & Crain, L. K. (2013). Act local or global? Comparing student experience in domestic and international service-learning programs. *Michigan Journal of Community Service Learning, 20*(1), 31–40.

Nigro, J. (2017). Community-based research. In C. Dolgon, T. K. Eatman, & T. Mitchell (Eds.), *The Cambridge handbook of service-learning and community engagement* (pp. 158–167). New York, NY: Cambridge University Press.

Nolting, W., Donohue, D., Matherly, C., & Tillman, M. (2013). *Internships, volunteering, and service-learning abroad.* Washington, DC: NAFSA: The Association of International Educators.

Nussbaum, M. (1992). Human functioning and social justice: In defense of Aristotelian essentialism. *Political Theory, 20*(2), 202–246.

Nussbaum, M. (1997). *Cultivating humanity: A classical defense of reform in liberal education.* Cambridge, MA: Harvard University Press.

Nussbaum, M. (2002). *For love of country?* Boston, MA: Beacon Press.

Oberg, K. (1960). Culture shock: Adjustment to new cultural environments. *Practical Anthropology, 7*, 177–182.

Oberhauser, A. M., & Daniels, R. (2017). Unpacking global service-learning in developing contexts. *Journal of Higher Education Outreach and Engagement, 21*(4), 139–170.

Ogden, A. (2007–2008, Winter). The view from the veranda: Understanding today's colonial student. *Frontiers: The Interdisciplinary Journal of Study Abroad, 15*, 35–55.

Ogden, A., Chieffo, L., & Hartman, E. (2017). *Student learning in short-term education abroad: Introducing new measures of global engagement.* Presented at The Forum on Education Abroad Annual Conference, Seattle, WA.

One Campaign. (2016). One. Retrieved from http://www.one.org/us/

Oppenheim, W. (2017). The problem with "placements": Why the dominant model for social impact internships abroad is ethically and pedagogically bankrupt, and why nobody wants to talk about it (PCDN Careers in Change Series). Retrieved from https://pcdnetwork.org/blogs/129174/

Oxfam. (2016). Food. Retrieved from http://www.oxfam.org.uk/what-we-do/issues-we-work-on/food

Paige, R. M. (1993). On the nature of intercultural experiences and intercultural education. In R. M. Paige (Ed.), *Education for the intercultural experience* (pp. 1–20). Yarmouth, ME: Intercultural Press.

Palmer, P. (2010). When philosophy is put into practice. In P. Palmer & A. Zanjonc (Eds.), *The heart of higher education: A call to renewal; Transforming the academy through collegial conversations* (pp. 35–51). San Francisco, CA: Jossey-Bass.

Palmer, P. (2016). Chutzpah and humility: Five habits of the heart for democracy in America. Retrieved from https://onbeing.org/blog/chutzpah-and-humility-five-habits-of-the-heart-for-democracy-in-america/

Perry, W. G., Jr. (1970). *Forms of intellectual and ethical development in the college years: A scheme.* New York, NY: Holt, Rinehart, and Winston.

Perry, W. G., Jr. (1981). Cognitive and ethical growth: The making of meaning. In A. W. Chickering & Associates (Eds.), *The modern American college* (pp. 76–116). San Francisco, CA: Jossey-Bass.

Perry Abello, O. (2016, February). Pittsburgh students asked to rethink volunteering. Retrieved from https://nextcity.org/daily/entry/pittsburgh-hill-district-amizade-volunteering-global-service-trips

Peterson, C. F. (2002, Winter). Preparing engaged citizens: Three models of experiential education for social justice. *Frontiers: The Interdisciplinary Journal of Study Abroad, VIII*, 165–206.

Piacitelli, J., Barwick, M., Doerr, E., Porter, M., & Sumka, S. (2013). Alternative break programs: From isolated enthusiasm to best practices; The Haiti Compact. *Journal of Higher Education Outreach and Engagement, 17*(2), 87–110.

Pigza, J. M., & Troppe, M. L. (2003). Developing an infrastructure for service-learning and community engagement. In B. Jacoby (Ed.), *Building partnerships for service-learning* (pp. 106–130). San Francisco, CA: Jossey Bass.

Plater, W. M., Jones, S. G., Bringle, R. G., & Clayton, P. H. (2009). Educating globally competent citizens through international service learning. In R. Lewin (Ed.), *The handbook of practice and research in study abroad* (pp. 62–74). Florence, KY: Taylor and Francis Books.

Poppendieck, J. (1999). *Sweet charity: Emergency food and the end of entitlement.* New York, NY: Penguin Books.

Porfilio, B. J., & Hickman, H. (Eds.). (2011). *Critical service-learning as a revolutionary pedagogy: A project of student agency in action.* Charlotte, NC: Information Age Publishing.

Porter, M. (2000). "Ayni" in the global village: Building relationships of reciprocity through global service-learning. *Michigan Journal of Community Service Learning, 8*(1), 5–17.

Porter Honnet, E., & Poulsen, S. J. (1989). *Principles of good practice for combining service and learning.* Racine, WI: Johnson Foundation.

Providence College. (2017). Global studies. Retrieved from http://www.providence.edu/global-studies

Punaks, M., & Feit, K. (2014). The paradox of orphanage volunteering: Combating child trafficking through ethical voluntourism. Retrieved from http://www.next-generationnepal.org/File/The-Paradox-of-Orphanage-Volunteering.pdf

Pusch, M. (2004). A cross-cultural perspective. In H. Tonkin (Ed.), *Service-learning across cultures: Promise and achievement* (pp. 103–129). New York, NY: International Partnership for Service-Learning and Leadership.

Rainbow Sig. (2018). NAFSA: Association of International Educators - Rainbow Special Interest Group. Retrieved from http://www.rainbowsig.org/

Rahnema, M., & Bawtree, V. (Eds.). (1997). *The post-development reader*. New York, NY: Zed Books.

Reardon, K. M. (1994). Undergraduate research in distressed urban communities: An undervalued form of service-learning. *Michigan Journal of Community Service Learning, 1*(1), 44–54.

Reardon, K., & Forester, J. (2016). *Rebuilding community after Katrina*. Philadelphia, PA: Temple University Press.

Reeb, R. N., & Folger, S. F. (2013). Community outcomes in service learning: Research and practice from a systems perspective. In P. H. Clayton, R. G. Bringle, & J. A. Hatcher (Eds.), *Research on service-learning: Conceptual models and assessment* (pp. 389–418). Sterling, VA: Stylus Publishing.

Reilly, D., & Senders, S. (2009, Fall). Becoming the change we want to see: Critical study abroad for a tumultuous world. *Frontiers: The Interdisciplinary Journal of Study Abroad, XVIII*, 241–267.

Reynolds, N. (2014). What counts as outcomes? Community perspectives of an engineering partnership. *Michigan Journal of Community Service Learning, 20*(1), 79–90.

Rhoads, R. A. (1997). *Community service and higher learning: Explorations of the caring self*. Albany, NY: SUNY Press.

Richards-Desai, S., & Lewis, L. (2017). The importance of cultural humility: Online module. Retrieved from https://compact.org/resource-posts/importance-cultural-humility-online-module/

Richter, L. M., & Norman, A. (2010). AIDS orphan tourism: A threat to young children in residential care. *Vulnerable Children and Youth Studies, 5*(3), 217–229.

Rorty, R. (1998). *Achieving our country: Leftist thought in twentieth-century America*. Cambridge, MA: Harvard University Press.

Ross, L. (2010). Notes from the field: Learning cultural humility through critical incidents and central challenges in community-based participatory research. *Journal of Community Practice, 18*(2–3), 315–335.

Rotabi, K. S., Roby, J. L., & Bunkers, M. K. (2016). Altruistic exploitation: Orphan tourism and global social work. *British Journal of Social Work*, 1–18. Retrieved from https://doi.org/10.1093/bjsw/bcv147

Sandmann, L. R., Kiely, R. C., & Grenier, R. S. (2009). Program planning: The neglected dimension of service-learning. *Michigan Journal of Community Service Learning, 15*(2), 17–33.

Sandmann, L., & Plater, W. (2013). Research on institutional leadership for service learning. In P. Clayton, R. Bringle, & J. Hatcher (Eds.), *Research on service learning: Conceptual frameworks and assessment, Vol. 2B: Communities, institutions, and partnerships* (pp. 505–535). Sterling, VA: Stylus.

Sandy, M., & Holland, B. (2006). Different worlds and common ground: Community partner perspectives on campus–community partnerships. *Michigan Journal of Community Service Learning, 13*, 30–43.

Savicki, V. (Ed.). (2008). *Developing intercultural competence and transformation: Theory, research, and application in international education*. Sterling, VA: Stylus.

Schattle, H. (2005). Communicating global citizenship: Multiple discourses beyond the academy. *Citizenship Studies, 9*(2), 119–133.

Schlabach, G. (2013). Lest good intentions become the enemy of the good. Retrieved from http://globalsl.org/lest-best-intentions-become-the-enemy-of-the-good/

Schroeder, S. A. (2007). We can do better: Improving the health of the American people. *The New England Journal of Medicine, 357,* 1221–1228.

Schwartz, J. (2008). *The future of democratic equality: Rebuilding social solidarity in a fragmented America.* New York, NY: Routledge.

Sexsmith, K., & Kiely, R. (2014, October 30). *Faculty experiences in global service-learning: A qualitative study.* Paper presented at the International Association for Research on Service-Learning and Community Engagement conference, New Orleans, LA.

Sigmon, R. (1979). Service-learning: Three principles. *Synergist, 8,* 9–11.

Singer, P. (2002). *One world.* New Haven, CT: Yale University Press.

Singer, P. (2006, December). What should a billionaire give—and what should you? *The New York Times Magazine.* Retrieved from http://www.nytimes.com/2006/12/17/magazine/17charity.t.html

Slimbach, R. (2010). *Becoming world wise: A guide to global learning.* Sterling, VA: Stylus.

Slimbach, R. (2016). Deschooling international education: Toward an alternative paradigm of practice. In B. Streitwieser & A. C. Ogden (Eds.), *International education's scholar-practitioners: Bridging research and practice* (pp. 195–209). Oxford, UK: Symposium Books.

Smith, A. (1993). *The wealth of nations.* Oxford, UK: Oxford University Press. (Original work published 1776)

Sobania, N. (Ed.). (2015). *Putting the local in global education: Models for transformative learning through domestic off-campus programs.* Sterling, VA: Stylus.

Sorrells, K. (2013). *Intercultural communication: Globalization and social justice.* Thousand Oaks, CA: SAGE.

Sorrells, K., & Nakagawa, G. (2008). Intercultural communication praxis and the struggle for social responsibility and social justice. In O. Swartz (Ed.), *Transformative communication studies: Culture, hierarchy, and the human condition* (pp. 17–43). Leicester, UK: Troubador.

Sparrow, L. M. (2000). Beyond multicultural man: Complexities of identity. *International Journal of Intercultural Relations, 24*(2), 173–201.

Spradley, J. P. (1979). *The ethnographic interview.* Fort Worth, TX: Harcourt.

Stanton, T. K., & Wagner, J. W. (2006). *Educating for democratic citizenship: Renewing the civic mission of graduate and professional education at research universities.* Stanford, CA: California Campus Compact.

Starr, K. (2016, January 27). Seduced by the "reductive seduction of other people's problems." *Stanford Social Innovation Review.* Retrieved from https://ssir.org/articles/entry/seduced_by_the_the_reductive_seduction_of_other_peoples_problems

Stoecker, R. (2016). *Liberating service learning and the rest of higher education civic engagement.* Philadelphia, PA: Temple University Press.

Stoecker, R., & Tryon, E. A. (2009). *The unheard voices: Community organizations and service learning.* Philadelphia, PA: Temple University Press.

Stoecker, R., Tryon, E. A., & Loving, K. (2011, Fall). A community development approach to service learning. *Research Digest.* University of Wisconsin, Center for Nonprofits.

Strand, K., Marullo, S., Cutforth, N., Stoecker, R., & Donohue, P. (2003). *Community-based research in higher education: Principles and practices.* San Francisco, CA: Jossey-Bass.

Sullivan, N. (2016). Hosting gazes: Clinical volunteer tourism and hospital hospitality in Tanzania. In R. Prince & H. Brown (Eds.), *Volunteer economies: The politics and ethics of voluntary labour in Africa* (pp. 140–163). Rochester, NY: James Currey.

Sumka, S., Porter, M. C., & Piacitelli, J. (2015). *Working side by side: Creating alternative breaks as catalysts for global learning, student leadership, and social change.* Sterling, VA: Stylus.

Swords, A., & Kiely, R. (2010). Beyond pedagogy: Service learning as movement building in higher education; Integrating teaching, research, and service through community engagement and partnership. *Journal of Community Practice, 18*(2), 148–170.

Talwalker, C. (2012). What kind of global citizen is the student volunteer? *Journal of Global Citizenship Equity and Education, 2*(2). Retrieved from http://journals .sfu.ca/jgcee/index.php/jgcee/article/viewArticle/51/46

Taylor, E. W. (1994). A learning model for becoming interculturally competent. *International Journal of Intercultural Relations, 3*(18), 389–408.

Taylor, E. W. (1998). *Transformative learning: A critical review* (Information Series No. 374). Columbus, OH: ERIC Clearinghouse on Adult, Career, and Vocational Education.

Taylor, M. C. (2009). End the university as we know it. *The New York Times.* Retrieved from http://www.nytimes.com/2009/04/27/opinion/27taylor.html

Tervalon, M., & Murray-García, J. (1998). Cultural humility versus cultural competence: A critical distinction in defining physician training outcomes in multicultural education. *Journal of Health Care for the Poor and Underserved, 9*(2), 117–125.

Tiessen, R., & Huish, R. (Eds.). (2014). *Globetrotting or global citizenship? Perils and potential of experiential learning.* Toronto, Canada: University of Toronto Press.

Tilley-Lubbs, G. A. (2009). Good intentions pave the way to hierarchy: A retrospective autoethnographic approach. *Michigan Journal of Community Service Learning, 16*(1), 59–68.

Toms, C. (2013). The economy of global service-learning and the problem of silence. Retrieved from http://globalsl.org/economy-global-service-learning-problem-silence/

Tonkin, H. (Ed.). (2004). *Service-learning across cultures: Promise and achievement.* New York, NY: International Partnership for Service-Learning and Leadership.

Torres, J. (Ed.). (2000). *Benchmarks for campus/community partnerships*. Providence, RI: Campus Compact.

Two Dollar Challenge. (2016). Sidekick manifesto. Retrieved from http://twodollarchallenge.org/sidekick-manifesto/

United Nations. (2016). Sustainable development knowledge platform. Retrieved from https://sustainabledevelopment.un.org/?menu=1300

United States Agency for International Development. (2016). Agriculture and food security. Retrieved from https://www.usaid.gov/what-we-do/agriculture-and-food-security

University of New Mexico School of Medicine. (2005). Effective use of performance objectives for learning and assessment (for use with Fink's and Bloom's taxonomies). Retrieved from http://engaged.cornell.edu/wp-content/uploads/2017/06/Designing-SMART-Learning-Objectives.pdf

Van Doore, K. E. (2016). Paper orphans: Exploring child trafficking for the purpose of orphanages. *The International Journal of Children's Rights, 24*(2), 378–407. https://doi.org/10.1163/15718182-02402006

Vande Berg, M., Paige, R. M., & Hemming Lou, K. (2012). *Student learning abroad: What our students are learning, what they're not, and what we can do about it.* Sterling, VA: Stylus.

Wahlberg, K. (2004). *CAFTA from a Nicaraguan perspective.* New York, NY: Global Policy Forum. Retrieved from https://www.globalpolicy.org/component/content/article/220/47242.html

Ward, C., Bochner, S., & Furnam, A. (2001). *The psychology of culture shock.* Philadelphia, PA: Routledge.

Watt, S. (2007). Difficult dialogues, privilege and social justice: Uses of the privileged identity exploration (PIE) model in student affairs practice. *The College Student Affairs Journal, 26*(2), 114–126.

Weber-Shirk, M. (May 2012). *AguaClara in Honduras.* Presentation at the 5th Annual Cornell University Global Service-Learning Institute. Ithaca, New York.

Weiler, K. (1991). Freire and a feminist pedagogy of difference. *Harvard Educational Review, 61*(4), 449–475.

Welch, M. (2016). *Engaging higher education: Purpose, platforms, and programs for community engagement.* Sterling, VA: Stylus.

Welcoming Rhode Island. (2017). Local stories. Retrieved from http://www.welcomingri.org/local-stories/

Wendel, A. (2013, May). Tools vs. textbooks: The academic and developmental impact of alternative break trips and classroom-based learning. Retrieved from http://globalsl.org/tools-vs-textbooks-the-academic-and-developmental-impact-of-alternative-break-trips-and-classroom-based-learning/

Westheimer, J., & Kahne, J. (2004). What kind of citizen? The politics of educating for democracy. *American Educational Research Journal, 41*(2), 237–269.

Wheatley, E. S., & Hartman, E. (2013). Participatory action research: Rethinking power dynamics and ethical engagement. In L. J. Shepherd (Ed.), *Critical approaches to security: Theories and methods* (pp. 146–157). Oxon, UK: Taylor and Francis.

Whitehead, D. (2015). Global service learning: Addressing the big challenges. *Diversity and Democracy, 18*(3). Retrieved from https://www.aacu.org/diversity-democracy/2015/summer/whitehead

Whitney, B. C., & Clayton, P. H. (2011). Research on and through reflection in international service learning. In R. G. Bringle, J. A. Hatcher, & S. G. Jones (Eds.), *International service learning: Conceptual frameworks and research* (pp. 145–187). Sterling, VA: Stylus.

Wiggins, G., & McTighe, J. (1998). *Understanding by design.* Alexandria, VA: Association for Supervision and Curriculum Development.

Willis, T. Y. (2012). *Rare but there: An intersectional exploration of the experiences and outcomes of Black women who studied abroad through community college programs* (Doctoral dissertation). Retrieved from PQDT Open (3533746).

Willis, T. (2015). "And still we rise...": Microaggressions and intersectionality in the study abroad experiences of Black women. *Frontiers: The Interdisciplinary Journal of Study Abroad, 26,* 209–230.

Wise, G. (1980). *American historical explanations: A strategy for grounded inquiry* (2nd rev. ed.). Minneapolis, MN: University of Minnesota.

Worcester Polytechnic Institute. (2017). Project-based learning at WPI. Retrieved from http://wp.wpi.edu/projectbasedlearning/proven-pedagogy/project-based-learning-at-wpi/

Worrall, L. (2007). Asking the community: A case study of community partner perspectives. *Michigan Journal of Community Service Learning, 17*(1), 5–17.

Yappa, L. (1996). What causes poverty? A postmodern view. *Annals of the Association of American Geographers, 86*(4), 707–728.

Yoder Clark, A., & Nugent, M. (2011). Power and service-learning: Salience, place, and practice. In B. J. Porfilio & H. Hickman (Eds.), *Critical-service learning as a revolutionary pedagogy* (pp. 3–27). Charlotte, NC: Information Age Publishing.

Your Fellow Americans. (2015). K-State. Retrieved from http://yourfellowamericans.com/category/your-fellow-students/k-state/

Zakaria, R. (2014). White tourist's burden. Retrieved from http://america.aljazeera.com/opinions/2014/4/volunter-tourismwhitevoluntouristsafricaaidsorphans.html

Zemach-Bersin, T. (2008). American students abroad can't be global citizens. *The Chronicle of Higher Education, 54*(26), A34.

Zierdt, G. L. (2009). Responsibility-centered budgeting: An emerging trend in higher education budget reform. *Journal of Higher Education Policy and Management, 31*(4), 346–353.

guide, this book will help you develop a daily practice of discovering assets in yourself and your community, and lead you to a destination that experiences community engagement as 'desire-centered' work." —***Chris Nayve***, *Associate Vice President for Community Engagement & Anchor Initiatives, Mulvaney Center, University of San Diego*

Learning Through Serving
A Student Guidebook for Service-Learning and Civic Engagement Across Academic Disciplines and Cultural Communities
Second Edition

Christine M. Cress, Peter J. Collier, and Vicki L. Reitenauer

"First published in 2005, *Learning through Serving* is a collection of critical thought on the nature of service learning, as well as a practical field guide for educators looking to expand their skills in this arena . . . . [It] offers a wealth of pedagogical advice for service-learning courses, but also situates service-learning within a larger commitment to civic engagement and building a more just society. It contains invaluable nuts-and-bolts course planning assistance, and gives wise counsel on how to develop enduring, reciprocal community partnerships that build capacity for the long haul. "—*Reflective Teaching (Wabash Center)*

22883 Quicksilver Drive
Sterling, VA 20166-2019

Subscribe to our e-mail alerts: www.Styluspub.com

Engaging Higher Education
Purpose, Platforms, and Programs for Community Engagement

Marshall Welch

Foreword by John Saltmarsh

"Welch provides an overview of the community engagement field in its current state, rooted in research and scholarly analysis. From its historical origins as a movement to the evolution of community engagement as a field, this volume extends an evidence-based synthesis of how higher education systems structure and implement community engagement, as well as a 'how-to' for higher education institutions. It will serve multiple purposes for higher education administrators, faculty, community engagement center directors, and graduate students in education." —***Patrick M. Green***, *Founding Director, Center for Experiential Learning, Loyola University Chicago; Past Board Chair, International Association for Research on Service-Learning and Community Engagement*

Building on the findings of the research undertaken by the author and John Saltmarsh on the infrastructure of campus centers for engagement that have received the Carnegie Classification for Community Engagement, this book responds to the expressed needs of the participating center directors for models and practices they could share and use with faculty and mid- and upper-level administrators to more fully embed engagement into institutional culture and practice.

The Student Companion to Community-Engaged Learning
What You Need to Know for Transformative Learning and Real Social Change

David M. Donahue and Star Plaxton-Moore

Foreword by Tania D. Mitchell

Afterword by Chris Nayve

"The authors face head on the most urgent issues that affect communities, and encourage us to embrace the notion that it is through reciprocal relationships that one earns the privilege of working alongside leaders in the community not as saviors but as partners. As you begin your journey in the community, this book will serve as a meditative companion and roadmap. When used as a

(Continues on preceeding page)

Also available from Stylus

Working Side by Side
Creating Alternative Breaks as Catalysts for Global Learning, Student Leadership, and Social Change

Shoshanna Sumka, Melody Christine Porter, and Jill Piacitelli

Foreword by Tanya O. Williams

"This is not a collection of stories about students who have miraculously transformed communities and themselves in a single week. While *Working Side By Side* inspires, it does so by thoughtfully raising and addressing the major complexities and challenges inherent to this type of community engagement. The authors provide many practical tools and frameworks for ethical and effective alternative breaks. This book signals the maturation of a movement while reminding us about potential pitfalls." —***Thomas Schnaubelt***, *PhD, Executive Director, Haas Center for Public Service, Assistant Vice Provost for Student Affairs, Resident Fellow, Branner Hall, Stanford University*

This book constitutes a guide for student and staff leaders in alternative break (and other domestic and international community engagement) programs, offering practical advice, outlining effective program components and practices, and presenting the underlying community engagement and global learning theory.

International Service Learning
Conceptual Frameworks and Research

Edited by Robert G. Bringle, Julie A. Hatcher, and Steven G. Jones

This book focuses on conducting research on international service learning (ISL), which includes developing and evaluating hypotheses about ISL outcomes and measuring its impact on students, faculty, and communities. The book argues that rigorous research is essential to improving the quality of ISL's implementation and delivery and provides the evidence that will lead to wider support and adoption by the academy, funders, and partners. It is intended for both practitioners and scholars, providing guidance and commentary on good practice. The volume provides a pioneering analysis of and understanding of why and under what conditions ISL is an effective pedagogy.

(Continues on preceeding page)